Democracy and Media Decadence

D1321755

We live in a revolutionary age of communicative abundance in which many media innovations – from satellite broadcasting to smart glasses and electronic books – spawn great fascination mixed with excitement. In the field of politics, hopeful talk of digital democracy, cybercitizens and e-government has been flourishing. This book admits the many thrilling ways that communicative abundance is fundamentally altering the contours of our lives and of our politics, often for the better. But it asks whether too little attention has been paid to the troubling counter-trends, the decadent media developments that encourage public silence and concentrations of unlimited power, so weakening the spirit and substance of democracy. Exploring examples of clever government surveillance, market censorship, spin tactics and back-channel public relations, John Keane seeks to understand and explain these trends, and how best to deal with them. Tackling some tough but big and fateful questions, Keane argues that 'media decadence' is deeply harmful for public life.

JOHN KEANE is Professor of Politics at the University of Sydney and at the Wissenschaftszentrum Berlin (WZB). He is also the Director of the Institute for Democracy and Human Rights (IDHR) at the University of Sydney. His online column 'Democracy Field Notes' appears regularly in the British- and Australian-based *The Conversation* (theconversation.com/uk). Among his best-known books are the best-selling *Tom Paine: A Political Life* (1995), *Violence and Democracy* (Cambridge University Press, 2004), *Global Civil Society?* (Cambridge University Press, 2003) and the highly acclaimed full-scale history of democracy, *The Life and Death of Democracy* (2009).

Democracy and Media Decadence

JOHN KEANE

CAMBRIDGE
UNIVERSITY PRESS

CAMBRIDGE
UNIVERSITY PRESS

University Printing House, Cambridge CB2 8BS, United Kingdom

Published in the United States of America by Cambridge University Press, New York

Cambridge University Press is part of the University of Cambridge.

It furthers the University's mission by disseminating knowledge in the pursuit of education, learning, and research at the highest international levels of excellence.

www.cambridge.org
Information on this title: www.cambridge.org/9781107614574

© John Keane 2013

First published 2013

Printed in the United Kingdom by TJ International Ltd. Padstow Cornwall

A catalogue record for this publication is available from the British Library

ISBN 978-1-107-04177-6 Hardback
ISBN 978-1-107-61457-4 Paperback

Contents

Acknowledgements and permissions

Generous research support provided by the University of Sydney, the Wissenschaftszentrum Berlin (WZB) and the ERC Project, Media and Democracy in Central and Eastern Europe, University of Oxford, is gratefully acknowledged.

Permission for the use of illustrations has been granted as follows:

Cover 'Dust', by Cong Lingqi (2008), courtesy of White Rabbit Contemporary Chinese Art Collection, Sydney.

1.1 Computer graphic ('splat map') of global Internet traffic, by Giovanni Navarria, with permission.

1.2 Marshall McLuhan, by Louis Forsdale, courtesy of Library and Archives Canada.

1.3 Ratio of media supply, courtesy of W. Russell Neuman, University of Michigan.

1.4 Patterns of Facebook usage, courtesy of Thomas Crampton.

1.5 Nellie Bly, courtesy of the Library of Congress, Prints and Photographs Division, LC-USZ62-75620.

1.6 Centralised, decentralised and distributed networks, by Giovanni Navarria, with permission.

1.7 Space Hijackers, courtesy of Guy Smallman.

1.8 Julian Assange, by John Keane.

2.1 Representative democracy, by Giovanni Navarria, with permission.

2.2 Monitory democracy, by Giovanni Navarria, with permission.

3.1 Planting the first pole on the overland telegraph line to Carpentaria, by Samuel Calvert, courtesy of National Library of Australia, an10328023.

4.1 China Carnival No. 1: Tiananmen (detail; 2007), by Chen Zhou and Huang Keyi, courtesy of the White Rabbit Gallery, Sydney.

4.2 'The Grass-mud Horse and the River Crab', by Jessi Wong (2010). Linocut on paper, edition of 10. Courtesy of the artist.

1 | *Communicative abundance*

In the beginning there was the first ever worldwide satellite television broadcast featuring the Beatles, Maria Callas, Marshall McLuhan and Pablo Picasso, all live, watched by an estimated 400 million people. Mountainous mainframe computers and host-based systems for sending messages by multiple users from remote dial-up terminals were already in use. Then along came electronic mail, fax machines, photocopiers, video recorders and personal computers. Now there are electronic books, cloud computing, scanners, smart watches and smart glasses, tweets and cell phones converted into satellite navigators, musical instruments and multi-person video chat sites. It is unclear even to the innovators what comes next, but these and other media inventions, commercially available only during recent decades, have persuaded more than a few people that we are living in a revolutionary age of communicative abundance.

In the spirit of the revolution, as in all previous upheavals in the prevailing mode of communication, fascination mixed with excitement is fuelling bold talk of the transcendence of television, the disappearance of printed newspapers, the withering of the printed book, even the end of literacy as we have known it. In the heartlands of the revolution, there is widespread recognition that time is up for spectrum scarcity, mass broadcasting and predictable prime-time national audiences, and that they have been replaced by spectrum abundance, fragmented narrowcasting and less predictable 'long tail' audiences.[1] Symbolised by the Internet, which is often portrayed through images that strongly resemble snowflakes (Figure 1.1), the revolutionary age of communicative abundance is structured by a new world system of overlapping and interlinked media devices. For the first time in history, thanks to built-in cheap microprocessors, these devices integrate texts, sounds and images in digitally

---

[1] The best-known work is Chris Anderson, *The Long Tail, or Why the Future of Business is Selling Less of More* (New York, 2006).

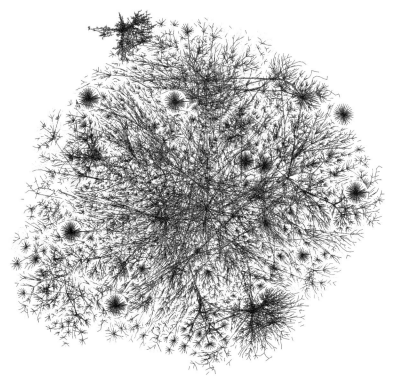

Figure 1.1 Computer graphic ('splat map') of global Internet traffic, shaded by ISP addresses, by Giovanni Navarria.

compact and easily storable, reproducible and portable form. Communicative abundance enables messages to be sent and received through multiple user points, in chosen time, either real or delayed, within modularised and ultimately global networks that are affordable and accessible to several billion people scattered across the globe.

The transformative potential of this new mode of communication is staggering, but its disruptive force and positive effects should not blindly be exaggerated. Communicative abundance does not bring paradise to Earth. Most of the world's people 'participate' within the global communications revolution on its sidelines. The cruel facts of communication poverty should not be ignored: a majority of the world's population (now totalling nearly 7 billion) are still too poor to buy a book; at least one-third have never made a phone call in their lives; and only around one-third have access to the Internet, whose distribution patterns are highly uneven and are marked in turn by great divides between those who have access to its tools and techniques and those who are 'Internet savvy'.[2] Within the most media-saturated settings, for instance, the societies of Iceland, South Korea and Singapore, digital divides based on differences of age, gender, class, ethnicity and disability are plainly observable. Even among young people, supposedly the most digitally sophisticated stratum of the population in wealthy societies, social inequalities of access and patterns of use of digital media are striking.[3]

These points should be sobering. Yet the fact remains that the communications revolution of our time is a worldwide phenomenon that defies simple talk of rich–poor and North–South divides. Many different regions witness the breathtaking growth of information flows. Measured globally, an estimated 2.5 quintillion bytes of new data are generated daily; some 90 per cent of the data that now exists has been created during the past two years; and in the years leading to 2020, thanks to the spreading use of smartphones, tablets, social media sites, email and other forms of digital communication, the global volume of digital information is expected to double every two years. Gripped by such dynamics, some local trends veer towards the perverse: for instance, more Africans now have access to mobile phones than to clean drinking water; while in South Africa, among the continent's most vibrant, but still deeply class-divided economies, with a high proportion (approximately 40 per cent) of its people living in poverty, aggregate mobile phone use has rocketed during the past decade by more than four times (from around 17 per cent in the year 2000 to 76 per cent in 2010), to the point where more South African citizens (when they can afford them) rank their use of mobile phones above their listening to radio, or watching television or using personal computers.[4] Elsewhere, in countries otherwise as different as India, the

---

[2] See the various data sets and figures cited at: www.internetworldstats.com/stats. htm, accessed 10 January 2012.

[3] J. C. Witte and S. E. Mannon, *The Internet and Social Inequalities* (New York, 2010); L. Nakamura, *Digitizing Race: Visual Cultures of the Internet* (Minneapolis, MN, 2008); Sonia Livingstone and E. Helsper, 'Gradations in Digital Inclusion: Children, Young People and the Digital Divide', *New Media & Society* 9 (2007): 671–96.

[4] Estimates of the growth of information flows are based on recent studies by IBM and the International Data Corporation, as reported in 'Technology Revolution

United States, South Korea and Brazil, and in the European Union member states, evidence is growing that many people routinely sense sideways motion and forward movement in the way that they communicate, even in the little things of life. Whether they like it or not, old media broadcasting habits are dying, or are already dead and buried. India is a striking case in point: until 1991, the country had only a single state-owned television channel, but the subsequent rapid expansion of independent satellite channels has resulted not only in multiple news channels, but a plethora of other genres, ranging from regular talk-shows focusing on political issues and the political satire of cartoons and puppetry, to daily opinion polls via SMS messages and the rise of 'citizen journalists' who send in video clips through computers and mobile phones.[5] In India, as in other democracies, radio, television and chit-chat continue to be the principal sources of news and entertainment for many citizens; in various parts of the world, these are the only media available to people. Yet in the heartlands of communicative abundance, mass audiences with pricked ears and wide eyes predictably glued to radio and television broadcasts have become exceptional. In their place, multiple audiences of many different shapes and sizes are flourishing, helped along by dispersed multimedia communications that radically multiply choices about when, how and at what distances people communicate with others.

The communications revolution that brought the world the telegraph and the telephone sparked tremendous excitement. The Boston Library feature panels, painted by the famous nineteenth-century artist Puvis de Chavannes, depicted the telegraph and telephone as two female figures flying above electric wires, adding the inscription: 'By the wondrous agency of electricity, speech flashes through space and swift as lightning bears tidings of good and evil.' Communicative abundance exudes the same feverish sense of ferment and fire captured in that image. The present seems charged with radical uncertainty about future trends.

Consider, to take a few brief examples, developments within the commercial music sector, where for some time copyright arrangements

---

Moves Mountains of Data', *International Herald Tribune*, 10 June 2013, pp. 1, 8; the data from South Africa is drawn from Jan Hutton, 'Mobile Phones Dominate in South Africa', 2011, http://blog.nielsen.com/nielsenwire/global/mobile-phones-dominate-in-south-africa, accessed 22 September 2011.

[5] Nalin Mehta, *Television in India: Satellites, Politics and Cultural Change* (London and New York, 2008).

(it is said by industry figures) have been ransacked by simple reproduction techniques and by freely available electronic download methods that threaten to erode music company earnings. The cassette tape replaced the eight-track, only to be replaced in turn by the compact disc, itself now being replaced by MP3 players. Or look at what has been happening within the field of electronic books. Despite reassurances that the 'book is like the spoon, scissors, the hammer, the wheel. Once invented, it cannot be improved,'[6] manufacturers of tablet reading devices and online retailers of hard-copy and e-books are putting heavy pressure on the prices and distribution methods of traditional book publishing business models. As with free or cheaply downloadable music, books delivered in digital form raise profound questions not just about the future role played by traditional book publishers, but also much fretting about whether books in any form and selective 'reading for the sake of reading' remain a powerful way of constructing meaning from life's experiences, the best and most pleasurable antidote against the anaesthetics of boredom and vacuity in an age of multimedia distraction.[7] Unsettlement and restructuring equally grip the newspaper world, where a combination of plummeting advertising revenues, takeovers and mergers, independent citizens' journalism, competition from digital devices and shifting public definitions of news and entertainment has prompted profound unease about the future of hard-copy, mass circulation newspapers. Some observers even predict their eventual disappearance from street news stands, cafés and kitchen tables.

The uneasy excitement triggered by the coming of communicative abundance is often hard to interpret; the predictions of pundits are equally difficult to assess. Yet with some certainty it can be said that the myriad disturbances in the field of communications hail an historic shift away from the era of limited spectrum radio and television broadcasting. Gone are the times, during the 1950s, when on American television an episode of the sitcom *I Love Lucy* was watched by over 70 per cent of all television households, or when even more households (nearly 83 per cent) watched Elvis Presley's appearance on the Ed Sullivan Show. The days are behind us (I recall) when children played with

---

[6] Umberto Eco, in conversation with Jean-Claude Carrière, in *This is Not the End of the Book: A Conversation about the Past, Present and Future* (London, 2011), p. 4.

[7] See Alan Jacobs, *The Pleasures of Reading in an Age of Distraction* (Oxford, 2011); the continuity between hard-copy books and e-books is emphasised by Andrew Piper, *Book Was There: Reading in Electronic Times* (Chicago, 2012).

makeshift telephones made from jam tins connected by string; or the evenings when they were compulsorily flung into the bath and scrubbed behind the ears, sat down in their dressing gowns and instructed to listen in silence to the radio. There are still moments when live-event television coverage (of sporting events, political dramas, catastrophic accidents and singing competitions) binds together splintered audiences, but memories of the age of mass broadcasting and its various tools of communication are fading fast.

In the heartlands of today's revolution, people no longer own telephone directories, or memorise telephone numbers by heart. Most people have had no direct experience of the nervous excitement triggered by making a pre-booked long-distance call. Old documentaries featuring interviews with people looking with nervous hostility at the camera are no more; once seen as an invasion of self, cameras are considered enhancers of self. Everybody chuckles when mention is made of the wireless; nobody thinks of the bakelite tube radio as the source of a retronym now used to describe cord-free connections among stationary and portable tools of communication, large and small. Typewriters belong in curiosity shops. Pagers have almost been forgotten. Old jokes at the expense of television, said to be chewing gum for the eyes, or called a medium because it is neither rare nor well done, now seem flat. Even the couch potato seems to be a figure from the distant past. Few people think twice about the transformation of the word text into a verb. Writing and receiving hand-written letters and postcards have become a rare, nostalgic pleasure, and such formal valedictions as 'Yours truly' and 'Yours faithfully' have long ago been supplanted by 'Best' or 'Thanks' or 'Cheers' – or a blank space.

For many busy, well-equipped people, dead time, the art of doing nothing while contemplating the world out of a window, is on the skids; the same fate, at least for those who can afford it, is suffered by the ancient pleasure of curling up with a good book, or taking a quiet stroll in the park, without a Samsung in hand, or an iPod plugged into an ear. Soon after the publication of this book, the examples it cites will seem dated, replaced (for instance) by mobile phones with laser keyboards and holographic displays, or by tiny computers worn like wristwatches, which will have the effect of confirming the underlying trend. In contexts as different as Seoul, London and Mumbai, many office workers meanwhile admit that they spend their lunch hours snaffling a snack while checking their email or browsing the Web, rather than taking a physical break from their desk; family members say that watching television in the company of others, except for sport and live reality shows, is now no match for the magnetic pull of mobile phones, tablets and desktop computers; and the younger generation, determined to prove the point with an iPod plugged into one ear, spends many hours each day and night online, often connecting through mobile applications with others, elsewhere in the so-called virtual world.

One key marker of the broad trend towards multimedia saturation is the perceived transformations taking place in the content and delivery of news.[8] Communicative abundance stirs up public disputes about the future of newspapers in hard-copy form. In their defence, some observers insist that while newspapers are bleeding revenues to online destinations, newspaper journalists working in well-equipped and well-connected newsrooms remain the 'content engines' (as American journalists say) of talkback radio, television news shows and blogs and tweets. The point is well made, for newspapers such as the *New York Times*, *El País* and *Yomiuri Shimbun* (the Japanese daily usually credited with having the largest circulation of any newspaper in the world) are probably not dinosaurs due for extinction. There is undoubtedly scope for their reinvention and ongoing redefinition in online form, for instance, using combinations of subscriptions and advertisements to deliver news to tablets.

Yet, in the age of communicative abundance, the ecology of news production and news circulation is undergoing rapid change.[9] News sources and streams diversify and multiply. Symptomatic is the way many media-savvy young people in countries otherwise as different as South Korea, Singapore and Japan are no longer wedded to traditional 'bundled' news outlets; they do not listen to radio bulletins, or watch current affairs or news programmes on television. 'Reading the morning newspaper', Hegel famously wrote in his daily journal, 'is the realist's morning prayer. One orients one's attitude toward *the* world.'[10] Digital

---

[8] See, for example, Leonard Downie Jr and Michael Schudson, 'The Reconstruction of American Journalism', *Columbia Journalism Review*, 19 October 2009.

[9] Michael Schudson, 'On Journalism and Democracy: Tocqueville's Interesting Error', public lecture delivered at the Centre for the Study of Democracy, London, 3 February 2010.

[10] *Miscellaneous Writings of G. W. F. Hegel*, ed. Jon Bartley Stewart (Chicago, 2002), p. 247; for the exodus of young people from conventional newspaper culture see Pew project for Excellence in Journalism, *The State of the News Media: An Annual Report on American Journalism* (Washington, DC, 2008).

natives, as they are sometimes known, are doing things differently. They refuse the old habit of mining the morning newspaper for their up-to-date information, as four out of every five American citizens once did (in the early 1960s). Internet portals have instead become their favoured destination for news. It is not that they are uninterested in news; it is rather that they want lots of it, news on demand, in instant 'unbundled' form and delivered in new ways, not merely in the mornings but throughout the day, and night.

Not surprisingly, pressured by such changes, plenty of observers, even from within the newspaper industry itself, have warned of the coming disappearance of newspapers. They point to mounting evidence that conventional newspaper business models are reaching crisis point, dragged down by online competitors (such as real-time sharing of YouTube and Twitter feeds) and the dramatic decline of classified and display advertising revenues.[11] Other observers make deliberately outlandish comments, designed to shock, for instance, through reminders that in the two years to 2009 the newspaper readership market in the United States fell by 30 per cent, more than 160 mastheads disappeared, along with 35,000 jobs; and through predictions that on current trends newspapers in the United States will no longer be printed after 2043.[12] More measured observers point out that although there are worrying developments (fewer than 20 per cent of Americans aged between 18 and 34 read a daily paper, for instance), overall trends are considerably more complicated; but, nevertheless, they agree that compared with the now-distant era of representative democracy, when print culture and limited spectrum audio-visual media were closely aligned with political parties, elections and governments, and flows of communication took the form of broadcasting confined within state borders, our times are different. The shift towards multimedia platforms and user-generated communication involves many more people listening, watching and talking directly to other people, rather than to traditional media sources. Or so most commentators now suppose.

[11] James Fallows, 'How to Save the News', *Atlantic Magazine* (June 2010); Hal Varian, 'A Google-Eye View of the Newspaper Business', *The Atlantic*, 10 May 2011.
[12] Compare Philip Meyer, *The Vanishing Newspaper: Saving Journalism in the Information Age* (Columbia, MO, 2009) with Charles M. Madigan (ed.), *The Collapse of the Great American Newspaper* (Lanham, MD, 2007) and the two reports by the Media, Entertainment and Arts Alliance, *Life in the Clickstream: The Future of Journalism* (2008; 2010) at www.alliance.org.au/documents/foj_report_final.pdf and www.thefutureofjournalism.org.au/foj_report_vii.pdf.

Novelties

As in every previous communication revolution – think of the upheavals triggered by the introduction of the printing press, or radio, film and television – the age of communicative abundance breeds exaggerations, false hopes, illusions. Thomas Carlyle expected the printing press to topple all traditional hierarchies, including monarchies and churches. 'He who first shortened the labor of copyists by device of movable types', he wrote, 'was disbanding hired armies, and cashiering most kings and senates, and creating a whole new democratic world.' Or to take a second example: D. W. Griffith predicted that the invention of film would ensure that schoolchildren would be 'taught practically everything by moving pictures' and 'never be obliged to read history again'.[13] Revolutions always produce fickle fantasies – and dashed expectations. This one is no different, or so it seems to wise minds. Yet, when judged in terms of speed, scope and complexity, the new galaxy of communicative abundance has no historical precedent. The digital integration of text, sound and image is a first, historically speaking. So also are the compactness, portability and affordability of a wide range of communication devices capable of processing, sending and receiving information in easily reproducible form, in vast quantities, across great geographic distances, in quick time, sometimes instantly.

Technical factors play a pivotal role in the seismic upheavals that are taking place. Right from the beginning of the revolution, computing hardware has been undergoing constant change, with dramatic world-changing effects on the everyday lives of users. The number of transistors that can be placed inexpensively on an integrated circuit is doubling approximately every two years (according to what is known as 'Moore's law'[14]). The memory capacity, processing speed,

---

[13] Thomas Carlyle, *Sartor Resartus* (London, 1833); the D. W. Griffith quotation is from Richard Dyer MacCann, *The First Film Makers* (Metuchen, NJ, 1989), p. 5.

[14] The law takes its name from the co-founder of Intel, Gordon E. Moore, whose classic paper on the subject noted that the number of components in integrated circuits had doubled every year from the invention of the integrated circuit in 1958 until 1965. Moore predicted (in 1965) that the trend would continue for at least another decade. See his 'Cramming more Components onto Integrated Circuits', *Electronics* 38(8) (1965): 4–7.

sensors and even the number and size of pixels in smart phones and digital cameras have all been expanding at exponential rates as well. The constant revolutionising has dramatically increased the usefulness and take-up of digital electronics in nearly every segment of daily life, and within markets and government institutions as a whole, to the point where time–space compression on a global scale is becoming a reality, sometimes a functional necessity, as in the transformation of stock exchanges into spaces where computer algorithms (known as 'algobots') are programmed automatically to buy and sell equities, currencies and commodities in less than 200 milliseconds. Cheap and reliable cross-border communication is the norm for growing numbers of people and organisations. The tyranny of distance and slow-time connections is abolished, especially in such geographically isolated countries as Greenland and Iceland, where the rates of Internet penetration (over 90 per cent of the population) are the highest in the world. The overthrow of that tyranny provides a clue as to why, in the most media-saturated societies, people typically take instant communications for granted. Their habits of heart are exposed by the curse uttered when they lose or misplace their mobile phones or when their Internet connections are down. They feel lost; they wallow in frustration; they curse.

The historical novelty of quick-time, space-shrinking media saturation is easy to overlook, or to ignore, but it should in fact be striking. When four decades ago Diane Keaton told her workaholic husband in Woody Allen's *Play it Again, Sam* (1973) that he should give his office the number of the pay phone they were passing in case they needed to contact him, it was a good frisky gag. But jest soon turned into today's reality. Growing numbers of people are now familiar with real-time communication; as if born to check their messages, they expect instant replies to instant missives. Their waking lives resemble non-stop acts of mediated quick-time communication with others. In the space of an hour, for instance, an individual might send several emails, text or twitter a few times, watch some television on- or offline, channel hop on digital radio, make an old-fashioned landline telephone call, browse a newspaper, open the day's post, and even find time for a few minutes of face-to-face conversation.

In practice, for reasons of wealth and income, habit and shortage of time, only a minority of people perform so many communication acts in quick time. For most individuals, 'ponder time' has not disappeared. Their mediated acts of communication are sporadic, unevenly distributed and snared in processes of constant change. The available data covering the trends, understandably, tends to be unreliable; it suffers from blunt-edged indicators, lack of historical nuance and built-in obsolescence. Yet, when examined carefully, and especially through the lens of broader trends, the aggregate figures suggest a long-term cumulative growth of personal involvement in the multimedia process of communicative abundance. Except for the invention of human language, described by Jean-Jacques Rousseau as the 'first social institution',[15] no previous mode of communication has penetrated so deeply, so comprehensively, so dynamically, into daily human experience. Newspapers circulated through parlours, coffee houses and kitchens, but still they could be ignored, or set aside, or used to line drawers and wrap meat and fish or to light fires. The telephone had its fixed place, in the office, kitchen or living room; while it had definite halo effects, in that it altered the daily habits and expectations of its users, they were always free to avoid its ring, often for reasons of cost.

The digital media tools that service the architecture of communicative abundance are different. They lie beyond the famous distinction drawn by Marshall McLuhan between 'hot' and 'cool' media (Figure 1.2).[16] McLuhan rightly saw that different media engage their users in different ways, and to different degrees. Some media (he gave printed works as an example) are 'hot', by which he referred not to their temperature or topicality ('hot off the press'), but to the way they involve users, yet keep them detached, as if at arm's length. They favour such qualities as logicality, linearity, analytical precision. Other media, television, for example, are 'cool' (McLuhan took the term from the jazz world) in the sense that they substantially depend upon user participation. The distinction between 'hot' and 'cool' media dovetailed with his thesis that all media invest our lives with artificial perceptions and arbitrary values, and that to a varying degree communication media extend our bodily and sensory capacities, some at the expense of others, so that in a

[15] Jean-Jacques Rousseau, Essai sur l'origine des langues, in *Collection complète des oeuvres de J-J. Rousseau, citoyen de Genève* (Geneva, 1782), vol. 8, ch. 1, p. 357.
[16] Marshall McLuhan, *Understanding Media: The Extensions of Man* (New York, 1964).

Figure 1.2 Marshall McLuhan: 'People don't actually read newspapers. They step into them every morning like a hot bath' (1972).

visceral sense they deliver 'amputations and extensions' to our sensory apparatus.

The thesis remains important, but striking is the way communicative abundance sweeps aside the distinction between 'hot' and 'cool' media. Communicative abundance in fact involves a double combination. By fusing, for the first time in human history, the means of communication centred on text, touch, sound and image, the era of communicative abundance draws together and stimulates *most* human senses (fortune and fame awaits the person or group who masters the art of communicating taste and smell). And it involves a second combination: in some circumstances (reading a novel or newspaper on a tablet) the new mode of communication fosters reflective detachment, whereas in other settings (using Skype or messaging a friend on the other side of the planet, or wearing smart glasses) it requires the deep participation of its users and stimulates their various senses, in different combinations.

In the age of communicative abundance, vision is no longer (as many claimed it was in the age of film and television) the principal medium of power and politics. Scholars who insist that democracy based on public debate, and therefore on 'voice', is now obsolete, superseded by a type of 'spectator democracy' in which citizens are mostly passive and 'relate to politics with their eyes',[17] are exaggerating. Talk and text are not fading from political life. The eyes do not always have it. In the unfinished revolution of communicative abundance, democratic politics is a multi-sensual business. Various multimedia techniques and tools of communication draw on text, touch, sound and image. They enter every nook and cranny of daily existence. They touch and transform people's inner selves. Unsurprisingly, communicative abundance triggers constant disputes about the blurry line between 'free communication' and personal insult and criminal blasphemy. For instance, the difference between what can legitimately be said about a person, particularly someone with a public reputation, and what can be said to a person, becomes publicly controversial. The wall separating, say, speaking from an old-fashioned soapbox and making threatening telephone calls is swept away. Twitter posts fuel charges of defamation, hacking of Facebook accounts stirs up cries of felony identity theft, while students who bombard teachers with emails are accused of disturbing the peace or cyberstalking. Such disputes are due partly to the compactness, user-friendliness, cheapness and portability of the new communication tools; they are equally an effect of their multi-sensual and multi-interactive qualities (their enabling of one-to-many and many-to-one communication) and the decision of users to deploy the new means of communication deep within the territories of their personal lives, and within the lives of others.

The historic novelty of these deep transformations is strongly evident in many global settings, including the United States, perhaps the most media-saturated of the old democracies. There communication with

[17] Edward Green, *The Eyes of the People* (Oxford, 2010), p. 4.

others forms the second largest category of action after paid work, and it is certainly the predominant household activity, whose patterns are distributed quite unevenly. Daily communication preferences are structured by income and wealth; they are also age- and gender-dependent, as suggested by figures (from January 2005 to September 2010) for SMS usage, which show, for instance, that women talk and text more than men do, and that 13–17-year olds do so more than any other age group.[18] The high density of daily communication is reinforced by the tendency of each formerly separate medium to merge with others, to become 'hybrid' media. Contrary to earlier predictions, the new digital media in the United States show no signs of cannibalising old media, such as television, radio and books. Two decades ago, according to one report, the average American household had the television set on for about 7 hours a day, with actual viewing time estimated to be 4.5 hours daily per adult; radio listening averaged 2 hours per day, most of it in the car; newspaper reading occurred for between 18 and 49 minutes daily; magazine browsing consumed between 6 and 30 minutes; and book reading, including schoolwork-related texts, took up around 18 minutes per day. The implication was that American society was firmly in the grip of its television sets, and would remain so. More recent evidence suggests a more complex trend, in which overall mediated communication grew, along with ever more complex and 'hybrid' patterns of usage. America's love affair with televisions continues unabashed, but in altered, multimedia form. The average number of televisions per US household is 2.5; nearly a third of households have four or more televisions. Each week, Americans watch roughly 35 hours of television and 2 hours of time-shifted television via DVR. In the last quarter of 2009, however, simultaneous use of the Internet while watching television reached 3.5 hours a month, up 35 per cent from the previous year; nearly 60 per cent now use the Internet while watching TV. Internet video watching is rising fast; so is the preference for watching videos on smart phones. The overall effect of these various trends is to transform households into media-saturated spaces. In 1960, there were typically 3.4 television stations per household, 8.2 radio

[18] Roger Entner, 'Under-aged Texting: Usage and Actual Cost', 27 January 2010, available at: http://blog.nielsen.com/nielsenwire/online_mobile/under-aged-texting-usage-and-actual-cost, accessed 10 February 2010; and 'Factsheet: The U.S. Media Universe', 5 January 2011, available at: http://blog.nielsen.com/nielsenwire.

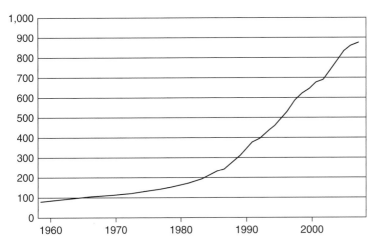

Figure 1.3 Ratio of media supply to consumption in minutes/day per household in the United States, 1960–2005, after W. Russell Neuman *et al.*

stations, 1.1 newspapers, 1.5 recently purchased books and 3.6 magazines; the ratio of media supply to actual household media consumption was 82:1 (see Figure 1.3). By 2005, that figure had risen to 884:1, that is, nearly 1,000 minutes of mediated content available for each minute available for users to access content of various kinds.[19]

The shift towards high-intensity, multimedia usage within the daily lives of people, or communicative abundance as it is called throughout this book, are by no means restricted to the United States. The Asia and Pacific region is arguably the laboratory of future patterns. Quite aside from its robust oral cultures,[20] the region currently accounts for

[19] W. Russell Neuman, Yong Jin Park and Elliot Panek, 'Tracking the Flow of Information into the Home', *International Journal of Communication* 6 (2012): 1022–41.

[20] The BBC's chief reporter for two decades in India, Mark Tully, notes the continuing importance of word-of-mouth communication within a society increasingly structured by various other means of communication: 'Anyone who has joined a group of villagers huddled over a transistor set in the dim light of a lantern listening to news from a foreign radio station knows that the spread of information is not limited to the number of sets in a village. Go to that village in the morning, and you will learn that the information heard on that radio has reached far beyond the listenership too' ('Broadcasting in India: An Under-Exploited Resource', in Asharani Mathur (ed.), *The Indian Media: Illusion, Delusion and Reality. Essays in Honour of Prem Bhatia* (New Delhi, 2006), pp. 285–6).

the highest global share of Internet users (more than 40 per cent of the total). Its telecommunications markets are rapidly expanding; and with cheaper, more reliable and faster connectivity rapidly becoming a reality throughout the region, the penetration of daily and institutional life by new tools of communication and user-generated information seems bound to grow, especially in democratic countries such as India and Indonesia, whose young people show a remarkable capacity for experimentation. Japan, whose citizens on average watch television 4 hours a day, is the country with the most avid bloggers globally, posting more than one million blogs per month. Each of its well-entrenched social networking sites and game portals – Mixi, Gree and Mobage-town – has over 20 million registered users. Everywhere in the region, the take-up rate of new media is striking. Micro-blogging (Twitter use in India, for instance) and social networking is all the rage. Australians spend more time on social media sites (nearly 7 hours per month) than any other country in the world. Every month in South Korea, the leading social networking site, Naver, attracts 95 per cent of Internet users. The trend is not confined to single territorial states; throughout the region, despite barriers of language, there are signs of rapidly thickening cross-border connections, with many global cross-links (Figure 1.4). The patterns of regional and global interconnectivity are helped along by many interesting and important trends, including the fact that three-quarters of the world's Internet population has now visited Facebook, Wikipedia, YouTube or some other social network/blogging site; that Internet users spend on average almost 6 hours per month on these sites in a variety of languages; and that some of these sites are now fully multilingual, as in the case of Wikipedia, which (by late 2012) contained more than 23 million entries, less than a fifth (4.1 million) of which were in the English language.

Wild thinking

Pushed here and there by such trends, it is unsurprising that the developing culture of communicative abundance stokes political visions. With more than a million new devices – desktop computers, mobile phones, televisions and other gadgets – hooked up each day to the Internet, the current revolution is said not only to have upset standard

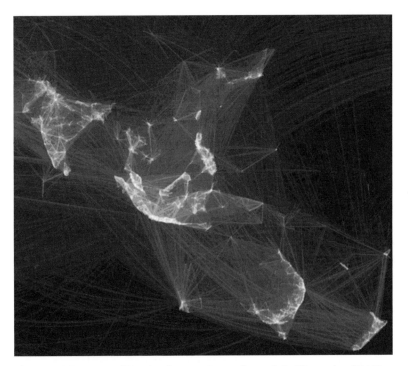

Figure 1.4 Patterns of Facebook usage in southeast Asia (December 2010).

business models, but also to have generated unexpected wealth and changed the lives of millions of people. Sometimes seen as a bulldozer or likened to a great flattener of the world, the new mode of communicative abundance is rated as a challenger of all settled hierarchies of power and authority.[21] It fuels hopeful talk of digital democracy, online publics, cybercitizens and Wiki-government. Some speak of a third stage of democratic evolution, in which the spirit and substance of ancient assembly democracy are reincarnated in wired form. 'Telecommunications', or so runs the argument, 'can give every citizen the opportunity to place questions of their own on the public agenda and participate in discussions with experts, policy-makers and fellow

---

[21] Thomas L. Friedman, *The World Is Flat: A Brief History of the Twenty-first Century* (New York, 2005).

citizens.'[22] Others promote visions of a 'connected' digital world where 'citizens hold their own governments accountable' and 'all of humanity has equal access to knowledge and power' (the words used by former US Secretary of State Hillary Clinton during an address at Washington's Newseum).[23] In the spirit of the revolution, some pundits venture further. They draw the conclusion that the 'advent and power of connection technologies', with their ever faster computing power, their accelerating shift from the one-to-many geometry of radio and television broadcasting towards many-to-many communication patterns, implies that there is something like a 'natural' affinity between communicative abundance and democracy, understood (roughly) as a type of government and a way of life in which power is subject to permanent public scrutiny, chastening and control by citizens and their representatives.[24] Communicative abundance and democracy are thought of as conjoined twins. The stunning revolutionary process and product innovations happening in the field of communications fuel the dispersal and public accountability of power, or so it is supposed.

There is much to be said (it seems) in support of the claim. There are indeed positive, important, exciting, even intoxicating things happening inside the swirling galaxy of communicative abundance. So let us look more carefully at the details. In examining the affinities between communicative abundance and democracy, a term that, so far, has been used loosely, several strictures need to be borne in mind, beginning with McLuhan's prudent warning: since every new communication medium tends to cast a 'spell' on its users, in effect imposing 'its own assumptions, bias, and values' on the unwary, seducing them into a 'subliminal state of Narcissus trance', a measure of analytic detachment and diffidence is necessary when analysing and evaluating its social and political impact.[25] The need for detachment implies something positive: the cool-headed analysis of a new historical mode of communication can

---

[22] Lawrence K. Grossman, *Electronic Republic: Reshaping Democracy in the Information Age* (New York, 1996).

[23] Former US Secretary of State Hillary Clinton, 'Remarks on Internet Freedom', an address delivered at the Newseum, Washington, DC, 21 January 2010, available at: www.state.gov/secretary/rm/2010/01/135519.htm, accessed 20 March 2010.

[24] See Eric Schmidt and Jared Cohen, 'The Digital Disruption: Connectivity and the Diffusion of Power', *Foreign Affairs* 89(6) (November/December 2010): 75–85.

[25] Marshall McLuhan, *Understanding Media: The Extensions of Man* (New York, 1964), p. 7.

alert us to its novelties, make (more) visible what previously was less than obvious, so alerting us, in matters of democracy, to its many positive and negative dynamics. That is not to say that interpretations of communicative abundance can 'master' its elusive qualities. Mastery is reserved for the deities; just as any speaker of a language can never comprehensively follow and practise its rules and anticipate and control its past and present and future effects, so the dynamic contours of communicative abundance will retain a measure of elusiveness. Hence, this book attempts nothing like what Germans call a *Gesamtdarstellung*, a complete picture of communicative abundance and its dynamics. Nor does it suppose that in future, in some other shape or form, a comprehensive account might be possible. There is much too much dynamic reality for that to happen. The complexity of communicative abundance is too complex, too elusive, to be captured in smooth or slick formulae, in propositions based on statistics extracted by using blunt-edged criteria, in hard-and-fast rules, in confident predictions based on the supposed truth of things. We could say that communicative abundance is a modest mistress. She prefers to keep more than a few of her secrets close to her chest.

When it comes to mediated communication with others, we live in a strange new world of confusing unknowns, a thoroughly media-saturated universe cluttered with means and methods of communication, whose dynamic social and political effects have the capacity to hypnotise us, even to overwhelm our senses. These puzzling novelties and unknowns are not easily decoded, partly for epistemological and methodological reasons. Put simply, the facts of communicative abundance do not speak for themselves; they do not reveal their riddles spontaneously, of their own volition, without our help. Contrary to those who think of the study of political communications as an empirical 'science', the confusing novelties of communicative abundance cannot be deciphered purely through 'objective' empirical investigation, that is, by cross-referring to so-called brute facts and the corresponding data sets that function as ultimate arbiters of what we do know and what we do not know about the world of communicative abundance. The so-called 'facts' cannot rescue us by guiding and putting right our heads from a distance. This is not just because there are just too many available 'facts' to be grasped as such, so that selective biases (the setting aside of certain 'facts') are inevitable in each and every effort to produce 'objective' knowledge of our media-saturated world (this was the conclusion famously drawn by Max Weber[26]). The problem runs deeper, for 'facts' are always artefacts. How the 'facts' of communicative abundance appear to us, and what strategic and normative significance they have for us, very much depends upon a combination of forces, including the language frameworks through which people who communicate see themselves and express their own situations, and through which the analysts of communicative abundance and its complex dynamics also structure their own research goals and methods. In the age of communicative abundance, 'thick' descriptions, with as many details of the context and the motives and moves of actors, are mandatory. Yet thick descriptions are themselves artefacts. They are always and inescapably structured by frameworks of theoretical interpretation. The key point is this: in efforts to grasp and make sense of complex realities, perspectives are not 'detachable' from empirical methods. Interpretative frameworks do not have a secondary or subsidiary status. They are not barriers to 'adequate' descriptions of 'objective realities' or dispensable luxuries. They are, rather, vitally important conditions of making sense of the webs of communicative abundance within which people interact, more or less purposefully and meaningfully, for multiple ends using multiple means. In matters of communication, the principle sketched by Einstein is about right: not everything that can be counted counts, and not everything that counts can be counted.

Since the age of communicative abundance brims with puzzling novelties, many old ways of thinking and interpreting media, power and politics are now rendered suspect. Sentimental longings for imaginary better times, when life supposedly was shaped by high-quality national newspapers and BBC-style public service broadcasting, are not an option, not even when accompanied by understandable complaints about how the age of communicative abundance fails to overcome language barriers, racist and nationalist hatreds, untamed corporate power and other ills of our time.[27] Awareness of the novelties of our age should not be drowned in outpourings of nostalgia or pessimism. We need as well to be aware that extrapolations from current trends and predictions about the ultimate uses of new communications technologies are fraught, especially when sustained by

---

[26] Max Weber, '"Objectivity" in Social Science and Social Policy', in *The Methodology of the Social Sciences* (New York, 1949), p. 110.
[27] James Curran, 'The Internet: Prophecy and Reality', public lecture, Justice and Police Museum, Sydney, 21 September 2011.

analogies to the past. When faced with unfamiliar situations, it is always tempting to suppose that new media will carry on doing familiar things (enabling us freely to communicate with others, for instance), but in more efficient and effective, faster and cheaper ways. Just as the railway was called the 'iron horse' and the automobile the 'horseless carriage', or telephones were viewed in terms of the telegraph, as tools for communicating emergencies or important news, rather than tools for other, more casual purposes, so it is tempting to interpret the new dynamics of communicative abundance through terms inherited from our predecessors. The enticement should be resisted. Presumptions that have outlived their usefulness must be abandoned. What is needed are bold new probes, fresh-minded perspectives, 'wild' concepts that enable different and meaningful ways of seeing things, more discriminating methods of recognising the novelties of our times, the democratic opportunities they offer and the counter-trends that have the potential to snuff out democratic politics.

But what does the call for 'wild' new perspectives actually imply? Minimally, it means abandoning dogmas, clichés and bland formulae, including (to take a short string of examples) the commonplace choice between naive, simple-minded 'cyber-utopian' beliefs in the liberating nature of online communication and the trite mirror-image verdict that communicative abundance is equally a tool of repression, that all techniques and tools of communication, including the Internet, can be used equally for good or bad purposes, and that everything depends upon the context in which they are used.[28]

In matters of method, 'wild' new perspectives certainly imply the need for suspicion of neologisms that have a false-start quality about them. A case in point is the word 'cyberspace'. An artefact of times when computerised digital networks had still not substantially penetrated everyday life and formal institutional settings, the term is not seriously used in this book simply because it misleadingly conveys the sense that things that happen in and through the Internet are not quite 'real', or 'real' in some different way, in a world governed by different principles than those of the corporeal world. Talk of cyberspace radically underestimates the growth of cutting-edge media technologies that are now structuring people's lives. Examples include sensors and microcomputers embedded in objects as varied as kitchen appliances, surveillance

---

[28] Evgeny Morozov, *The Net Delusion: The Dark Side of Internet Freedom* (New York, 2011).

cameras, cars and mobile phone apps; and smart glasses that enable wearers, with a touch of the frame or shake of the head or verbal command, to take pictures, record and send videos, search the Web, or receive breaking news or walking directions, without so much as lifting a finger. Other examples include wearable wireless gadgets known as 'sociometers', gadgets attached to the human body or seamlessly integrated into human clothing for the purpose of measuring and analysing people's communication patterns (an example is the name tag device called 'HyGenius', used in hospital and restaurant bathrooms to check that employees are properly washing their hands). And there are wired-up 'smart' cities, such as Korea's Songdu and Portugal's PlanIT Valley, where 'smart' appliances pump constant data streams into 'smart grids' that measure and regulate flows of people, traffic and energy use.[29] In the face of such trends, old-fashioned talk of cyberspace is just that: old-fashioned. It goes hand-in-hand with mistaken questions like 'what effect is the Internet having on democratic politics?' when the priority is, rather, to understand the institutional world from which digital communication networks and tools originally sprang, how they have subsequently taken root within a range of other institutions, and which new power dynamics and power effects their revolutionary techniques and tools are having on the worlds in which they operate.

Wild perspectives imply the need for something more: questioning and abandoning outdated clichés, including all descriptions of communication media as the 'fourth estate', a misleading metaphor that originated with Edmund Burke and the pamphlet and newspaper battles of the French Revolution. Contemporary accounts of communication media that suppose the continuing validity of that metaphor, for instance, analyses of the ideal functions of 'media systems' as 'gatekeepers', independent 'agenda setters', or as 'the fourth branch of government', or even the 'Fifth Estate',[30] are less than persuasive.

---

[29] These various trends are discussed in Stefano Marzano *et al.* (eds), *New Nomads: An Exploration of Wearable Electronics by Philips* (Rotterdam, 2001); Alex Pentland, *Honest Signals: How They Shape Our World* (Cambridge, MA, 2008). For a striking experimental view, using machine vision footage, of how electronic sensors and robots view the world, see http://vimeo.com/36239715, accessed 22 October 2012.

[30] Hannah Arendt, 'Lying in Politics: Reflections on the Pentagon Papers', in *Crises of the Republic* (New York, 1972), p. 45; W. H. Dutton, 'The Fifth Estate Emerging through the Network of Networks', *Prometheus* 27(1) (2009): 1–15.

Their sense of the political geography of media is downright misleading. Communicative abundance dissolves divisions between 'the media' and other institutions. All spheres of life, from the most intimate everyday milieux through to large-scale global organisations, operate *within* heavily mediated settings in which the meaning of messages is constantly changing and is often at odds with the intentions of their creators.[31] To say this is not to indulge contemporary talk of 'the media', which is much too abstract and all too loose; in matters of media everything matters, certainly, but not everything connects simply or is distributed in complex ways that can be figured out easily.

The complex dynamics of contemporary forms of connectivity is a strong reason why disciplinary divisions between political science and communications and other scholarly fields need to be bridged. It is also why democracy and media must be analysed simultaneously, and in new ways, in part by leaving behind worn-out concepts and perspectives that we have inherited from the era of print culture, radio, television and Hollywood cinema. The following pages show, for instance, why talk of 'the informed citizen' has become an unhelpful cliché. Engaged citizens whose heads are stuffed with unlimited quantities of 'information' about a 'reality' that they are on top of: that is an utterly implausible and – yes – anti-democratic ideal that dates from the late nineteenth century. Favoured originally by the champions of a restricted educated franchise, and by interests who rejected partisan politics grounded in the vagaries and injustices of everyday social life, the ideal of the 'informed citizen' was elitist. It remains an intellectualist ideal, unsuited to the age of communicative abundance, which needs 'wise citizens' who know that they do not know everything, or so this book argues. It proposes as well the need to set aside once fashionable presumptions, popular among intellectuals, for instance, that the decline of print culture and the advent of electronic media has been an unmitigated disaster; or the prejudices that all television is children's television; or that the only likeable thing about television is its fleetingness; or that televisions are dream machines that remove citizens, tragically, far from the reality of what is actually happening in the world;[32] or that television-led mass media transform 'the public' into

---

[31] John Thompson, *The Media and Modernity: A Social Theory of the Media* (Cambridge, 1995), pp. 34–41.

[32] Pierre Bourdieu, *On Television* (New York, 1996).

an apathetic blob, 'a black hole into which the political efforts of politicians, advocates of causes, the media, and the schools disappear with hardly a trace'.[33] This book casts doubt on such presumptions, which draw silently upon the older, wider prejudice that 'modern' broadcasting systems breed listless people who live off daily doses of unreality. It is no longer (if it ever was) accurate to say, as the famous American philosopher John Dewey once said, that we 'live exposed to the greatest flood of mass suggestion that any people has ever experienced'. The arts of creating, manipulating and controlling public opinion through media still pose serious problems for democracy. But the warnings issued during the early years of mass broadcasting, during the 1920s and 1930s, need to be fundamentally rethought. It is no longer straightforwardly the case, as Edward Bernays, the godfather of propaganda, put it, that 'propaganda is the executive arm of the invisible government'; or that 'propaganda is to a democracy what violence is to a dictatorship'; or that if 'the people' want to be 'free of chains of iron' and in the name of democracy refuse blindly to 'love, honor, and obey' leaders, then the people must accept the 'chains of silver' produced by organised seduction and propaganda, what Adorno and Horkheimer later called the 'culture industry'.[34]

---

[33] Murray Edelman, *Constructing the Political Spectacle* (Chicago and London, 1988), p. 8.

[34] John Dewey, 'The United States, Incorporated', in *The Later Works, 1925–1953* (Carbondale, IL, 2008), vol. 5, p. 61; Edward L. Bernays, *Propaganda* (New York, 1928), p. 48; Harold D. Laswell, *Propaganda Technique in the World War* (London, 1927), p. 227; Jacques Ellul, *Propaganda: The Formation of Men's Attitudes* (New York, 1965), p. 132: 'Governmental propaganda suggests that public opinion demand this or that decision; it provokes the will of a people, who spontaneously would say nothing. But, once evoked, formed, and crystallized on a point, that will becomes the peoples' will; and whereas the government really acts on its own, it gives the impression of obeying public opinion – after first having built that public opinion. The point is to make the masses demand of the government what the government has already decided to do'; Theodor Adorno and Max Horkheimer, 'The Culture Industry: Enlightenment as Mass Deception', in *Dialectic of Enlightenment* (New York, 1972). Bertrand Russell ('China's Entanglements', in *Uncertain Paths to Freedom: Russia and China, 1919–22* (London and New York [1922] 2000), p. 360) summed up the old view of propaganda thus: 'It is much easier than it used to be to spread misinformation, and, owing to democracy, the spread of misinformation is more important than in former times to the holders of power. Hence the increase in circulation of newspapers.'

So here is the rub: just as in the sixteenth century, when the production of printed books and the efforts to read codex type required a fundamental shift of perspective, so today, in the emergent world of communicative abundance, a whole new mental effort is required to make sense of how democracies in various regions of the world are being shaped and re-shaped by the new tools and rhetoric of communication – and why our very thinking about democracy must also change.

But how should we proceed? Which are the key trends that we need to note, to interpret, to internalise in our thinking about democracy in the age of communicative abundance? A handful of trends seem pivotal. They cry out for careful analysis with a strong sense of its own historicity.

Democratisation of information

Let us begin with the most obvious political effect of communicative abundance: the democratisation of information. Thanks to cheap and easy methods of digital reproduction, we live in times of new information banks and what has been called information spreading, a sudden marked widening of access to published materials previously unavailable to publics, or formerly available only to restricted circles of users. The democratisation process involves the dismantling of information privileges formerly available only on a restricted basis to elites. It operates simultaneously on three intersecting planes.

One flank involves users gaining access from a distance to materials that were once available only within a restricted geographical radius, or only to users prepared to travel great distances and to foot the costs of living locally for a time, in order to make use of the otherwise inaccessible materials. Symbolised by the online editions of the *New York Times*, *The Hindu*, *El País* and *Der Spiegel*, democratisation in this sense refers to a dramatic reduction of the tyranny of distance, the radical widening of spatial horizons, a dramatic expansion of the catchment area of possible users of published materials. It is practically reinforced by a second sense of information democratisation: a great expansion in the numbers of potential users of materials, so that anyone with a computer and Web access, perhaps using tools such as Kindles, Nooks, iPads, or whatever tools succeed them, can now gain access to materials simply at the click of a mouse. The online music search engine Grooveshark and Piratebay.org, a Swedish website that hosts torrent files, is representative of this sense of democratisation, which means the enhanced availability of materials to people, often at zero cost, on a common access basis instead of a privileged, private right basis. Then there is a third and perhaps most consequential sense of the democratisation of information: the process of assembling scattered and disparate materials that were never previously available, formatting them as new data sets that are then made publicly available to users through entirely new pathways. Well-known examples include the multi-million entry encyclopaedia Wikipedia; the Computer History Museum (located in Mountain View, California); YouTube, whose users uploaded at least 35 hours of video footage per minute in 2010; the most popular Farsi-language website balatarin.com (a crowd-sourced platform that enables registered users to post and rank their favourite articles); and theeuropeanlibrary.org, which is a consortium of libraries of the nearly fifty member states in the Council of Europe, accessed through a single search engine, in three dozen languages.

Do these instances of democratised information have a wider historical significance? They do, but not because they signal the replacement of old-fashioned modern 'narrative' by new computer-age 'databases', as some scholars have proposed.[35] True, the new databases are not normally arranged as intelligible narratives. They do not tell stories structured by a beginning and an end. They are, indeed, disparate collections of 'information', multimedia materials arranged so that within the collection each item tends to have the same significance as all the others. Yet it does not follow that 'database and narrative are natural enemies'. Just the opposite: exactly because the new information sources are not presented as moral sermons, they are more amenable to being used as the 'raw material' of chosen narratives by publics that enjoy access to them. It is, therefore, unsurprising that the contemporary use of digital networks to spread all kinds of informative material to ever wider publics has politically enlivening effects. The democratisation of information serves as power steering for hungry minds previously handicapped by inefficient communication. Some observers

---

[35] Lev Manovich, *The Language of New Media* (Cambridge, MA, 2001), p. 225: 'database and narrative are natural enemies. Competing for the same territory of human culture, each claims an exclusive right.'

even hail the advent of times in which citizens regularly 'stand on the shoulders of a lot more giants at the same time'.[36] Such claims invite comparisons with the Reformation in Europe, which was triggered in part by the conviction of dissident Christian believers that access to printed copies of the Bible could be widened, that there were no spiritual or Earthly reasons why reading its pages should be restricted to a select few who were proficient in Latin, and that those who could read or had ears to hear were entitled to join reading groups and to savour the pleasures of pondering and disputing printed sermons, spiritual autobiographies and ethical guides to life in all its stages and forms.[37] Such comparisons are probably overdrawn, but there can be little doubt that when measured in terms of equal and easy accessibility to materials whose availability was formerly restricted, communicative abundance opens gates and tears down fences separating producers and users of information, some of which is highly specialised, so that new and vitally important information banks become accessible to many more users, often at great distances, more or less at the same time, at zero or low cost.

The trend is for the moment especially powerful in digitally reproduced collections of rare or hard to obtain materials. Some developments affect quite particular user groups. Each year, for instance, the electronic collection known as Romantic Circles distributes around 3.5 million pages of material to users living in more than 160 countries. Art historians now have ready access to the Digital Michelangelo Project, which aims to make available to researchers high-quality laser copies of the artist's three-dimensional works. Scholars and members of the general public from around the world have access to collections such as the East London Theatre Archive of many thousands of theatre programmes, the Catalogue of Digitised Medieval Manuscripts and the Prehistoric Stones of Greece Project. Then there are databanks that, potentially, have wide public appeal because they affect collective memories. Examples include an initiative called American Memory, sponsored by the Library of Congress, which aims digitally to preserve sound

---

[36] William Calvin, 'The Shoulders of Giants', in John Brockman (ed.), *How is the Internet Changing the Way You Think?* (New York, 2011), pp. 66–9.
[37] See Andrew Cambers, *Godly Reading: Print, Manuscript and Puritanism in England, 1580–1720* (Cambridge and New York, 2011).

recordings, maps, prints and images that form part of the history of the United States. Harvard University Library is planning to digitise its vast collection of Ukrainian-language material, the world's largest, much of it otherwise destroyed or lost in Ukraine during a twentieth century of horrific violence. Other examples include the Holocaust Collection of audio clips, maps, texts, photographs and images of artefacts; and the databases built by citizen networks such as the Association for the Recovery of Historical memory in Spain. All these exemplify the importance of democratised information in combating the twin political dangers of amnesia and confabulation. By preserving details of past traumas, publicly accessible information banks keep alive the politics of memory, in effect extending votes to a constituency that is normally neglected: the dead.

Equally impressive are the 'born digital' collections that are being formed to combat the possible permanent loss of certain materials circulated through the Web itself. Its birth and growth has been synonymous with the higgledy-piggledy proliferation of websites, many of which are ephemeral, structured by different and incompatible metadata and often resistant to search engines – hence, prone to easy disappearance into the thin air of what some still call cyberspace. In the United States, where government agencies were using email from the mid-1980s, available evidence suggests that for the following two decades most White House correspondence has been lost (on average 6 million email messages were generated annually by the two Clinton administrations alone). The disappearance of electronic data from lower levels of government, from non-governmental organisations (NGOs) such as universities and in general from private users of various parts of the Web, has been even more extreme. Alarm bells have rung about the dangers of obliterating memories from civil society and government; and, despite shortages of money and technical and legal difficulties, plans for storing and saving digital material are flourishing, along with initiatives such as the Arthur and Elizabeth Schlesinger Library's 'Capturing Women's Voices', a collection of postings by women from a wide range of blogs.[38]

---

[38] The background is summarised in Robert Darnton, 'The Future of Libraries', in *The Case For Books: Past, Present, and Future* (New York, 2009), pp. 50–3.

Google

The contemporary democratisation of digital information triggers bitter disputations. Complex and politically difficult issues to do with copyright ownership, and whether, or to what extent, it is legitimate to commercialise information, are fiercely contested. Consider the stalled business venture known as the Google Book Search. The world's boldest attempt (so far) to produce a giant online library of books, much bolder than anything conceived since the ancient library of Alexandria, the venture involved digital scanning many millions of books, to be made publicly available online, either free of charge or via annual subscriptions to the database. Controversial details of the future for-profit mega-library were revealed and amended during several rounds (2005–2011) of legal challenge initiated by a group of authors, publishers and governments, who insisted that copyright laws would be violated by Google's plans to digitise books from research libraries and display snippets of these books online. Critics railed against the hunger for advertising revenues and not-so-disguised profit motives of Google; accused of monopoly practices geared to cornering the online book market, the company was portrayed as hostile to the long-standing not-for-profit principle of libraries committed to the preservation and diffusion of knowledge for the use and enjoyment of reading publics.

Behind this objection stood the understandably embittered realisation of a lost opportunity that first arose in the early 1990s: the potential that had existed at the time for developing a genuinely open-access, public service library, a super-library modelled on the British Library or Library of Congress or Bibliothèque nationale and funded, for instance, by a consortium of government agencies and networks of philanthropic organisations dedicated to serving the principle carved on the entrance stone of the Boston Public Library: 'Free to All'. There were other objections to the Google scheme. Some critics underscored the loss of control by authors of copyright and the royalties to which they are entitled. Others criticised the failure of Google's proposed governing arrangements to extend a voice for either libraries or members of the general reading public. Still others pointed out that Google, through its use of secret algorithmic relevance rankings, could easily abuse the rights to privacy of individual readers; or they worried that just as 80 per cent of silent films and most radio programmes have permanently disappeared, all texts 'born digital' depend upon hardware and software systems that are vulnerable to the forces of built-in obsolescence.

These and other complaints made their mark in a proposed final legal settlement (October 2008) that saw Google reiterate its mission statement 'to organize the world's information and make it universally accessible and useful'.[39] The lengthy class-action settlement was supposed to confirm Google's right to create and sell access to a digital database comprising many millions of books currently housed within American libraries – primarily out-of-print and copyrighted books. The scope of the proposed settlement was broad. The class-action deal covered the entire category of authors and publishers in the United States (and Canada, the United Kingdom and Australia as well). It also contained a most-favoured-nation clause designed to prevent any potential future competitor of Google from winning better terms for authors and publishers. The deal was thus in effect supposed to be exclusive; even though in-copyright and in-print books were excluded unless their authors choose to make them available for scanning, the deal was to lock all American publishers, authors and readers into a complex four-tiered subscription system. Books already in the public domain, for instance, Adam Smith's *Wealth of Nations*, Thomas Paine's *Common Sense* and Antoine Laurent Lavoisier's *Essays Physical and Chemical* (books all published in the year 1776), would have been available free of charge to online readers, who could also download and print off a copy for their own personal use. Organisations such as universities and private research institutes meanwhile would have been required to pay an 'institutional licence'. Public libraries which paid a 'public access licence' would have gained access to the giant databank, made freely available to library users at a single computer terminal. Individuals who took out a 'consumer licence' were being offered the chance of reading and printing off books from the database, with the added opportunity to explore and analyse books in depth, either through simple word searches or more complex methods of text mining. Access arrangements were to be provided for readers with disabilities. The settlement would have created a body called the Book Rights Registry. Its proposed remit was to represent the overall concerns and

---

[39] The 134-page text of the proposed settlement and the fifteen legal appendices are available at: http://thepublicindex.org/docs/amended_settlement/opinion.pdf, accessed 19 June 2013.

interests of copyright holders and to disburse the revenues generated (37 per cent to Google; 63 per cent to copyright holders). Individual readers among the general public and participating organisations such as libraries would not have enjoyed a right of representation.

The proposed landmark legal settlement was rejected (by the US District Court for the South District of New York, in March 2011[40]) as not conforming to 'fair, adequate and reasonable' standards. The finding pointed to inadequate representation of the rights of copyright owners and authors to grant or refuse their consent; it also underscored concerns that Google would develop 'a *de facto* monopoly' over unclaimed titles (so-called 'orphan works', whose copyright holders are unknown or cannot be found) and online book searches. The court's decision left the door open to a new settlement agreement, so flinging the contending parties into an unexpected state of suspended animation. Only one outcome seemed virtually guaranteed: the world of books, many of them previously inaccessible, will eventually be brought within close reach of citizens who enjoy online access. At the time of the court's decision, Google had digitised less than a fraction of the 550 million books currently housed in American research libraries. That left scope for new proposals to supplement and go beyond the Google scheme. Plans are afoot to develop a 'digital public library of America' that includes the Library of Congress; the national libraries of Norway and the Netherlands are actively digitising their entire collections of books, newspapers, photographs and radio and television programmes; and Google itself has negotiated 'co-habitation' arrangements with several European national libraries.

It is easy to imagine the lateral replication and global conjoining of such cross-border schemes. If that came to pass, then the lattice network universe of books would be brought to many hundreds of millions of people living at various points on Earth by way of participating libraries. It might be thought that there is nothing much that is new in this vision. From the time of Gutenberg, the objection might run, books never knew borders. Books were often compared with bees, carrying the pollen of ideas and sentiments from one reader to another, across vast distances; or

[40] *Authors Guild et al.* v. *Google Inc.*, United States District Court, South District of New York, Opinion 05 Civ. 8136 (DC), 22 March 2011, available at: www.scribd.com/doc/51331062/Google-Settlement-Rejection-Filing, accessed 15 September 2011.

(in a common nineteenth-century refrain) likened to compasses and tele-
scopes, sextants, charts and lighthouses vital for helping humans to
navigate the confusing and dangerous seas of the world. Houses without
books were said to be like rooms without windows. Books were seen as
not being bound by linguistic and national differences; authors thought
of themselves as bound to other authors by invisible threads, as contributors to an international republic of letters; publishers struck deals with
booksellers in different countries; and translators made texts come alive
for readers unfamiliar with their original language of publication. All that
is true, but early twenty-first century efforts to leverage and popularise
digital books uniquely belong to the age of communicative abundance. In
support of the worldliness of books, these early experiments harbour an
unprecedented vision: the same book (or newspaper or radio and television programme copy) will be available on an open-access basis simultaneously, say, to readers and audiences in the richest cities and poorest
townships of South Africa, to students at universities in Hong Kong, Tel
Aviv, Chicago and Montevideo, and to bookish types and lovers of pulp
fiction in places otherwise as different as the outback towns of Australia,
the villages of India and Pakistan and the nested high-rise apartment
complexes of Bangkok and Jakarta.

The new publicity

Let us return to the political effects of the unfinished communications
revolution, for there is a second salient trend, one so far mentioned only
in passing: communicative abundance stirs up disputes among citizens
and their representatives about the definition and ethical and political
significance of the public–private division. Publicity is now directed at all
things personal; the realm that used to be called 'private' becomes publicly contested; and backlashes in defence of the 'private' develop. Under
conditions of communicative abundance, privacy battles are constantly
fought, lost and won. Awash in vast oceans of circulating information
that is portable and easily reproduced, individuals daily practise the art of
selectively disclosing and concealing details of their private selves; anxiety
about privacy is commonplace; decisions about whether and to whom
they give out their 'coordinates' remain unresolved.[41]

---

[41] Christena Nippert-Eng, *Islands of Privacy: Selective Concealment and Disclosure
in Everyday Life* (Chicago and London, 2010).

Whatever is thought of the disadvantages of the whole process, the rough-riding or 'outing' of private life ensures not only that the public–private boundary is the source of constant legal, political and ethical disputes. Controversies about the private have a long-term positive effect: they teach citizens that the personal is political, that the realm of the private, once hidden away from the eyes and ears of others, but still said by many to be necessary for getting risky and dodgy things done in life, is embedded in fields of power in which rogues take refuge and injustices result. Gone are the days when privacy could be regarded as 'natural', as a given bedrock or substratum of taken-for-granted experiences and meanings. More than a generation ago, the Moravian philosopher Edmund Husserl thought in that way about the 'world of everyday life' (*Lebenswelt*). He proposed that daily interactions among people are typically habitual. Everyday life has a definite '*a priori*' quality. It is social interaction guided by acts of *empathy* among people who believe and expect others to behave more or less like themselves. This inter-subjectivity is structured by unquestioned presumptions of mutual familiarity. Actors suppose a 'natural attitude' to themselves and to the world about them; they interact on a bedrock of taken-for-granted beliefs that their own way of seeing and doing things is 'naturally' shared by others.[42]

Whatever its level of former plausibility, this way of thinking about the everyday world is now obsolete. Those who still think in terms of everyday life as a barrier against the outside world, perhaps even as a safe and secluded haven of freedom in a world dominated by large-scale, powerful institutions, are out of touch. The reality is that everyday life is no longer a substratum of taken-for-granted things and people. In the age of communicative abundance, for instance, users of the Internet find their personal data is the engine fuel of a booming Web-based market economy; traditional methods of matching advertising to the content of people's interests is rapidly giving way to a world structured by digital 'cookies', small pieces of software installed on personal computers that function as unique identifiers of what users are looking at, and can store the tracked information, so building up a picture of the

---

[42] Edmund Husserl, *The Crisis of European Sciences and Transcendental Phenomenology*, trans. D. Carr (Evanston, IL, [1936] 1970). Compare the line of analysis of contemporary trends by Phil Agre and Marc Rotenberg (eds), *Technology and Privacy: The New Landscape* (Boston, MA, 1997), especially http://polaris.gseis.ucla.edu/pagre/landscape.html, accessed 16 October 2011.

demographics and interests of users that are of high market value to companies such as Facebook and Google, and to their advertising clients. The 'de-siloing' (as they say) of personal data allows advertisers to track users with precision; a class-action lawsuit settled out of court by Facebook revealed that even the 'likes' posted by its users can be deployed as 'sponsored stories' (advertisements) for marketing purposes.[43] Such tactics are part of a deepening trend in which no private matter or intimate topic is left unmediated, that is, cordoned off from media coverage. The more 'private' experiences are, the more 'publicity' they seem to get, especially when what is at stake are matters of taste and consumption, sex and violence, birth and death, personal hopes, fears, skulduggery and tragedy. It is as if we have entered a twenty-first century version of the court of Louis XVI, a world where the waking (*le lever*) as well as the going to bed (*le coucher*) and other intimate details of the king were regarded as 'public' events that induced a sense of wondrous astonishment among all who witnessed them (Asian court societies, such as that of imperial Japan, whose monarchy is a modern European import, also defined the public realm as the courtly household of the ruler, whose 'private' world, as we would see it, was deemed worthy of display to intrigued and sometimes admiring others[44]).

The comparison of our times with the age of Louis XVI is far-fetched, of course; but there is little doubt that in today's media-saturated societies private life is becoming ever less private. Government agencies create systems of online content filtering; install 'black box' surveillance devices within Internet traffic; build up data mountains and engage in large-scale data-mining of the lives of citizens; and track individuals' exact location, moment to moment, using pioneer techniques known as trilateralisation. Digital identities of individuals are meanwhile mined and tracked by companies. Personal data is big business. Techniques of 'data capture' develop traction. We live in a surveillance economy, in which companies known as data brokers, also called information

---

[43] See Somini Sengupta, 'On Facebook, "Likes" Become Ads', available at: www.nytimes.com/2012/06/01/technology/so-much-for-sharing-his-like.html?_r=0, accessed 3 November 2012; and Dan Levine, 'Facebook "Sponsored Stories" Class Action Settled', available at: www.huffingtonpost.com/2012/05/22/facebook-sponsored-stories-class-action-settlement_n_1537182.html, accessed 20 October 2012.

[44] T. Fujitani, *Splendid Monarchy: Power and Pageantry in Modern Japan* (Berkeley, CA and London, 1996).

re-sellers, gather and then market to other companies, including advertisers, hundreds or thousands of details about the consumption patterns, racial or ethnic identity, health concerns, social networks and
financial arrangements of most individuals who go online. Meanwhile,
cheap and user-friendly methods of reproduction and access to portable
networked tools of communication ensure that we live in the age of
hyper-coverage. Everything that happens in the fields of power stretching from the bedroom and bathroom to the boardroom to the battlefield
seems to be up for media grabs. With the flick of a switch or the click of a
camera button, the world of the private is suddenly public. Unmediated
privacy has become a thing of the past.

These are times in which the private lives of celebrities – their romances, parties, health, quarrels and divorces – are the interest and fantasy
objects of millions of people. There is, thanks to genres such as Twitter,
television talk shows and talkback radio, an endless procession of
'ordinary people' talking publicly about what privately turns them on,
or off. We live in times when millions of people feel free to talk publicly
about their private fears, fantasies, hopes and expectations, and to act
as if they are celebrities by displaying details of their intimate selves on
Facebook. We live in an age when things done in 'private' are big public
stories. It is the era in which, say, so-called reality TV cuts from a
scheduled afternoon programme to an armed and angry man; holding
a hostage, he turns his shotgun on himself, or fires at the police, live,
courtesy of a news helicopter or outside broadcasting unit. There are
moments when citizens themselves take things into their own hands, as
when a woman spits racist comments to other passengers on a packed
London tram, the incident is filmed and posted online, then after spark-
ing a Twitter trend goes viral, attracting 10 million viewers within a
week. These are times in which things that were once kept quiet, for
instance, the abuse of children by priests of the Roman Catholic
Church, are publicly exposed by newspapers and other media, with
the help of the abused, who manage to unearth details of their molesters,
sometimes quite by accident, thanks to the new tools of communication.
And we live in an age when privately shot video footage proves that
soldiers in war zones fired on their own side, or tortured prisoners,
robbed innocent civilians of their lives, raped women and terrorised
children.

The culture and practices of communicative abundance cut deeply
into everyday life in other ways. Nurtured by aggressive and prying

styles of journalism, and by easy-to-use portable media tools, communicative abundance destroys the early modern, originally European, supposition that property ownership, market conditions, household life, the emotions and biological events like birth and death are givens, or God-given. All these dimensions of life lose their 'naturalness'. Their contingency comes to the fore; they become potentially the subjects of public questioning and political action. For the same reason, communicative abundance cuts to shreds the older, originally Greek, presumption that democratic public life requires pre-political foundations, the tight-lipped privacy (literally, as the Greeks thought of it, the idiocy) that marks the *oikos*, the realm of household and market life in which life's basic needs are produced, distributed and consumed. In the age of media saturation, the privacy of the realm of the so-called private market economy disappears. The injustices and inequalities it harbours are no longer seen as necessary or inevitable, as being nobody else's business.

Just as the democratisation of information stirs up public controversies, so the de-privatisation and democratisation of the private power of daily life is both a complicated and heavily contested process. It disturbs lived certainties and presumptions that once seemed to be 'natural'. Yet while the supposed *a priori* qualities of everyday life are questioned and challenged, backlashes against the whole process develop. Political objections to the destruction of privacy flourish. Some observers argue, extending and upending an eighteenth-century simile, that communicative abundance robs citizens of their identities, that it resembles not a goddess of liberty, but a succubus, a female demon supposed to rape sleeping men and collect and pass on their sperm to other women. Switching similes, some denounce the mounting pressures to expose the secrets of the private as 'totalitarian'.[45] Other critics express things differently by denouncing the killer instincts of high-pressure media coverage of the private; famously spelled out by Janet Malcolm in *The Journalist and the Murderer* (1990), the accusation of media murder is

---

[45] See the comment of Jacques Derrida, in Jacques Derrida and Maurizio Ferraris, *A Taste for the Secret*, eds Giacomo Donis and David Webb (Malden, MA, 2001), p. 59: 'I have a taste for the secret, it clearly has to do with not-belonging; I have an impulse of fear or terror in the face of a political space, for example, a public space that makes no room for the secret. For me, the demand that everything be paraded in the public square and that there be no internal forum is a glaring sign of the totalitarianization of democracy.'

sometimes literally the leitmotif of media events, as when intense publicity tracked the death of Princess Diana following a high-speed car chase by journalists dubbed *paparazzi*.[46] Still other critics, sensing that a private life is vital for cultivating a sound sense of self, deliberately choose *not* to send tweets, *not* to purchase a smart phone or *not* to use email. Running in the same direction are calls for journalists to respect others' privacy, to raise their ethical standards and to exercise moral self-restraint as defined by established codes of conduct; challenges to spam and other types of invasive messages; data vault schemes (offered by companies such as Reputation.com) that allow individuals, for a price, to store and manage their private data; and legal cases that aim to prevent journalists from unlimited digging and fishing expeditions, as in the controversies surrounding the 2011/12 Murdoch press 'hacking' scandal and the major (unsuccessful) appeal brought before the European Court of Human Rights by Max Mosley against the British newspaper *News of the World* for its headline story that he had engaged in a 'sick Nazi orgy with five hookers'.[47]

---

[46] See, for example, Tina Brown, *The Diana Chronicles* (New York, 2007). The ethical dangers of media prying into the intimate lives of others are articulated by Janet Malcolm, *The Journalist and the Murderer* (New York, 1990), p. 1, where the professional journalist is seen as 'a kind of confidence man, preying on people's vanity, ignorance or loneliness, gaining their trust and betraying them without remorse. Like the credulous widow who wakes up one day to find the charming young man and all her savings gone, so the consenting subject of a piece of nonfiction learns – when the article or book appears – *his* hard lesson. Journalists justify their treachery in various ways according to their temperaments. The more pompous talk about freedom of speech and "the public's right to know"; the least talented talk about Art; the seemliest murmur about earning a living.'

[47] See the judgment of the European Court of Human Rights (Fourth Section), *Case of Mosley* v. *United Kingdom* (Application No. 48009/08; Strasbourg, 10 May 2011), paragraphs 131–2. Referring to Articles 8 and 10 of the European Convention on Human Rights, the court recognised the fundamental importance of situations where 'information at stake is of a private and intimate nature and there is no public interest in its dissemination'. It noted as well that 'the private lives of those in the public eye have become a highly lucrative commodity for certain sectors of the media'. The court nevertheless warned of the 'chilling effect' of pre-notification requirements and reaffirmed the principle, which it applied to this particular case, that the 'publication of news' about persons holding public office 'contributes to the variety of information available to the public'. It concluded with a reminder of the 'limited scope' for applying 'restrictions on the freedom of the press to publish material which contributes to debate on matters of general public interest'.

Some critics of de-privatisation meanwhile call publicly for the legal right of citizens to delete all present-day traces of their past 'private' communications with others. Digital communications technologies are seen as double-edged sharp swords: while individuals find themselves taking full advantage of communicative abundance, their lives are potentially harmed by digitisation, cheap storage, easy retrieval, global access and increasingly powerful software, which together conspire to increase the dangers of everlasting digital memory of our private lives, for instance, outdated information taken out of context, or compromising photos or messages accessed by employers or political foes. According to these champions of privacy, whereas the invention of writing enabled humans to remember across generations and vast swathes of time, communicative abundance does something altogether different: it potentially threatens our individual and collective capacity to forget things that need to be forgotten. The past becomes ever present, ready to be recalled at the flick of a switch or the click of a mouse. The trouble with digital systems, runs this line of criticism, is not only that they remember things that are sometimes better forgotten. It is that they hinder our ability to make sound decisions unencumbered by the past.[48] Meanwhile, acting on that point, a new generation of technically savvy privacy activists associated with networked bodies like Privacy International and the Open Rights Group has launched various public campaigns, for instance, in favour of stricter application of expiration dates and the development of privacy-enhancing technologies (so-called PETs), and against publicly available geospatial information about private dwellings, government initiatives to regulate access to strong cryptography, the corporate abuse of consumer databases and unregulated wiretapping and hacking powers of media organisations.[49]

All these developments centred on the 'right to privacy' confirm the point that communicative abundance exposes the contingency and deep ambiguity of the private–public distinction famously defended, philosophically speaking, as a sacrosanct First Principle by nineteenth-century liberal thinkers, such as the English political writer and parliamentarian John Stuart Mill and Germany's greatest philosopher of

---

[48] Viktor Mayer-Schönberger, *Delete: The Virtue of Forgetting in the Digital Age* (Princeton, 2011).
[49] Phil Agre and Marc Rotenberg (eds), *Technology and Privacy: The New Landscape* (Cambridge, MA, 1997).

liberty, Wilhelm von Humboldt.[50] Their insistence that there are clear distinctions to be drawn between 'the private' (conceived as the sphere of self-regarding actions) and 'the public' (the sphere of other-affecting actions) no longer rings true. In the age of communicative abundance, privacy, defined as the ability of individuals to control how much of themselves they reveal to others, their 'right to be let alone',[51] is seen as a complicated and publicly contestable right. Disputes about privacy and its 'invasion' have a long-term political significance. They underscore not only growing public awareness of the contingent and reversible character of the public–private distinction, which is to say that the distinction is no longer readily seen, as it was seen by many nineteenth- and twentieth-century European liberals, as either a binary opposite set in stone or as having a divine, mysterious validity. Thanks to the communications revolution of our time, the private–public distinction is regarded instead as a precious, but ambivalent, inheritance from former times.

The sphere of 'the private' is seen as a fragile 'temporary resting place'[52] that usefully serves as a refuge from interference by others, but that can function just as well as a refuge for scoundrels. Put differently, communicative abundance exposes deep ambiguities within the private–public distinction. It encourages individuals and groups within civil society to think more flexibly and contextually about the public and the private. Citizens are forced to become aware that their 'private' judgements about matters of public importance can be distinguished from both actually existing and desirable norms that are shared publicly. They learn as well to accept that there are times when embarrassing publicity given to 'private' actions – 'outing' – is entirely justified, for instance, when confronted with mendacious politicians, or with men who are duplicitous about their sexual preference or even leaders (as in Berlusconi's Italy) desperate to confirm that they are men.[53] Finally,

---

[50] John Stuart Mill, *On Liberty*, in *Essays on Politics and Society*, ed. J. M. Robson (Toronto and Buffalo, [1859] 1977), pp. 213–310; Wilhelm von Humboldt, 'Of the Individual Man and the Highest Ends of his Existence', in *The Limits of State Action* (London and New York, 1969), pp. 16–21.

[51] See the oft-cited Samuel D. Warren and Louis D. Brandeis, 'The Right to Privacy', *Harvard Law Review* 4(5) (15 December 1890): 193.

[52] Richard Rorty, 'Introduction: Pragmatism and Philosophy', in *Consequences of Pragmatism* (Minneapolis, MN, 1982), pp. xiii–xlvii.

[53] Confronted by magistrates with evidence of his involvement in an alleged prostitution ring, including wiretap evidence in which he boasted that he was only

citizens come to see that some things are definitely worth keeping private. They learn there are times when privacy – ensuring that certain matters are nobody else's business, that individuals and groups should not freely witness or comment upon their actions – is a precious inheritance. That is why they favour keeping certain areas of social and political life 'private', for instance, through efforts by journalists to protect the identity of their sources, and by means of public campaigns against governments' use of closed-circuit TV cameras and other forms of unauthorised surveillance.

The new muckraking

Aside from the democratisation of access to information and the politicisation of definitions of the private–public distinction, a third democratic trend is noteworthy: high-intensity efforts by citizens, journalists and monitory institutions to bombard power holders with 'publicity' and 'public exposure'. This third trend might be described as muckraking, a charming Americanism, an earthy neologism from the late nineteenth century, when it referred to a new style of journalism committed to the cause of publicly exposing corruption.[54] Writers like Lincoln Steffens, Ida Tarbell and Jacob Riis pictured themselves as public journalists writing for a public hungry for the facts of life in contemporary America. True to their name, they saw nothing sacrosanct about privacy. Publicity must be given to the private lives of the rich and powerful wherever and whenever 'the public interest' was at stake, they thought. To this end, they used new investigative techniques, such as the interview; under hails of protest (they were often condemned as busybodies and meddlers) they took advantage of the widening circulation of newspapers, magazines and books made possible by advertising, and by cheaper, mass methods of production and distribution, to write long

---

'prime minister in my spare time', as well as complaining that he needed to reduce the flow of women in the face of a 'terrible week' ahead in which he would be seeing leaders such as Pope Benedict, Nicolas Sarkozy, Angela Merkel and Gordon Brown, Prime Minister Silvio Berlusconi defended himself in a letter published in the Milan-based newspaper *Il Foglio*, whose editor served as minister in one of his former governments: 'I did nothing for which I must be ashamed . . . My private life is not a crime, my lifestyle may or may not please, it is personal, reserved and irreproachable' (17 September 2011).

[54] John Keane, *The Life and Death of Democracy* (London and New York, 2009), pp. 341–7.

and detailed articles, even entire books, to provide often sensational exposés of grimy governmental corruption and waste, business fraud and social deprivation.

Along these lines, the Pennsylvania-born journalist Nellie Bly (1864–1922) (Figure 1.5) did something daring but dangerous: for Joseph Pulitzer's newspaper the *New York World* she faked insanity to publish an undercover exposé of a woman's lunatic asylum. Other muckrakers openly challenged political bosses and corporate fat cats. They questioned industrial progress at any price. The muckrakers took on profiteering, deception, low standards of public health and safety. They complained about child labour, prostitution and alcohol. They called for the renewal of urban life – for an end to slums in cities. By around 1905, the muckrakers were a force to be reckoned with, as William Randolph Hearst demonstrated with his acquisition of *Cosmopolitan* magazine; its veteran reporter, David Graham Phillips, quickly launched a much-publicised series, called 'The Treason of the Senate', which poured scorn on senators, portraying them as pawns of industrialists and financiers, as corruptors of the principle that representatives should serve all of their constituents.

In the age of communicative abundance, the new muckrakers keep these themes alive, and they do so by putting their finger on a perennial problem for which democracy is a solution: the power of elites always thrives on secrecy, silence and invisibility. Gathering behind closed doors and deciding things in peace and private is their specialty. Little wonder then that in media-saturated societies, to put things paradoxically, unexpected 'leaks' and revelations become predictably commonplace. Everyday life is constantly ruptured by mediated 'events'.[55] They pose challenges to both the licit and the illicit. It is not just that stuff happens; media users ensure that shit happens. Muckraking becomes rife. There are moments when it even feels as if the whole world is run by rogues.

Muckraking has definite political effects on the standard institutions of representative democracy. It arguably deepens the already wide divisions that have opened up between parties, parliaments, politicians and the available means of communication. In recent decades, an accumulation of survey evidence suggests that citizens in many established democracies, although they strongly identify with democratic ideals,

[55] Alain Badiou, *Being and Event* (New York, 2005).

Figure 1.5 Nellie Bly, pseudonym of Elizabeth Cochrane Seaman, *c.* 1890, by H. J. Myers.

have grown more distrustful of politicians, doubtful about governing institutions and disillusioned with leaders in the public sector.[56] The patterns of public disaffection with official 'politics' have much to do with the practice of muckraking under conditions of communicative abundance. Politicians are sitting ducks. The limited media presence and media vulnerability of parliaments is striking. Despite efforts at

[56] Pippa Norris, *Democratic Deficit: Critical Citizens Revisited* (New York, 2011).

harnessing new digital media, parties have often been left flat-footed; they neither own nor control their media outlets and they have lost much of the astonishing energy displayed at the end of the nineteenth century by political parties, such as Germany's Social Democratic Party (SPD), which at the time was the greatest political party machine on the face of the Earth, in no small measure because it was a powerful champion of literacy and a leading publisher of books, pamphlets and newspapers in its own right.

The overall consequence is that under conditions of communicative abundance the core institutions of representative democracy become easy targets of rough-riding. Think for a moment about any current public controversy that attracts widespread attention: the news and commentaries it generates typically begin *outside* the formal machinery of representative democracy. The messages become memes quickly relayed by many power-scrutinising organisations, large, medium and small. In the world of communicative abundance, that kind of latticed or networked pattern of circulating controversial messages is typical, not exceptional. It produces constant feedback effects: unpredictably non-linear links between inputs and outputs. The trend renders obsolete once influential propositions in the field of political communications, especially the claim that democracies are principally defined by 'band-wagon effects', 'running with the pack' and 'spirals of silence' fuelled by fears of isolation among citizens.[57] The viral effects of public scrutiny have profound implications as well for the state-framed institutions of the old representative democracy, which find themselves outflanked by webs of mediated criticisms that often hit their target, sometimes from long distances, often by means of boomerang effects.

Consider a few samples of muckraking from a twelve-month media cycle (2008/9) within the world's democracies: a male legislator in the Florida state assembly is spotted watching online porn while fellow legislators are debating the subject of abortion. During a fiercely fought presidential election campaign in the United States one of the candidates (Barack Obama) switches to damage control mode after calling a female journalist 'sweetie'; he leaves her a voicemail apology: 'I am duly chastened'. In Japan, a seasoned Japanese politician (Masatoshi

---

[57] The influential thesis that public opinion is loneliness turned inside out was developed at length in the classic work by Elisabeth Noelle-Neumann, *The Spiral of Silence. Public Opinion: Our Social Skin* (Chicago and London, 1984).

Wakabayashi) is forced to resign from the Diet after being caught on camera during a budget debate pressing the voting button of a parliamentary colleague who had earlier left the chamber; the disgraced legislator, who had evidently supposed that he was sitting in the blind spot of cameras, later confessed to breaking the parliamentary rules: 'I wasn't thinking straight. It was an unforgivable act, and I'd like to apologise.'[58] While on a state visit to Chile, the President of the Czech Republic was caught on camera at a signing ceremony pocketing a golden ballpoint pen. In Finland, a senior politician was brought down with the help of a mobile telephone. His private text messages rebounded publicly, to reveal his duplicity and force the resignation of a government minister, as happened in April 2008, after *Hymy* magazine revealed that the Minister of Foreign Affairs Ilkka Kanerva had sent several hundred text messages, some of them raunchy, to an erotic dancer, who first sold the messages to the magazine, then failed to win a court injunction to stop their publication. He tried unsuccessfully to defend himself by saying: 'I would not present them in Sunday school, but they are not totally out of line either.' In the age of communicative abundance, Sony hand-held cameras are meanwhile used by off-air reporters and amateur users to file ongoing videos and blogs featuring politicians live, unplugged and unscripted. This is exactly that happened in recent years in France; according to video footage quickly uploaded onto LeMonde.fr, the Interior Minister (Brice Hortefeux) agreed to be photographed with a young Arab supporter and responded to an onlooker's joke about 'our little Arab' as a symbol of integration with heartfelt words: 'There always has to be one. When there's one, it's ok. It's when there are a lot of them that there are problems.'

It is not only elected politicians and formal political institutions that come in for stick. Oiled by communicative abundance, it seems as if no organisation or leader within the fields of government, business or social life is immune from political trouble. Our great grandparents would find the whole process astonishing in its democratic intensity. It certainly spells trouble for 'bad news' accounts of contemporary media, those that are convinced that democracy is going to the dogs because 'the media' is 'dumbing down' or 'entertaining to death' its citizens, for instance, by churning out materials of a poisonously low quality. Such

---

[58] Alex Martin, 'Wakabayashi exits Diet due to Illicit Votes', *Japan Times*, 3 April 2010.

pessimism contains a fundamental flaw: it misses the brawling, rowdy, rough-and-tumble qualities of communicative abundance, its propensity to stir up public troubles by exposing hidden discriminations and injustices.

But who or what drives all this muckraking? Certainly, they are not the effect of the medium alone, as believers in the magical powers of technology suppose. Individuals, groups, networks and whole organisations make muckraking happen. Yet buried within the infrastructures of communicative abundance are technical features that enable muckrakers to do their work of publicly scrutinising power. From the end of the 1960s, as we have seen, product and process innovations have happened in virtually every field of an increasingly commercialised media, thanks to technical factors, such as electronic memory, tighter channel spacing, new frequency allocation, direct satellite broadcasting, digital tuning and advanced compression techniques.[59] These technical factors have made a huge difference, but within the infrastructure of communicative abundance there is something special about its distributed networks. In contrast, say, to the centralised state-run broadcasting systems of the past, the spider's web linkages among many different nodes within a distributed network make them intrinsically more resistant to centralised control (Figure 1.6). The network functions according to the logic of packet switching: flows of information pass through many latticed points en route to their destination. Initially broken down into bytes of information that are then re-assembled at the point of delivery, these flows readily find their way through censorship barriers. If messages are blocked at any point within the latticed system, then the information is diverted automatically, re-routed in the direction of their intended destination.

This packet-switched and networked character of media-saturated societies ensures that messages go viral, even when they come up against organised resistance. Media-saturated societies are thus prone to contestability and dissonance. Some observers claim that a new understanding of power as a 'mutually shared weakness' is required in order to make sense of the impact of networks on the distribution of

---

[59] For treatments of the background, see Manuel Castells, *The Rise of the Network Society* (Oxford and Malden, MA, 1998), especially ch. 5; Manuel Castells, *The Internet Galaxy: Reflections on the Internet, Business, and Society* (Oxford and New York, 2003); Manuel Castells, *Networks of Outrage and Hope: Social Movements in the Internet Age* (Cambridge, 2012).

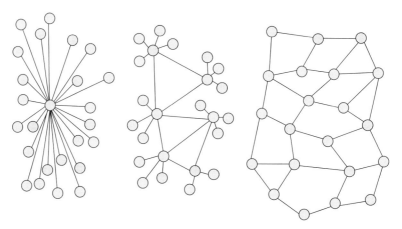

Figure 1.6 Centralised, decentralised and distributed networks, by Giovanni Navarria.

power within any given social order. The claim is that those who are in positions of power over others are subject constantly to unforeseen setbacks, reversals and revolts. Manipulation and bossing and bullying of the powerless become difficult; the powerless readily find the net-worked communicative means through which to take their revenge on the powerful. Unchecked power becomes harder to win, much easier to lose. Exemplified by online political initiatives such as the South Korean citizens' journalism site OhmyNews, UK Uncut, the Indian online tool I Paid A Bribe, the American campaigning network MoveOn.org Political Action, and SMS activism of the kind that contributed to the fall of Philippines President Joseph Estrada, the trend is summarised by the American scholar and activist Clay Shirky: when compared with the eras dominated by newspapers, the telegraph, radio and television, the age of communicative abundance, he says, is an era when 'group action just got easier'. Thanks to networked communications and easy-to-use tools, the 'expressive capability' of citizens is raised to unprecedented levels. 'As the communications landscape gets denser, more complex, and more participatory', he writes, 'the networked population is gain-ing greater access to information, more opportunities to engage in public speech, and an enhanced ability to undertake collective action.' Others speak of the rising predilection for 'self-organizing' and 'con-nective action' spurred on by the belief that 'life can be more participatory, more decentralized, less dependent on the traditional models of organization, either in the state or the big company'.[60] Still others experiment with the principle in the field of party politics, for instance, by trying to outflank mainstream political parties using the techniques of 'liquid democracy'. Beppe Grillo's 5 Star Movement in Italy and the Pirate Party in Germany are examples. So is Iceland's Best Party, which, in 2012, won enough votes to co-run Reykjavik City Council, partly on the promise that it would not honour any of its promises, that since all other political parties are secretly corrupt it would be openly corrupt.

Caution is required at this point because, to repeat, the changes catalysed by networked innovations are not the product of technical design and networked communicative abundance alone. It should go without saying, but it is often forgotten, that the changes that are going on have been driven by a variety of technical causes *and* human causers, including radical alterations to the ecology of public affairs reporting and commentary. As the revolution in favour of communicative abundance has taken root, the whole media infrastructure through which news of worldly events is produced and publicly circulated has become ever more complicated and cluttered. It is much more rough and tumble, to the point where professional news journalism is now just one of many different types of power-scrutinising institution. Within all democracies, many hundreds and thousands of monitory institutions now skilfully trade in the business of stirring up questions of power, often with political effect. Human rights reports, blogs, courts, networks of professional organisations and civic initiatives are just a few examples of the watchdog, guide-dog and barking-dog mechanisms that are fundamentally altering the spirit and dynamics of democracy.

These public monitors thrive within the new galaxy of communicative abundance. They do not simply give voice to the voiceless; they produce

---

[60] Giovanni Navarria, 'Citizens Go Online: Probing the Political Potential of the Internet Galaxy', PhD dissertation, University of Westminster, 2010; Clay Shirky, *Here Comes Everybody* (London, 2008); Clay Shirky, *Cognitive Surplus: Creativity and Generosity in a Connected Age* (London, 2010); Clay Shirky, 'The Political Power of Social Media', *Foreign Affairs* (January/ February 2011); Yochai Benkler, as quoted in Nicholas Kulish, 'As Scorn for Vote Grows, Protests Surge Around Globe', *New York Times*, 27 September 2011; W. Lance Bennett and Alexandra Segerberg, 'The Logic of Connective Action: Digital Media and the Personalization of Contentious Politics', *Information, Communication & Society* (2012): 1–30.

echo effects. An important case in point is the Spanish *Los Indignados* (15-M) movement, which used a wide range of new media tools to monitor and resist police brutality, welfare budget cuts, house evictions, corruption within the credit and banking system, unfair electoral laws, antiquated parliamentary procedures and the suppression of 'inconvenient' news by mainstream media.[61] The political work of such movements is strengthened by the growth of aggressive new forms of professional and citizens' journalism. The days of journalism proud of its commitment to the principles that 'comment is free, but facts are sacred' (that was the phrase coined in 1921 by the *Manchester Guardian*'s long-time editor C. P. Scott) and fact-based 'objectivity', ideals that were born of the age of representative democracy, ideals that were always the exception in practice, are fading. In place of the 'rituals of objectivity'[62] we see the rise of adversarial and 'gotcha' styles of commercial journalism, forms of writing that are driven by ratings, political affiliation, sales and hits. There is biting political satire, of the deadly kind popularised in India by STAR's weekly show *Poll Khol* using a comedian anchorman, an animated monkey, news clips and Bollywood soundtracks (the programme title is translated as 'open election', but is actually drawn from a popular Hindi metaphor which means 'revealing the hidden story'). All these criteria sit poorly with talk of 'fairness' (a criterion of good journalism famously championed by Hubert Beuve-Méry, the founder and first editor of *Le Monde*). We witness as well open challenges to professional 'embedded' journalism bound up with the spread of so-called citizen journalism and enclaves of self-redaction.[63] The forces of professional and citizen journalism often intersect, and when that happens (as at *The Guardian*) they are understandably proud of their contribution to the muckraking trend. They like to emphasise that they refuse to take no for an answer, that their job is to uncover things that were previously hidden, to report things as they are, to slam

---

[61] The best account is Ramón Andrés Feenstra, *Democracia monitorizada en la era de la nueva galaxia mediática. La propuesta de John Keane* (Barcelona, 2012).
[62] C. P. Scott, 'A Hundred Years', [1921], reprinted in *The Guardian*, 29 November 2002; Gaye Tuchman, 'Objectivity as Strategic Ritual: An Examination of Newsman's Notions of Objectivity', *American Journal of Sociology* 77(4) (January 1972): 660–79.
[63] John Hartley, 'Communicative Democracy in a Redactional Society: The Future of Journalism Studies', *Journalism: Theory, Practice & Criticism* 1(1) (2000): 39–47.

the foolish, to give liars and thieves a hard time. They are sure that the function of journalism is to produce neither pleasure nor harm nor 'objectivity' nor 'balance'. Its purpose, rather, is to point cameras at wounds, to find words to confront injustice, to let victims of power speak in their own voices. Sometimes they say journalism should be guided by killer instincts – even if that means that there must be victims. Such talk is sometimes simple self-justification and (as we shall soon see) we need to be more sceptical of the way many professional and citizen journalists like to see themselves as the midwives of 'truth'. But given this gutsy style of independent journalism there is little wonder that public objection to corruption and wrongdoing nowadays has become commonplace.

We shall soon see that the new age of communicative abundance is blighted by trends that contradict the basic democratic principle that all citizens are equally entitled to communicate their opinions, and periodically to give representatives a rough ride. Yet rough-riding happens – on a scale and with an intensity never before witnessed. Speaking figuratively, one could say that communicative abundance cuts like a knife into the power relations of government, business and the rest of civil society. In the era of media saturation there seems to be no end of scandals; and there are even times when so-called '-gate' scandals, like earthquakes, rumble beneath the feet of whole governments. The frequency and intensity of media-shaped '-gate' scandals are greatly feared by power wielders; and although scandals can have damaging effects on the spirit and institutions of democracy, they provide a sober reminder of a perennial problem facing any political system: that there are never shortages of organised efforts by the powerful to manipulate people beneath and around them.

That is why the political dirty business of dragging power from behind curtains of secrecy remains fundamentally important. Nobody should be seduced into thinking that media-saturated societies, with their latticed networks, multiple channels, tough-minded journalism and power-scrutinising institutions, are level playing fields in the democratic sense. Yet even though societies shaped by communicative abundance are not paradises of open communication, historical comparisons show just how distinctive is their permanent flux, their unending restlessness driven by complex media combinations of different interacting players and institutions, permanently heaving and straining, sometimes working together, at other times in contrarian ways. The powerful routinely strive to define and to determine who gets what, when and how; but the less powerful, taking advantage of communicative abundance, keep tabs on the powerful – sometimes with great drama and surprising success.

The consequence is that media-saturated societies are richly conflicted, political orders in which, contrary to some pessimists and purists, politics does not wither away. Nothing is ever settled, or straightforward. In striking contrast to galaxies of communication that were structured by the printing press, the telegraph, radio and television, media-saturated societies enable actors to cut through habit and prejudice and hierarchies of power much more easily. They stir up the sense that people can shape and re-shape their lives as equals; not surprisingly, they often bring commotion into the world. Media-saturated societies have a definite 'viral' quality about them. Power disputes are often bolts out of the blue; they follow unexpected pathways and reach surprising destinations that have unexpected outcomes.

The phone-hacking scandal that hit News Corporation in mid-2011 is a striking case in point: it began with investigative reporting by *The Guardian* newspaper, which revealed that the company's publication *News of the World* had hacked into the voicemail messages of a 13-year-old murder victim, Milly Dowler. Public indignation suddenly flared. The global company suffered reputational damage. In quick succession there followed several arrests of News Corporation executives; the closure of the *News of the World*, which had been in business for 168 years; parliamentary hearings; and a public apology by Rupert Murdoch, the company's chairman and chief executive. He was forced to watch the public embarrassment of his political friends and to witness the collapse of his plans to buy control of a multi-billion pound major satellite television provider, British Sky Broadcasting. Soon afterwards came recommendations to shake up the management of the firm by a major investor advisory organisation that criticised News Corporation's senior executives for their 'striking lack of stewardship and failure of independence' by a board unable to set a strong tone at the top about unethical business practices; and the public inquiry led by Lord Justice Leveson into the culture, practices and ethics of British media.[64]

---

[64] The materials gathered by the Leveson Inquiry are available at: www. levesoninquiry.org.uk; see also Michael J. de la Merced, 'Advisory Firm Urges Ouster of Murdoch and his Sons', *International Herald Tribune*, 12 October

Other examples of unexpected power disputes spring readily to mind. Groups using mobile phones, bulletin boards, news groups, wikis and blogs sometimes manage, against considerable odds, to heap embarrassing publicity on their opponents. Corporations are given stick (by well-organised, media-savvy groups such as Adbusters) about their services and products, their investment plans, how they treat their employees and the size of their impact upon the biosphere. Power-monitoring bodies such as Human Rights Watch, Avaaz.org, Global Witness and Amnesty International regularly do the same, usually with help from networks of supporters spread around the globe. There are initiatives such as the World Wide Web Consortium (known as W3C) that promote universal open access to digital networks. There are even bodies (such as the Democratic Audit network, the Global Accountability Project and Transparency International) that specialise in providing public assessments of the quality of existing power-scrutinising mechanisms and the degree to which they fairly represent citizens' interests. Politicians, parties and parliaments get much stick from dot.org muckrakers like California Watch and Mediapart (a Paris-based watchdog staffed by a number of veteran French newspaper and news agency journalists). And, at all levels, governments are grilled on a wide range of matters, from their human rights records, their energy production plans to the quality of the drinking water of their cities. Even their arms procurement policies – notoriously shrouded in secrecy – run into trouble, thanks to media-savvy citizens' initiatives guided by the spirit, and sometimes the letter, of the principle that in 'the absence of governmental checks and balances … the only effective restraint upon executive policy and power in the area of national defense and international affairs may lie in … an informed and critical public opinion which alone can … protect the values of democratic government'.[65]

WikiLeaks

These are times in which terrifying state violence directed at citizens is witnessed and, against tremendous odds, publicly confronted by

2011, p. 21; Tom Watson and Martin Hickman, *Dial M for Murdoch: News Corporation and the Corruption of Britain* (London, 2012).
[65] These are the words used by Justice Potter Stewart in the United States Supreme Court's famous opinion in *New York Times Co. v. United States* (1971), the so-called *Pentagon Papers* case.

Figure 1.7 Demonstration by the Space Hijackers against an arms fair in east London (September 2007).

citizen-uploaded videos, digital sit-ins, online 'hacktivist' collectives and media-savvy monitory organisations, such as the Syrian Observatory for Human Rights, Anonymous and Burma Watch International. There are small citizen groups, such as the Space Hijackers, which manage to win big publicity by acts of daring, for instance, driving a second-hand UN tank to Europe's largest arms fair in London's Docklands, ostensibly to test its 'roadworthiness', then to auction it to the highest market bidder, in the process offering prosthetic limbs for sale to arms dealers (Figure 1.7).

Then there are global headline-making initiatives that lunge non-violently at the heart of highly secretive, sovereign power. WikiLeaks is so far the most talked-about experiment in the arts of publicly probing secretive military power. Pundits at first described it as the novel defining story of our times, but the point is that its spirit and methods belong firmly and squarely to the age of communicative abundance. Engaged in a radical form of muckraking motivated by conscience and supported by a shadowy band of technically sophisticated activists led by a charismatic public figure, Julian Assange (Figure 1.8), WikiLeaks took full advantage of the defining qualities of communicative abundance: the

Figure 1.8 WikiLeaks founder and publisher, Julian Assange, London (February 2013).

easy-access multimedia integration and low-cost copying of information that is then whizzed around the world through digital networks. Posing as a *lumpen* outsider in the world of information, aiming to become a watchdog with a global brief, WikiLeaks sprang to fame by releasing video footage of an American helicopter gunship crew cursing and firing on unarmed civilians and journalists. It then sent shock waves throughout the civil societies and governments of many countries by releasing sprawls, hundreds of thousands of top-secret documents appertaining to the diplomatic and military strategies of the United States and its allies and enemies.

With the help of mainstream media, WikiLeaks produced pungent effects, in no small measure because of its mastery of the clever arts of 'cryptographic anonymity', military-grade encryption designed to protect both its sources and itself as a global publisher. For the first time on a global scale, WikiLeaks created a viable custom-made mailbox that enabled disgruntled muckrakers within any organisation to release classified data on a confidential basis, initially for storage in a camouflaged cloud of servers. WikiLeaks then pushed that bullet-proofed information into public circulation, as an act of radical transparency and 'truth'.

WikiLeaks was guided by a theory of hypocrisy and democracy. Its attempt to construct an 'intelligence agency of the people' supposed that individual employees within any organisation are motivated to act as whistleblowers not just because their identities are protected by encryption, but especially because their organisation suffers intolerable gaps between its publicly professed aims and its private *modus operandi*. Hypocrisy is the night soil of muckrakers, whose rakes in the Augean stables of government and business have a double effect: they multiply the amount of muck circulated under the noses of interested or astonished publics, whose own sense of living in muck is consequently sharpened. Muckraking in the style of the WikiLeaks platform has yet another source, which helps to explain why its attempted criminalisation and forcible closure is already spawning many similar offspring, such as BalkanLeaks, a Bulgarian-based initiative to publicise organised crime and political corruption in the region; and the International Consortium of Investigative Journalists, a global network campaigning to end the secrecy that protects capital assets held in offshore havens. Put simply, WikiLeaks feeds upon a contradiction deeply structured within the digital information systems of all large-scale complex organisations. States and business corporations and other organisations take advantage of the communications revolution of our time by going digital and staying digital. They do so to enhance their internal efficiency and external effectiveness, to improve their capacity for handling complex, difficult or unexpected situations, swiftly and flexibly. Contrary to Max Weber, the databanks and data-processing systems of these organisations are antithetical to red tape, stringent security rules and compartmentalised data sets, all of which have the effect of making these organisations slow and clumsy. So they opt for dynamic and time-sensitive data sharing across the boundaries of departments and whole organisations. Vast streams of classified material flow freely – which serves to boost the chances that leaks into the courts of public opinion will happen. If organisations then respond by tightening internal controls on their own information flows, a move that Julian Assange has described as the imposition of a 'secrecy tax', the chances are that these same organisations will both trigger their own 'cognitive decline', their reduced capacity to handle complex situations swiftly and effectively, as well as increase the likelihood of resistance to the secrecy tax by motivated employees who are convinced of the hypocrisy and injustice of the organisations which are unrepresentative of their views.[66]

Unelected representatives

The subject of representation brings us to a fourth trend that has significant implications for democracy in representative form: in the age of communicative abundance, unelected representatives multiply, sometimes to the point where their level of public support casts shadows over the legitimacy and viability of elected representation (politicians and parliaments) as the central organising principle of democracy. The phrase 'unelected representatives' refers to champions of public causes and values, public figures whose authority and power base are located outside the boundaries of electoral politics. It is, of course, an unfamiliar phrase. Taking us back in time (it seems) to the age of Thomas Carlyle and Ralph Waldo Emerson, and to contentions about the importance of great men and heroes,[67] it grates on democratic ears. Hence, it is important to understand carefully its meaning, and the ill-understood trend it describes.

Our ignorance of the past inevitably breeds misunderstandings of our present, so let us go back to the age when the grafting of the principle and practice of representation onto democracy irreversibly changed the original meaning of both.[68] Representation, once conceived by Hobbes and other political thinkers as simply equivalent to the actual or virtual authorisation of government, had to make room for equality, accountability and free elections. For its part, at least in theory, democracy had to find space for the process of delegation of decisions to others and, hence, open itself up to matters of public responsiveness and the public

---

[66] Julian Assange, 'The Non-linear Effects of Leaks on Unjust Systems of Governance', 31 December 2006, available at: http://web.archive.org/web/20071020051936/ http://iq.org/#Thenonlineareffectsofleaksonunjustsystemsofgovernance; cf. 'State and Terrorist Conspiracies', 10 November 2006, available at: http://cryptome.org/ 0002/ja-conspiracies.pdf, both accessed 18 January 2011.

[67] Thomas Carlyle, *On Heroes, Hero-Worship and The Heroic in History* (London, [1840] 1870); Ralph Waldo Emerson, *Representative Men: Seven Lectures* (Boston, MA, 1850).

[68] An extended account of the complex historical origins of representative democracy is found in John Keane, *The Life and Death of Democracy* (London and New York, 2009), Pt 2.

accountability of leaders. From roughly the last quarter of the eighteenth century, democratic representation came to mean a process of re-presenting the interests and views of electors who are absent from the chambers and forums where decisions are made. Representatives decide things on behalf of, and in the physical absence of, those who are affected.

But that was only one side of the complex, dynamic equation. For under conditions of democracy, or so many observers pointed out, those who are rendered absent from the making of decisions must periodically step forward and make their presence felt by raising their hands in public, or (in our times) by touching a screen or placing a cross on a ballot paper in private. Under democratic conditions, representation is a process of periodically rendering or making present what is absent; it is not simply (as Burke supposed) an act of delegation of judgements to the few trustees who make decisions on behalf of those whom they represent. Representation is, ideally, the avoidance of *misrepresentation*. By that is meant that representation is accountability, an ongoing tussle between representatives who make political judgements and the represented, the citizens who also make political judgements.

The upshot of this dialectic was that representative democracy became a distinctive form of government that simultaneously distinguished and linked together the source of political power – the people or *dēmos* – and the use made of political power by representatives who are periodically chastened by the people whose interests they are supposed to serve. The downside was that the election of representatives became a dynamic process subject to what can be called the disappointment principle.[69] Today, elections are still seen as a method of apportioning blame for poor political performance: a way of ensuring the rotation of leadership, guided by merit and humility, in the presence of electors equipped with the power to trip leaders up and throw them out of office if and when they fail, as often they do. Every election is as much a beginning as it is an ending. The whole point of elections is that they are a means of disciplining representatives who have disappointed their electors, who are then entitled to throw harsh words, and paper or electronic rocks, at them. If representatives were always virtuous,

---

[69] John Keane, 'A Productive Challenge: Unelected Representatives can Enrich Democracy', *WZB-Mitteilungen* 31 (March 2011): 14–16.

impartial, competent and responsive then elections would lose their purpose.

The disappointment principle coded into the principles and practice of representative democracy not only helps to explain why elected political representatives periodically come in for tough public criticism, or become scapegoats or targets of satire and sarcasm. The factor of disappointment helps to explain why, under conditions of communicative abundance, alternative forms of representation become attractive; and why unelected representatives attract great media attention and public support. Thomas Carlyle spotted that the fame of 'heroes' such as Shakespeare, Luther, Goethe and Napoleon was made possible by the modern printing press; he would be dumbfounded by the amplifying effects of communicative abundance. Media-saturated societies multiply the variety, scope and sophistication of publicity outlets hungry for 'stars'. An unsurprising consequence is the rapid growth and diffusion, well beyond the reaches of elected government, of famous individuals, groups and organisations who stand up for causes and carve out public constituencies that are often at odds with the words and deeds of established political parties, elected officials, parliaments and whole governments. Whatever may be thought of their particular brand of politics, or the merits of the particular issues for which they stand, unelected representatives alter the political geography and political dynamics of democracies. These respected public personalities with a difference add to the commotion of democratic politics – while often causing established representative mechanisms serious political headaches.

But who exactly are unelected representatives? What does the unfamiliar phrase mean? In the most elementary sense, unelected representatives are authoritative public figures who win public attention and respect through various forms of media coverage. Documentaries are made about their lives; interviews with them go viral; they have websites and they blog and tweet. Often extroverted characters, they sometimes seem to be everywhere, even though they usually have a strong sense of contract with the citizens who admire them, who see in themselves what they would like to become. These representatives have to be media savvy. They enjoy notoriety and they are good at its arts. They are famous, but they are not simply 'celebrities', a term which is too wide, too loose and too normatively burdened to capture their core quality of being unelected representatives of others' views. Unelected representatives are not mindless fame seekers who have climbed the ladders of renown. They are not 'million-horsepowered entities' (McLuhan), individuals well known for their 'well-knownness'.[70] And they are not in it for the money. They are not exaltations of super-ficiality; they do not thrive on smutty probes into their private lives; and they do not pander to celebrity bloggers, gossip columnists and tabloid *paparazzi*. The figure of the unelected representative is not what Germans call a *Hochstapler* (a 'high piler'), an impostor who brags and boasts a lot. Unelected representatives instead bear the marks of humility. Their feet are on the ground. They stand for something outside and beyond their particular niche. More exactly: as public representatives they simultaneously 'mirror' the tastes and views of their public admirers as well as fire their imaginations and sympathies by displaying leadership in matters of the wider public good, seen from their and others' point of view.

Unelected representatives have the effect of widening the horizons of the political, even though they are not chosen in the same way as parliamentary representatives, who are subject to formal periodic elections. It is true that there are times and places where unelected representatives decide (for a time) to reinvest their fame, to make a lateral move into formal parliamentary politics and a ministerial position. An example is Wangari Maathai (1940–2011), the first African woman to win the Nobel Peace Prize and the founder of the pan-African grass-roots Green Belt Movement.

Other figures do exactly the reverse, by pursuing public leadership roles after elected office.[71] Many examples spring to mind. Among them are the efforts of former German Chancellor Helmut Schmidt, who

---

[70] Marshall McLuhan, in *Explorations 3*, republished in *Marshall McLuhan Unbound 1* (Toronto, 2005); Daniel Boorstin, *The Image, Or, What Happened to the American Dream* (New York, 1962), p. 57. Treatments of the phenomenon of the celebrity include, Daniel Boorstin, *The Image: A Guide to Pseudo-Events in America* (New York, 1961; 1971); Joshua Gamson, *Claims To Fame: Celebrity in Contemporary America* (Berkeley, 1994); Nick Couldry, *The Place of Media Power: Pilgrims and Witnesses of the Media Age* (London, 2000); Chris Rojek, *Celebrity* (London, 2001); G. Turner, *Understanding Celebrity* (London, 2004); Chris Hedge, *Empire of Illusion: The End of Literacy and the Triumph of the Spectacle* (New York, 2009).

[71] John Keane, 'Life after Political Death: The Fate of Leaders after Leaving High Office', in John Kane, Haig Patapan and Paul 't Hart (eds), *Dispersed Leadership in Democracy: Foundations, Opportunities, Realities* (Oxford, 2009).

helped to found (in 1983) the InterAction Council, a group of over thirty former high office holders; Mikhail Gorbachev's and Nelson Mandela's running commentaries on world affairs; Al Gore's *An Inconvenient Truth* campaign; the Africa Progress Panel and peace negotiation efforts of former UN Secretary General Kofi Annan, for instance, during the violently disputed elections of 2007/8 in Kenya; and the multiple public activities of Jimmy Carter, whose self-reinvention as an advocate of human rights makes him the first ex-president of the United States to insist that the world is so shrinking that it needs new ways of doing politics in more negotiated and principled ways, nurtured by bodies like The Elders, which he helped to found in 2007.

It is hard to interpret the long-term viability and significance of these unelected representatives who once occupied high office (let alone what to say about those figures, like ex-president George W. Bush, whose first priority after leaving the executive was self-rehabilitation, using Facebook[72]). These public figures arguably demonstrate positively that the age is over when former elected leaders lapsed into mediocrity, or spent their time 'taking pills and dedicating libraries' (as Herbert Hoover put it), sometimes bathed in self-pity ('after the White House what is there to do but drink?', Franklin Pierce reportedly quipped). What is clear is that elections or governmental politics are not the normal destiny or career path of unelected representatives. Fascinating is the way they most often shun political parties, parliaments and government. They do not like to be seen as politicians. Paradoxically, that does not make them any less 'chosen' or legitimate in the eyes, hearts and minds of their followers. It often has the opposite effect.

Untainted by office, unelected representatives walk in the footsteps of Mahatma Gandhi: beyond the confines of government, they carve out constituencies and win over supporters who, as a consequence, are inspired to act differently, to strive to be better than they currently

---

[72] See at: www.facebook.com/georgewbush#!/georgewbush, accessed 7 June 2010. His page lists his location as 'Dallas, TX', his birthday as 'July 6, 1946' and he has 73,289 friends (more than the uncharitable might have imagined). A first status update read: 'Since leaving office, President Bush has remained active. He has visited 20 states and 8 countries; given over 65 speeches; launched the George W. Bush Presidential Center; participated in 4 policy conferences through The Bush Institute; finished the first draft of his memoir, "Decision Points"; and partnered with President Clinton to establish the Clinton Bush Haiti Fund. More on his activities in future posts.'

are. The upshot is that in their role as public representatives they often cross swords with elected authorities. They put the represented on trial as well: they challenge them to hold fast to their convictions and/or urge them to take a stand on an issue. And despite the fact that they are not mandated by periodic votes, unelected representatives most definitely have a strong sense of being on trial, above all by acknowledging their 'contractual' dependence upon those whom they represent. Their supporters and admirers are in effect their creators. That is why they have to handle their self-importance carefully: their fame requires them to be both different from their admirers and yet similar enough so that they are not aloof or threatening. Unelected representatives are in this sense not to be confused with 'oligarchs' or 'demagogues' or scheming demiurges such as Vladislav Surkov, the style architect of 'sovereign democracy' in contemporary Russia.[73] The grip of unelected representatives on popular opinion is much more tentative. Their fame can be thought of as the democratic descendant of aristocratic honour. It does not come cheaply. It has its price: since their reputation for integrity depends upon a strong media profile, unelected representatives can find, sometimes with surprising speed, that their private lives and public reputation are quickly ruined by the active withdrawal of the support of the represented. The old maxim, a favourite of Harry Truman when he was out of office, that money, craving for power and sex are three things that can ruin political leaders, applies with real force to unelected leaders. Unlike celebrities, who can thrive on bad press, they find scandals fatal, ruinous of their whole public identity. They know the meaning of the old maxim: reputations are hard won and easily lost.

Unelected representatives draw breath from communicative abundance, but by no means does this imply that they are 'second best' or 'inferior' or 'pseudo-representatives' when compared with their formally elected counterparts. Emerson noted how the printing press made it seem that some great men had been elected. 'As Sir Robert Peel and Mr. Webster vote, so Locke and Rousseau think for thousands', he wrote.[74] In the age of multimedia culture, unelected representatives similarly enjoy robust public reputations, and they exercise a form of 'soft' or 'persuasive' power over others, including their

---

[73] Peter Pomerantsev, 'Putin's Rasputin', *London Review of Books*, 20 October 2011.
[74] Emerson, *Representative Men*, in Porte (ed.), *Essays and Lectures*, p. 715.

opponents. They are listened to, admired, sometimes adored, often mimicked or followed; and to the extent that they are influential in these ways they may, and often do, present challenges to formally elected representatives, for instance, by confronting their claims or questioning their actions. So what is the basis of their unelected fame? How do they manage to produce political effects? To put things simply: what is the source of their popularity and how are they able to use it to stand apart from elected representatives, either to praise their work or to call their actions into question?

There are many different types of unelected representatives. Some draw their legitimacy from the fact that they are widely regarded as models of *public virtue*. Figures such as Martin Luther King Jr, Princess Diana and Aamir Khan (a Bollywood film star and television presenter known for spotlighting festering issues such as domestic violence and caste injustice) are seen to be 'good', or 'decent', or 'wise' or 'daring' people who bring honesty, fairness and other valuable things to the world. Their reputations are untarnished by allegations of corruption; although they are not presumed to be angels they are widely supposed to be living illustrations of alternative pathways, a challenge for people to aspire to greater moral heights, to inspire them to live differently. Other unelected representatives – Mother Teresa or Desmond Tutu – win legitimacy because of their *spiritual or religious commitments*. There are unelected representatives whose status is based instead on *merit*; they are former nobodies who become somebody because they are reckoned to have achieved great things. Amitabh Bhachan (India's screen star whose early reputation was built on playing the role of fighter against injustice), Colombian-born Shakira Mebarak and the Berliner Philharmoniker (the latter two are Goodwill Ambassadors of UNICEF) belong in this category of achievers. Still other figures are deemed to be representatives of *suffering, courage and survival* in this world (His Holiness the fourteenth Dalai Lama of Tibet is an example). There are other unelected representatives – in marked contrast to political party leaders and governments who 'fudge' issues – who draw their legitimacy from the fact that they have taken a principled stand on a particular issue, on which they campaign vigorously, in the process appealing for public support in the form of donations and subscriptions. Bodies like Amnesty International or initiatives such as the Live 8 benefit concerts are of this type: their legitimacy is mediated not by votes, but by means of *moral monetary contracts* that can be cancelled at any time by admiring supporters and subscribers who are equipped with the power to draw the conclusion that these ad hoc representatives are no longer representative or worthy of their financial support.

Whatever is thought of their stardom, unelected representatives play a vital democratic role in the age of communicative abundance. They certainly refute the old presumption, championed by Thomas Carlyle and Ralph Waldo Emerson, that unelected leaders serve to reinvent monarchical and aristocratic standards of proper behaviour and greatness, that, in effect, 'representative men' stand outside time and can be its master, re-binding the fractured polities of the modern world. This way of thinking about unelected leaders no longer makes sense; their dynamic effects are different. Unelected representatives can do good works for democracy, especially when politicians as representatives suffer a mounting credibility gap. They stretch the boundaries and meaning of political representation, especially by putting on-message parties, parliaments and government executives on their toes. Sometimes posthumously (Gandhi is a prime example), their figure draws public attention to the violation of public standards by governments, their policy failures, or their general lack of political imagination in handling so-called 'wicked' or 'devilish' problems that have no readily agreed upon definition, let alone straightforward solutions. Unelected representatives also force existing democracies to think twice, and more deeply, about what counts as good leadership. They serve as an important reminder that during the course of the past century the word leadership was excessively politicised, to the point where we have forgotten that the words *leader* and *leaderess*, from the time of their first usage in English, were routinely applied to those who coordinated such bodies as singing choirs, bands of dancers and musicians and religious congregations.

Unelected leaders can have profoundly transformative effects on the meaning of leadership itself. They serve not only as an important corrective to the undue dominance of state-centred definitions of leadership; and not only do they multiply and disperse different and conflicting criteria of representation that confront democracies with problems (such as whether unelected leaders can be held publicly accountable for their actions using means other than elections) that were unknown to the earliest champions and architects of representative democracy. Thanks to their efforts, leadership no longer means (as it meant ultimately in Max Weber's classic state-centred analysis) bossing and strength backed ultimately by cunning and the fist and other means of state power, a *Realpolitik* understanding of leadership that slides towards political authoritarianism (and until today has given the words *Führer* and *Führerschaft* a bad name in countries such as Germany).[75] Leadership also no longer means manipulation through the bully pulpit (a peculiarly American term coined by Theodore Roosevelt to describe the use by leaders of a 'superb' or 'wonderful' platform to advocate causes and agendas). Leadership instead comes to be understood as the capacity to mobilise 'persuasive power' (as Archbishop Desmond Tutu likes to say). It is the ability to motivate citizens to do things for themselves.

Unelected leadership is certainly challenging. 'A determination to be courageous; an ability to anticipate situations; the inclination to drama-tise political effects, so as to warn citizens of actual or potential prob-lems; above all, the willingness to admit that mistakes have been made, to urge that they must be corrected, without ever being afraid of making

---

[75] Max Weber's famous account of the qualities of competent political leadership (*Führerschaft*) in parliamentary democracies is sketched in 'Politik als Beruf' (originally delivered as a speech at Munich University in the revolutionary winter of 1918/19), in *Gesammelte Politische Schriften* (Tübingen, 1958), pp. 493–548. During the speech, Weber said that democracies require leaders to display at least three decisive qualities. Genuine leadership, first of all, necessitates a passionate devotion to a cause, the will to make history, to set new values for others, nourished from feeling. Such passion must not succumb to what he called (Weber here drew upon Georg Simmel) 'sterile excitation'. Authentic leaders – this is the second imperative – must avoid 'self-intoxication' all the while cultivating a sense of personal responsibility for their achievements, and their failures. While (finally) this implies that leaders are not merely the mandated mouthpieces of their masters, the electors, leaders' actions must embody a 'cool sense of proportion': the ability to grant due weight to realities, to take them soberly and calmly into account. Passionate, responsible and experienced leaders, Weber urged, must be relentless in 'viewing the realities of life' and must have 'the ability to face such realities and . . . measure up to them inwardly'. Effective leadership is synonymous with neither demagoguery nor the worship of power for its own sake. Passionate and responsible leaders shun the blind pursuit of ultimate goals; such blindness, Weber noted sarcastically, 'does rightly and leaves the results with the Lord'. Mature leaders must be guided instead by the 'ethic of responsibility'. Recognising the average deficiencies of people, they must continually strive, using state power, to take account of the foreseeable effects of particular actions that aim to realise particular goals through the reliance upon particular means. Responsible leaders must therefore incorporate into their actions the prickly fact, in many contexts, that the attainment of good ends is dependent upon (and therefore jeopardised by) the use of ethically doubtful or (in the case of violence) even dangerous means.

yet more mistakes,' is how one unelected leader explains it.[76] Unelected leadership is many things. It involves flat rejection of the devils of blind ambition, what Carlyle called 'Lionism'. It is the learned capacity to communicate with publics about matters of public concern, to win public respect by cultivating 'narrative intelligence' that includes (when unelected representatives are at their best) a mix of formal qualities, such as level-headed focus, inner calm, courteousness, the refusal to be biddable, the ability to listen to others, poking fun at oneself and a certain radiance of style (one of the confidants of Nelson Mandela once explained to me his remarkable ability to create 'many Nelson Mandelas around him'; the same thing is still commonly said of Jawaharlal Nehru). The qualities of unelected leadership also include the power to use media to combine contradictory qualities (such as strength and vulnerability; singularity and typicality) simultaneously, and apparently without effort, as if leadership is the art of gestalt switching. Above all, unelected leadership demands awareness that true leaders are not the elect, that they are always deeply dependent upon the people known as the led – that true leaders lead because they manage to get people to look up to them, rather than hauling them by the nose.

Cross-border publics

One other distinctive trend within contemporary democracy must be noted: communicative abundance makes possible the growth of large-scale publics whose footprints are potentially or actually global in scope, and whose membership cuts across and underneath the boundaries of territorial states, thus complicating the dynamics of opinion formation and representative democracy within those states.

The trend should not be underestimated: the unfolding communications revolution of our time features the growth of networked globe-girdling media whose time–space conquering effects are of epochal

---

[76] From an interview with Emílio Rui Vilar, former senior minister of the first democratic governments after the defeat of the Salazar dictatorship, former Deputy Governor of the Bank of Portugal and Director-General of the Commission of the European Union, and director of the Calouste Gulbenkian Foundation, a non-governmental foundation known for its active support for public accountability and pluralism in matters ranging from political power to aesthetic taste (Lisbon, 27 October 2006).

significance. The Canadian scholar Harold Innis famously noted the time- and distance-shrinking effects of the wheel, the printing press and other communications media, but genuinely global communication systems only began, during the nineteenth century, with inventions like overland and underwater telegraphy and the early development of international news agencies, such as Reuters.[77] In recent decades, the globalising process has been undergoing an evolutionary jump, thanks to the development of a combination of forces. Wide-footprint geostationary satellites (of the kind that broadcast the Beatles and Maria Callas to the world, in real time) have played an important role; equally important has been the growth of global journalism and the networked flows of international news, electronic data exchange and entertainment and education materials controlled by giant firms like TimeWarner, News International, the BBC, Al Jazeera, Disney, Bertelsmann, Microsoft, Sony and Google.

The rapid expansion of global media linkages has triggered talk of abolishing barriers to communication, which in some quarters functions as a misleading ideology of digital networks. Among the earliest and most influential example was John Perry Barlow's *A Declaration of the Independence of Cyberspace* (1996). It claimed that computer-linked networks were creating a 'global social space', a borderless 'global conversation of bits', a new world 'that all may enter without privilege or prejudice accorded by race, economic power, military force, or station of birth'.[78] Such talk is complicated and contradicted by real-world trends, but it underscores correctly the way global communication networks have done what the world maps and globes of Gerardus Mercator (1512–1594) manifestly failed to do: these networks strengthen the intuition of millions of people (perhaps somewhere between 5 per cent and 25 per cent of the world's population) that our world is 'one world', and that this worldly interdependence beckons humans to share some responsibility for its fate. The trend is in a sense self-reinforcing; it has more than a passing resemblance, but on a vastly expanded scale, to the way newspapers, as Tocqueville put it, played the role of 'beacons' of common activity by dropping 'the same

---

[77] Harold Innis, The Bias of Communication (Toronto, 1951); Peter J. Hugill, Global Communications since 1844: Geopolitics and Technology (Baltimore and London, 1999).

[78] John Perry Barlow, *A Declaration of the Independence of Cyberspace* (8 February 1996), available at: http://www.eff.org.

thought into a thousand minds at the same moment'.[79] By imagining
that their work is targeted at potentially global audiences whom they
will otherwise never physically encounter, professional and citizen
journalists, book publishers, radio and television broadcasters, tweeters, emailers and bloggers till the ground in which actual publics of
listening, reading, watching, chatting citizens take root – on a global
scale, in opposition to time and space barriers that were once taken for
granted, considered 'natural' or technically unbridgeable.

The process is not straightforward, nor is it uncontested. Though
critics and commentators alike seem to agree that global media networks
foster a common sense of worldly interdependence, some sceptical
observers ask: exactly what kind of worldly interdependence are we
talking about? They note that today's global communications market is
disproportionately controlled by ten or so vertically integrated media
conglomerates, most of them based in the United States.[80] These media
conglomerates are no longer 'homespun' (to use Keynes' term for describing territorially bound, state-regulated markets). Bursting the bounds of
time and space, language and custom, media big business is better
described in terms of complex global commodity chains, or global
flows of information, staff, money, components and products. Not surprisingly, so runs the argument, journalism associated with the global
media conglomerates gives priority to advertising-driven commercial
ventures: to saleable music, videos, sports, shopping, children's and
adults' filmed entertainment. In the field of news, for instance, special
emphasis is given to 'news-breaking' and 'block-busting' stories that
concentrate upon accidents, disasters, political crises and violence. The
material that is fed to editors by journalists who report from or around

---

[79] Alexis de Tocqueville, 'Of the Relation between Public Associations and the
Newspapers', in Phillips Bradley (ed.), *Democracy in America* (New York,
1945), vol. 2, bk 2, ch. 6: 'A newspaper is an adviser that does not require to be
sought, but that comes of its own accord and talks to you briefly every day of the
common weal, without distracting you from your private affairs . . . The effect of a
newspaper is not only to suggest the same purpose to a great number of persons,
but to furnish means for executing in common the designs which they may have
singly conceived.'

[80] The following points are taken up in more detail in my *Global Civil Society?*
(Cambridge and New York, 2003), especially pp. 65 ff. See also R. Burnett, *The
Global Jukebox* (London, 1996); Ali Mohammadi (ed.), *International
Communication and Globalization* (London, 1997); Edward S. Herman and
Robert W. McChesney, *The Global Media: The New Missionaries of Corporate
Capitalism* (London and Washington, DC, 1997).

trouble spots ('clusterfucks' they are called in the trade) is meanwhile shortened, simplified, repackaged and transmitted in commercial form. Staged sound bites and 'live' or 'catchy' material are editors' favourites; so, too, are flashy presentational technologies, including the use of logos, rapid visual cuts and 'stars' who are placed centre stage. The picture is then completed by news exchange arrangements, whereby subscribing news organisations exchange visual footage and other material, so ensuring a substantial deracination and homogenisation of news stories in many parts of the globe, circulated at the speed of light.

The trends dispirit some observers. Far from nurturing freedom of communication and democracy, they complain, global media companies produce bland commercial pulp for audiences who become politically comatose. 'McWorld' is the end result: informed citizenship is replaced by a universal tribe of consumers dancing to the music of logos, advertising slogans, sponsorship, brand names, trademarks and jingles.[81] Other critics slam 'global cultural homogenisation' in the form of 'transnational corporate cultural domination': a world in which 'private giant economic enterprises' pursue 'capitalist objectives of profit making and capital accumulation'.[82] Still others complain that the overall effect is a silent takeover by markets, a world 'where corporate interests reign, where corporations spew their jargon on to the airwaves and stifle nations with their imperial rule. Corporations have become behemoths, huge global giants that wield immense political power.'[83]

The criticisms are sobering; the complainants have a point. Corporate power is aggressively innovative, but it also poses threats to freedom of communication and democracy: media markets tend to restrict freedom and equality of communication by generating barriers to entry, monopoly restrictions upon choice, and by shifting the definition of communication with others as a publicly meaningful good to *commercial speech* and the consumption of commodities.[84] Yet this is not the

---

[81] Benjamin Barber, *Jihad vs. McWorld: How Globalism and Tribalism are Reshaping the World* (New York, 1995).

[82] Herbert Schiller, 'Not Yet the Post-Industrial Era', *Critical Studies in Mass Communication* 8 (1991): 20–1.

[83] Noreena Hertz, *The Silent Takeover: Global Capitalism and the Death of Democracy* (London, 2001), p. 8.

[84] See Owen Fiss, 'Why the State?' in Judith Lichtenberg (ed.), *Democracy and the Mass Media* (Cambridge and New York, 1990), pp. 136–54; John Keane, *The Media and Democracy* (Oxford and Cambridge, MA, 1991), esp. pp. 51–92.

whole story. Thanks to communicative abundance, there are signs that the grip of commodity fetishism upon citizens is not absolute, and that from roughly the time of the worldwide protest of young people against the Vietnam War global media integration has had an unanticipated *political* effect: by erecting a world stage, global media conglomerates, helped along by the practice of global journalism, have slowly but surely massaged into life cross-border media events and, with them, a plurality of differently sized public spheres, some of them genuinely global, in which many millions of people scattered across the Earth witness mediated controversies about who gets what, when and how, on a world scale, often in real time.

Things are, again, not straightforward or unproblematic, for it remains true that even the most media-saturated societies, such as the United States, are riddled with pockets of parochialism. Citizens who read local 'content engine' newspapers like *The Desert Sun* in Palm Springs, Cheyenne's *Wyoming Tribune-Eagle* or the *Gainesville Sun* are fed a starvation diet of global stories, which typically occupy no more than about 2 per cent of column space.[85] Citizens' horizons are narrowed further by budget cuts for foreign news desks, excessive dependence on English-language sources, and recycled wire-service reporting and regional news exchanges that feed tabloid newspapers. Not to be overlooked, is the way that governments stick their noses into global information flows. Protected by dissimulation experts, or what in Washington are called 'flack packs', governments cultivate links with trusted or 'embedded' journalists, organise press briefings and advertising campaigns, so framing global events, wilfully distorting and censoring them, to suit their own interests.

It should be noted, by way of definition, that not all global media events, such as sporting fixtures, blockbuster movies and international media awards, nurture global publics, which is to say that audiences are not the same as publics, and that public spheres are not simply domains of entertainment or play. So what does it mean to speak of global publics? Are they sober spaces of rational-critical deliberation in search of truth and calm agreement, as the followers of Jürgen

---

[85] John Keane, 'Journalism and Democracy Across Borders', in Michael Schudson (ed.), *Institutions of Democracy: The Press* (Oxford and New York, 2005).

Habermas suppose?[86] There are moments when rational communication in that sense sometimes happens, but, strictly speaking, global publics are scenes of the political, spaces within which millions of people, living at various points on the Earth, witness power conflicts and attempts to resolve them. Global publics become aware of characters, events, governing arrangements and NGOs. They observe them being publicly named, praised, challenged and condemned – courtesy of media networks and professional, and citizen and 'hybrid' journalists, whose combined effect, however temporary, is to attract the attention of millions of otherwise unconnected citizens, across borders, in defiance of the old tyrannies of time and space.

The conscious targeting and interpellation of global audiences by melding worldwide forms and themes with localised interests in real-time was pioneered by such English-language channels as CNN. Launched in 1980, it was the first American channel to provide all-news television coverage, and on a twenty-four-hour basis. Its international counterpart, CNN International, began as 5 hours a week of material submitted by 100 broadcast stations around the world, some professional and some amateur; ironically, the whole operation was backed by owner Ted Turner's now legendary prohibition of the word 'foreign' on air. Using alternative banners, such as 'Go Beyond Borders', CNN International is now available to audiences in several languages (Spanish, Turkish and English) within over 200 countries and territories. It played a vital role in covering the drama of the 1989 Tiananmen Square crisis where, for the first time, live feeds were watched globally by government diplomats and policymakers to decide what their next moves should be. CNN's coverage of the first Gulf War and other crises of the early 1990s, particularly the battle of Mogadishu, led many observers to speak of 'the CNN effect' to describe the perceived impact on decision-makers of real-time, twenty-four-hour news coverage on a global basis.

---

[86] Some limits of the rational communication model of the public sphere, originally outlined in the important work of Jürgen Habermas, *Strukturwandel der Öffentlichkeit: Untersuchungen einer Kategorie der bürgerlichen Gesellschaft* (Neuwied, 1962), are sketched in John Durham Peters, 'Distrust of Representation: Habermas on the Public Sphere', *Media, Culture and Society* 15 (1993): 541–71; John Keane, 'Structural Transformations of the Public Sphere', *Communication Review* 1(1) (1995): 1–22.

The global–local media dialectics typical of the age of communicative abundance are often much less spectacular, and with less immediate effect, helped along by bodies such as the Internet-based Earth Watch, the World Association of Community Radio Broadcasters (AMARC), and public accountability initiatives such as Transparency International and Human Rights Watch. Then there are times when the same dialectics produce explosions. The dramatic media events that enveloped the overthrow of dictatorships in Tunisia, Egypt and Libya in 2011 certainly ran in this direction, with radical democratic effects. The struggles for public space for a time proved infectious throughout the region. These were not straightforwardly 'Twitter' rebellions or 'Facebook revolutions'[87]; they were equally rebellions of the poor and powerless against the unjust recent deregulation of rapacious global markets. Yet these uprisings were marked by an unusual public awareness of the political importance of digitally networked media. Thanks to outlets such as al-Arabiya and Al Jazeera (it has 3,000 staff members and more than 50 million household viewers in the Arab world), never before had so many people instantly witnessed dramatic political events on a global scale. Citizens understood that news is by definition powerful information still unknown to others, which helps to explain the remarkable first-time experiments in the arts of gathering and circulating news. Huge crowds in Alexandria watched themselves live on satellite television, hoping the coverage would protect them from police or military annihilation. Helped by Web platforms operated by exiles, tweets and blogs and video footage uploaded on to the Internet powerfully described situations both terrible and hopeful. Everything, even the shooting of protesters and innocent bystanders at point-blank range, was recorded for posterity in real-time.

Global media events are becoming 'normal' in the age of communicative abundance; not surprisingly, so is the intrusion of global publics within the domestic settings of many democracies. What happens elsewhere, what the world's people think and how they react in the circumstances begins to matter to their citizens and representatives. Within the democratic world, but even more so within autocratic regimes, global

---

[87] Wael Ghonim, *Revolution 2.0. The Power of the People is Greater than the People: A Memoir* (New York, 2012).

publics are certainly vulnerable to state interference.[88] Through no fault of their own, these global publics are also highly vulnerable to implosion, above all because they enjoy neither strong institutional protection nor effective channels of representation and accountability, for instance, through the mechanisms of elected representative government. Global publics donate money, spread news, circulate information and stage events, many of them targeted at the doings of elected representatives, but they remain, for the time being, echoing voices without a coherent body politic to acknowledge and act on their concerns. The age when public spheres were typically contained within the territorial boundaries of democratic states is passing, yet the trouble for democratic politics is the homelessness of the new global publics. Think of the example of global opinion polls, efforts to sample and measure what the world's people in different countries think about, say, American presidential candidates or, say, whether Palestinians are entitled to their own territorial state. Such polls are more than make-believe or 'fictional' exercises. They are forms of interpellation that suppose what is not yet a reality. By calling upon the world's people to shrug off their insularity, by measuring their opinions and giving them a voice, they feed the growth of new cross-border publics. But their voice cries out for – it implies – the need for new institutions. Global publics invite the world to see that it resembles a chrysalis capable of hatching the butterfly of cross-border democracy – despite the fact that we currently have no good account of what 'regional', or 'global' or 'cross-border' democratic representation might mean in practice.[89]

---

[88] Monroe Price, *Media and Sovereignty: The Global Information Revolution and its Challenge to State Power* (Cambridge, MA and London, 2002); Nancy Morris and Silvio Waisbord (eds), *Media and Globalization: Why the State Matters* (Lanham, MD, 2002).

[89] The difficult task of drawing clearer pictures of the contours and dynamics of a more democratic global order is made all the more difficult by the fact that there are not only vast numbers of governmental and non-governmental organisations that know little or nothing of democratic procedures and manners. The world is structured as well by an agglomeration of governmental and legal structures – a cosmocracy comprising bodies such as the European Union, the United Nations, the World Bank – that defies the textbooks of traditional political science and political theory (see John Keane, *Global Civil Society?* (Cambridge and New York, 2003), pp. 175 ff). Many structures of the cosmocracy escape the constraining effects of electoral and parliamentary supervision, which is why the sceptics of extending democratic procedures and ways of life across territorial state borders raise strong objections. Consider the doubts of the doyen of

These are powerful constraints, yet, in spite of their daunting force, global publics still make their political mark, for instance, on the suit-and-tie worlds of diplomacy, global business and meetings of NGOs and inter-governmental officials. Every great global issue that has surfaced since 1945 – human rights, the dangers of nuclear war, discrimination against women and minorities, the greening of politics, the domination of politics by the very rich – first crystallised as 'hot topics' within and by means of these publics, which, in turn, have had the effect of heightening the sense of contingency of global power relations. Public spheres tend to denature the codes of power inscribed in cross-border settings. Helped along by tit-for-tat conflicts among various media (the ongoing spats between Al Jazeera and American television news media since the US invasion of Iraq in 2003 is a case in point), these publics set or shape the agendas of various socioeconomic and political-legal institutions of our globally interdependent world. They put them on the spot, shake up their dogmas and sometimes inject them with legitimacy. They heighten the sense that they are transformable – that they are unfinished business.

Global publics have other effects, sometimes 'subpolitical' effects, in the sense that they work in favour of *creating* citizens of a new global order, in effect telling people that unless they find some means of showing that the wider world is not theirs, they are witnesses and participants in this wider world.[90] The speech addressed to 'global

democratic thought in the United States, Robert A. Dahl, who considers as utterly unrealistic the vision of democracy beyond state borders (see Robert A. Dahl, 'The Past and Future of Democracy', revised manuscript version of a lecture at the symposium, Politics from the 20th to the 21st Century, University of Siena, 14–16 October 1999; and *On Democracy* (New Haven, CT and London, 1998), pp. 114–17). The growing complexity of decision-making, for instance, in the field of foreign affairs, renders impossible the 'public enlightenment' so necessary for democracy, he argues. Meanwhile, legal and illegal immigration, combined with a new politics of identity within and beyond territorial states, lead to growing 'cultural diversity and cleavages', which undermine 'civil discourse and compromise', Dahl says. Worldwide threats of terrorist attacks make it even less likely that civil and political liberties could flourish within 'international organizations'.

[90] Martin Heidegger famously wrote: 'Dwelling is the manner in which mortals are on the earth' ('Building, Dwelling Thinking', in *The Question Concerning Technology and Other Essays* (New York, 1982), p. 146), but the implication in that passage that mortals are confined to local geographic places misses the new spatial polygamy that global publics make possible. Within global public spheres, people rooted in local physical settings travel to distant places, without ever

citizens' by Barack Obama at the Siegessaule in Berlin's Tiergarten, in July 2008, was a powerful case in point, a harbinger of a remarkable trend in which those who are caught up within global publics learn that the boundaries between home and abroad, native and foreigner, are blurred, negotiable and subject permanently to osmosis.[91] By witnessing far-away events, they learn that their commitments have become a touch more worldly. They become footloose. They live here and there; they learn to distance themselves from themselves; they discover that there are different temporal rhythms, other places, other problems, many different ways of living. They discover the 'foreigner' within themselves; they are invited to question their own dogmas, even to extend courtesy, politeness, respect and other ordinary standards of civility to others whom they will never meet.

Global publics centred on ground-breaking media events like Live Aid (in 1985 it attracted an estimated 1 billion viewers) can be spaces of fun, in which millions taste the joy of acting publicly with and against others for some defined common purpose. When they come in the form of, say, televised world news fixed on the suffering of distant strangers caused by man-made disasters and episodes of state violence, global publics also highlight injustice and cruelty. Media representation spreads awareness among millions of others' damned fates; global publics function as sites for handling unjust outcomes, bitter defeat and the tragedy of ruined lives. True, witnessing the pain and suffering of others can produce numbing effects, so that instead of active public engagement acts of witnessing by citizens turn out to be the prelude to

leaving home, to 'second homes' within which their senses are stretched. That they become a bit less parochial, a bit more cosmopolitan is no small achievement, especially considering that people do not 'naturally' feel a sense of responsibility for faraway events. Ethical responsibility often stretches no further than their noses. Yet when they are engaged by stories that originate elsewhere – when they are drawn into the dynamics of a global public sphere – their interest in the fate of others is not based simply on prurience, or idle curiosity or *Schadenfreude*. They rather align and assimilate these stories in terms of their own existential concerns, which are thereby altered. The world 'out there' becomes 'their' world.

[91] Addressing a vast global audience and a local crowd gathered at the Victory Column at Tiergarten Park, Berlin (24 July 2008), Senator Barack Obama said: 'I come to Berlin as so many of my countrymen have come before, not as a candidate for president but as a citizen – a proud citizen of the United States and a fellow citizen of the world.'

turning their backs on those who suffer.[92] Yet the equation between suffering and witnessing has no automaticity. Media representations of terrible suffering do not necessarily produce ethically cleansed cynics, mindless lovers of entertainment slumped on sofas, enjoying every second of the blood and tears. There is plenty of evidence, to the contrary, that global publics that gather around the stages of cruelty and humiliation scrap the old rule that good and evil are typically local affairs. Global initiatives such as 'One Billion Rising', a cross-border protest (February 2013) against gender-based violence, prove that the old maxim that half the world never knows how the other half lives is rendered false. Publics come to feel that the suffering of others is contagious.

By circulating images, sounds and stories of physical and emotional suffering in symbolic form, global publics make possible what Hannah Arendt once called a 'politics of pity'.[93] Witnessing the suffering of others at a distance, millions can be shaken and disturbed, sometimes to the point where they are prepared to exercise their sense of long-distance responsibility by speaking to others, donating time or money, or adding their voice to the general principle that the right of human-itarian intervention, the obligation to assist someone in danger, can and should override the old crocodilian formula that might equals right. And especially during dramatic media events – like the nuclear melt-down at Chernobyl; the Tiananmen massacre; the 1989 revolutions in central-eastern Europe; the overthrow and arrest of Slobodan Milošević; the terrorist attacks on New York, Pennsylvania and Washington; massive earthquakes in Chile and China; the overthrow of dictatorships in Tunisia, Egypt and Libya – public spheres intensify audiences' shared sense of living their lives contingently, on a knife edge.

---

[92] See the important work of Barbie Zelizer, *Remembering to Forget: Holocaust Memory Through the Camera's Eye* (Chicago and London, 1998); and her 'Journalism, Photography, and Trauma', in Barbie Zelizer and Stuart Allan (eds), *Journalism after September 11* (London and New York, 2002), pp. 48–68.

[93] Hannah Arendt, *On Revolution* (Harmondsworth, 1990), pp. 59–114; and the development of Arendt's ideas on the subject by Luc Boltanski, *La Souffrance à distance: morale humanitaire, médias et politique* (Paris, 1993), translated as Luc Boltanski, *Distant Suffering: Morality, Media and Politics* (London and New York, 1999); Clifford Christians and Kaarle Nordenstreng, 'Social Responsibility Worldwide', *Journal of Mass Media Ethics* 19(1) (2004): 3–28; Toni Erskine, *Embedded Cosmopolitanism: Duties to Strangers and Enemies in a World of 'Dislocated Communities'* (Oxford, 2008).

The witnesses of such events (contrary to McLuhan and others) do not enter a 'global village' dressed in the skins of humankind and thinking in the terms of a primordial 'village or tribal outlook'.[94] When they share a public sphere, audiences do not experience uninterrupted togetherness. As witnesses of worldly events, they instead come to feel the pinch of the world's power relations; they sense that our 'small world' is an arena of struggle, the resultant of moves and counter-moves, controversy and consent, resistance and compromise, war and peace.

Global publics feed upon the exposure of malfeasance. They keep alive words like freedom and justice by publicising manipulation, skul-duggery and brutality in other countries. Global publics, of the kind that in recent years have monitored the fates of Nelson Mandela, Aung San Suu Kyi, Osama bin Laden or George W. Bush, muck with the messy business of exclusion, racketeering, ostentation, cruelty and war. They chart cases of intrigue, lying and double-crossing. They help audiences across borders to spot the various figures of top-down power on the world scene: slick and suave managers and professionals who are well practised at the art of deceiving others through images; fools who prey on their citizens' fears; quislings who willingly change sides under pressure; thugs who love violence; and vulgar rulers, with their taste for usurping crowns, assembling and flattering crowds, or beating, tear-gassing or shooting and bombing them into submission.

Exactly because of their propensity to monitor the exercise of power, global publics, when they do their job well, put matters like representation, accountability and legitimacy on the political agenda. They are, in effect, challenges to the thickets of powerful cross-border business, inter-governmental and judicial institutions that increasingly shape the destiny of our world. These publics pose important questions: who benefits and who loses from the contemporary global order? Who currently speaks for whom in its multiple and overlapping power structures? Whose voices are heard, or half-heard, and whose interests and concerns are ignominiously shoved aside? And these publics imply more

---

[94] See the introduction to Edmund Carpenter and Marshall McLuhan (eds), *Explorations in Communication* (Boston, MA, 1966), p. xi : 'Postliterate man's [sic] electronic media contract the world to a village or tribe where everything happens to everyone at the same time: everyone knows about, and therefore participates in, everything that is happening the minute it happens ... This simultaneous sharing of experiences as in a village or tribe creates a village or tribal outlook, and puts a premium on togetherness.'

positive and far-reaching questions: in the push–pull of cross-border politics, can there be greater equality among the voices that emerge from the nooks and crannies of our global order? Through which institutional procedures could these voices be represented? Might it be possible to design alternatives that could inch our small blue and white planet towards greater openness and humility, potentially to the point where power, whenever and wherever it is exercised across borders, would come to feel more publicly accountable, more responsive to those whose lives it currently shapes and reshapes, secures or wrecks?

2 | *Monitory democracy*

It was noted earlier that the emergent world of communicative abundance demands a fresh sense of how real-world democracies are being affected by the new techniques and tools of communication. The shorthand recommendation harboured a sense of urgency: it implied the need to stop thinking in terms of the dead concepts and worn-out formulae of our predecessors; to become more attuned to the novelties, achievements and promise of our own times; to ask fresh and more imaginative questions, including how we understand democracy itself. In order to explore the point further, let us suppose for a moment that the handful of trends sketched above are by no means transitory, such that new information banks, changes in the public–private relationship and the growth of muckraking, unelected representatives and cross-border publics are together having real effects on the spirit and institutional dynamics of democracy. The questions then surface: with which kind of democracy are they interwoven?; and what exactly is their impact?

Most observers would reply by acknowledging that important things are happening in the field of democracy and communications. But diffuse agreement beyond that elementary point quickly crumbles into divisions of opinion about the meaning of democracy and the extent of the changes. Some observers draw the conclusion that the changes are proving to be minimal because traditional 'offline' political actors and organisations are moving online and slowly but surely colonising the new world of 'cyberspace', so that the new situation mirrors what came before and online politics remains 'politics as usual'.[1] A prime example, say these observers, is the way that the campaigning strategies of political parties now include teams of political strategists, video producers, code writers, data analysts, corporate marketers and Web producers sifting information gleaned from Facebook, Twitter subscribers,

---

[1] M. Margolis and D. Resnick, *Politics as Usual: The Cyberspace 'Revolution'* (Thousand Oaks, CA, 2000).

voter logs and feedback from telephone and in-person conversations.[2] Opposite views are championed by those for whom communicative abundance brings into being a new architecture of politics, a flourishing world of 'liquid democracy', active 'e-citizenship' in direct and participatory form, a form of 'e-democracy' that resembles, in higher form, the assembly democracy enjoyed by Greek democrats. In between these extremes stand observers who praise communicative abundance for the modest ways it breathes life into 'liberal democracy' by enabling better 'informed citizens' to find a new or stronger voice in public affairs.

A fundamental weakness of these interpretations is their amnesiac qualities, their poor grasp, or outright lack of awareness, of the bigger historical trends and comparative novelties of our times. Consideration is rarely given to the shifting temporal forms and patterns of intersection between media and democracy; suggestions that communicative abundance is having unique transformative effects on the spirit and dynamics of democracy, helping to remould its contours into a brand new historical mode of handling and controlling power, seem just too 'wild' to be taken seriously. But is this way of thinking so far-fetched? What if things were considered in the following way?

Every historical era of democracy is intertwined with a specific mode of communication. Assembly-based democracy in the ancient Greek city states belonged to an era dominated by the spoken word, backed up by laws written on papyrus and stone, and by messages dispatched by foot, or by donkey and horse. Eighteenth-century representative democracy, a new historical form of democracy understood as the self-government of people by means of elected representatives, sprang up in the era of print culture, within the world of the book, pamphlet and newspaper, and telegraphed and mailed messages. Representative democracy in this sense stumbled and fell into crisis during the advent of early mass broadcasting media, especially radio and cinema and (in its infancy) television. By contrast, or so the line of thinking runs, democracy in our times is tied closely to the growth of multimedia-saturated societies, whose structures of power are continuously questioned by a multitude of monitory or 'watchdog' mechanisms operating within a new media galaxy defined by the ethos of communicative abundance.

---

[2] Jim Rutenberg and Jeff Zeleny, 'Obama Mines for Voters with High-tech Tools', *New York Times*, 8 March 2012.

This way of thinking requires a fundamental shift of perspective – a gestalt switch – in the way contemporary democracies are understood. Compared with the era of representative democracy, when print culture and limited spectrum audio-visual media were much more closely aligned with political parties, elections and governments, contemporary democracies experience constant public scrutiny and spats about power, to the point where it seems as if no organisation or leader within the fields of government or business and social life is immune from political trouble. It is easy to see that prevailing ways of describing and analysing contemporary democracy – talk of the 'end of history' (Francis Fukuyama) and a 'third wave' of democracy (Samuel Huntington) – are either inadequate or downright misleading, too bound to the surface of things, too preoccupied with continuities and aggregate data to notice that political tides have begun to run in entirely new directions, to see that the world of actually existing democracy is experiencing an historic sea change, one that is taking us away from the assembly-based and representative models of democracy of past times towards a form of democracy with entirely different contours and dynamics. It is much harder to find an elegant name for this new historical form of democracy, let alone to describe in just a few words its workings and political implications.

Elsewhere, and at some length, the case has been made for introducing the strange-sounding term *monitory democracy* as the most exact for describing the big transformation that is taking hold in many regions of the world.[3] Monitory democracy is a new historical form of democracy, a variety of 'post-electoral' politics and government defined by the

---

[3] See my *The Life and Death of Democracy* (London and New York, 2009), pp. 648–747. The adjective 'monitory' derives from the medieval *monitoria* (from *monere*, to warn). It entered Middle English in the shape of *monitorie* and from there it wended its way into the modern English language in the mid-fifteenth century to refer to the process of giving or conveying a warning of an impending danger, or an admonition to someone to refrain from a specified course of action considered offensive. It was first used within the Church to refer to a letter or letters (known as 'monitories') sent by a bishop, or a pope or an ecclesiastical court who acted in the capacity of a 'monitor'. The family of words 'monitor', 'monition' and 'monitory' was soon used for more secular, this-worldly purposes. The monitor was one who, or that which, admonishes others about their conduct. The word 'monitor' was also used in school settings to refer to a senior pupil expected to perform special duties, such as that of keeping order, or (if the pupil was particularly bright or gifted) acting as a teacher to a junior class. A monitor also came to mean an early warning device; it was said as well to be a species of African,

rapid growth of many different kinds of extra-parliamentary, power-scrutinising mechanisms. Supposing the existence of independent publics, to whom their messages are addressed, these monitory bodies take root within the 'domestic' fields of government and civil society, as well as in 'cross-border' settings once subject to the arbitrary power of empires, states and businesses. In consequence, the architecture and dynamics of self-government is changing. The central grip of elections, political parties and parliaments on citizens' lives is weakening. Democracy is coming to mean much more than free and fair elections, although nothing less. Within and outside states, independent monitors of power begin to have major tangible effects on the dynamics and meaning of democracy. By putting politicians, parties and elected governments permanently on their toes, monitory institutions complicate their lives and question their power and authority, often forcing them to chop and change their agendas – sometimes by smothering them in political disgrace.

   Whether or not the trend towards this new kind of democracy is a sustainable, historically irreversible development remains to be seen; like its two previous historical antecedents, the assembly-based democracy of the ancient world and modern representative democracy in territorial form, monitory democracy is not inevitable. It did not have to happen, but it happened nonetheless; the whole issue of whether it will live, or fade away or die suddenly remains an open question, well beyond the scope of this book, a matter for the verdicts of future

---

Australian and New Guinean lizard that was friendly to humans because it gave warning of the whereabouts of crocodiles. Still later, the word 'monitor' came to be associated with communication devices. It referred to a receiver, such as a speaker or a television screen, that is used to check the quality or content of an electronic transmission; and in the world of computing and computer science, a 'monitor' either refers to a video display or to a program that observes, or supervises or controls the activities of other programs. In more recent years, not unconnected with the emergence of monitory democracy, 'to monitor' has become a commonplace verb to describe the process of systematically checking the content or quality of something, as when a city authority monitors the local drinking water for impurities, or a group of scientific experts monitors the population of an endangered species. Such usages helped to inspire the theory of 'monitorial democracy' developed by the American scholar, Michael Schudson (interview, New York City, 4 December 2006). See his 'Changing Concepts of Democracy', *MIT Communications Forum*, 8 May 1998, and the fuller version in *The Good Citizen: A History of American Public Life* (New York, 1998), to which my use of the term monitory democracy is indebted.

historians.[4] Yet when judged by its institutional contours and inner dynamics, monitory democracy is without doubt the most complex form of democracy known to us. Those with a taste for Latin would say that it is the *tertium quid*, the not fully formed successor of the earlier historical experiments with assembly-based and representative forms of democracy. In the name of 'people', 'the public', 'public accountability', 'the people' , 'stakeholders' or 'citizens' – the terms are normally used interchangeably in the age of monitory democracy – power-scrutinising institutions spring up all over the place, both within the fields of government and beyond, often stretching across borders. Elections, political parties and legislatures neither disappear nor decline in importance; but they most definitely lose their pivotal position in politics. Contrary to the orthodox claims of many political scientists, many of whom have unwittingly plunged themselves into deep seas of forgetfulness, democracy is no longer simply a way of handling the power of elected governments by electoral and parliamentary and con-stitutional means, and no longer a matter confined to territorial states.[5] Gone are the days when democracy could be described (and in the next breath attacked) as 'government by the unrestricted will of the majority' (Friedrich von Hayek). Whether in the field of local, national or supra-national government, or in the world of business and other NGOs and networks, some of them stretching down into the roots of everyday life and outwards towards the four corners of the earth, people and organ-isations that exercise power are now routinely subject to public mon-itoring and public contestation by an assortment of extra-parliamentary bodies.

Monitory mechanisms

Symptomatic of the historical shift is the appearance, during recent deca-des, of scores of new types of power-scrutinising and power-checking

---

[4] The subject of counter-trends and dysfunctions of monitory democracy is taken up in my *The Life and Death of Democracy*. A full range of related materials is to be found at www.thelifeanddeathofdemocracy.org.

[5] Examples include Adam Przeworski *et al.* (eds), *Democracy, Accountability, and Representation* (New York, 1999); Adam Przeworski, *Democracy and the Limits of Self-Government* (New York, 2010); and the review essay by Gerardo L. Munck, 'Democratic Theory after *Transitions from Authoritarian Rule*', *Perspectives on Politics* 9(2) (June 2011): 333–43.

mechanisms unknown to previous democrats, or whole systems of democracy. These monitory mechanisms have appeared in many different global settings. They are not exclusively 'American', or 'European', or 'OECD' or 'Western' inventions, but have diffused around the globe, from all points on the globe. They operate in different ways, on many different fronts, including groups and networks (such as the Alberta Climate Dialogue, BirdLife International and the World Glacier Monitoring Service) dedicated to scrutinising and defending our biosphere against wanton destruction by humans. Some scrutinise power primarily at the level of *citizens' inputs* to government or civil society bodies; other monitory mechanisms are preoccupied with monitoring and contesting what are sometimes called *policy throughputs*; still others concentrate on scrutinising the *policy outputs* of governmental bodies or NGOs. Quite a few of the inventions concentrate simultaneously upon all three dimensions, doing so in different rhythms and through different spatial settings. Monitory mechanisms are often long-haul institutions. Yet some of them are remarkably evanescent; in a fast-changing media world, like strong gusts of wind, they suddenly make their presence felt, stirring things up before dissolving into thin air, leaving things not quite as they were before. Power-monitoring mechanisms also assume different sizes and operate on various spatial scales; they range from 'just round the corner' bodies with quite local footprints to global networks aimed at keeping tabs on those who exercise power over great distances.

Given such variations, it should not be surprising that a quick short list of the inventions resembles, at first sight, to the untrained eye, a magpie's nest of randomly collected items. The list includes: citizen juries, bioregional assemblies, participatory budgeting, advisory boards and focus groups. There are think tanks, consensus conferences, teach-ins, public memorials, local community consultation schemes and open houses (developed, for instance, in the field of architecture) that offer information and advisory and advocacy services, archive and research facilities, and opportunities for professional networking. Citizens' assemblies, public occupations, justice boats, democratic audits, brainstorming conferences, conflict of interest boards, global associations of parliamentarians against corruption and constitutional safaris (famously used by the drafters of the new South African constitution to examine best practice elsewhere) are on the list. Included as well are consumer testing agencies and consumer councils, online petitions and chat rooms, democracy clubs and democracy cafés, public vigils and peaceful sieges, summits, protestivals (a South Korean specialty) and global watchdog organisations set up to bring greater public accountability to business and other civil society bodies. The list of innovations extends to deliberative polls, independent religious courts, public 'scorecards' and consultation exercises, electronic civil disobedience, and websites, weblogs and Twitter feeds dedicated to monitoring the abuse of power. And the list of new inventions includes unofficial ballots (text-messaged straw polls, for instance), international criminal courts, truth and reconciliation commissions, global social forums and the tendency of increasing numbers of NGOs to adopt written constitutions, with an elected component.

Let us pause, if only because the inventory is disjointed and potentially confusing. Clear-headed thinking is needed to spot the qualities that these inventions share in common. Monitory institutions play several roles. Some monitors, electoral commissions, anti-corruption bodies and consumer protection agencies, for instance, use their avowed neutrality as 'guide dog' institutions to protect the rules of the democratic game from predators and enemies. Other monitors are committed to providing publics with extra viewpoints and better information about the performance of various governmental and non-governmental bodies. Since they typically contest imbalances of power by appealing to publics, monitory institutions (to scotch a common misunderstanding) must not be confused with top-down surveillance mechanisms that operate in secret, for the privately defined purposes of those who are in charge of government or civil society organisations. The public monitoring of unequal power stands in opposition to internal audits, closed-circuit surveillance ('for quality and training purposes, your call may be monitored') and other managerial techniques of administrative power.[6]

---

[6] There are clear differences in this respect between public monitors and the 'regulatory' agencies of the kind analysed by Frank Vibert, *The Rise of the Unelected: Democracy and the New Separation of Powers* (Cambridge and New York, 2007). While monitory bodies are often unelected, their wide appeals for public attention mark them off from bodies, such as independent central banks, economic regulators, risk managers and auditors, whose principal function is to demarcate boundaries between the market and the state, and to resolve conflicts of interest and to allocate resources, even in sensitive ethical areas, such as those involving biotechnology. Vibert argues that such regulatory bodies, taken together, should be viewed as a new branch of government with its own sources of legitimacy and held to account through a new separation of powers. Vibert's belief that such unelected regulatory bodies help to promote a more informed citizenry

Monitory mechanisms are geared as well to the definition, scrutiny and enforcement of public standards and ethical rules for preventing corruption, or the improper behaviour of those responsible for making decisions, not only in the field of elected government, but in a wide variety of power settings, banks and other business included. The new institutions of monitory democracy are sometimes geared to altering the time frame of official politics; in such fields as the environment, pensions and health care, they publicise long-term issues that are neglected, or dealt with badly, by the short-term mentality encouraged by election cycles. Monitory institutions are further defined by their overall commitment to strengthening the diversity and influence of citizens' voices and choices in decisions that affect their lives. Especially in times when substantial numbers of citizens believe that politicians are not easily trusted, and in which governments are often accused of abusing their power or being out of touch with citizens, or simply unwilling to deal with their concerns and problems, monitory democracy serves as a brake upon majority-rule democracy and its worship of numbers. It proves (contrary to twentieth-century advocates of so-called free markets) that democracy does not necessarily crush minorities. Monitory democracy also defies descriptions of democracy as essentially a matter of elite-led party competition dressed up in the razzamatazz of elections.[7] Freed from

because they provide a more trustworthy and reliable source of information for decisions rather seriously understates their tendency to wilful blindness and hubris, of the kind that enveloped banking and credit sector institutions on the eve of the post-2007 great recession.

[7] Ludwig von Mises, for whom markets unfailingly cater for minority interests, strongly objected to representative democracy, seeing it as a recipe for the tyranny of the majority. 'In the political democracy', he wrote, 'only the votes cast for the majority candidate or the majority plan are effective in shaping the course of affairs. The votes polled by the minority do not directly influence policies. But on the market no vote is cast in vain. Every penny spent has the power to work upon the production processes. The publishers cater not only to the majority by publishing detective stories, but also to the minority reading lyrical poetry and philosophical tracts. The bakeries bake bread not only for healthy people, but also for the sick on special diets' (*Human Action: A Treatise on Economics* (San Francisco, 1963, 1949), p. 271). The view that democracy in representative form is, in essence, oligopolistic rule by manipulative political party machines was famously defended by Joseph Schumpeter, *Capitalism, Socialism, and Democracy* (New York and London, 1942), p. 283: 'The psycho-technics of party management and party advertising, slogans and marching tunes, are not accessories. They are the essence of politics. So is the political boss.'

the measured caution and double-speak of political parties and official politics, monitory institutions in fact boost the chances of democracy with a small 'd', 'minoritarian' democracy. Regardless of the outcome of elections, and sometimes in direct opposition to the principle of majority rule, monitors give a voice to the losers and provide independent representation for minorities, for instance, to Indigenous, disabled and other peoples who cannot ever expect to lay claim to being or becoming a majority.

One person, many representatives

By making room for representations of ways of life that people feel strongly about, despite their neglect or suppression by parties, parliaments and governments, or by powerful organised private interests, the new monitory inventions have the combined effect of raising the level and quality of public awareness of power, including power relationships 'beneath' and 'beyond' the institutions of territorial states. It is little wonder that in many democracies the new power-monitoring inventions have changed the language of contemporary politics. They prompt much talk of 'empowerment', 'high energy democracy', 'stakeholders', 'participatory governance', 'communicative democracy' and 'deliberative democracy'; and they help to spread a culture of voting and representation into many walks of life where previously things were decided by less-than-democratic methods. Monitory democracy is the age of surveys, focus groups, deliberative polling, online petitions and audience and customer voting. There are even simulated elections, in which, for instance, television audiences granted a 'vote' by media companies are urged to lodge their preference for the star of their choice, by acclamation, cell phone or the Internet. Whether intended or not, the spreading culture of voting, backed by the new power-monitoring mechanisms, has the effect of interrupting and often silencing the soliloquies of parties, politicians and parliaments. With the help of new information banks, unelected representatives, muckraking and cross-border publics, the new power-scrutinising innovations tend to enfranchise many more citizens' voices. The number and range of monitory institutions have so greatly increased that they point to a world where the old rule of 'one person, one vote, one representative' – the central demand in the struggle for representative democracy – is replaced with the new principle of monitory democracy: 'one person, many interests, many voices, multiple votes, multiple representatives'.

A different way of putting the same point is to say that what is distinctive about monitory democracy is that potentially *all fields of social and political life* come to be publicly scrutinised, not just by the standard machinery of representative democracy, but by a whole host of *non-party, extra-parliamentary and often unelected bodies* operating within, underneath and beyond the boundaries of territorial states. In the era of monitory democracy, it is as if the principles of representative democracy – public openness, citizens' equality, selecting representatives – are superimposed on representative democracy itself. This has many practical consequences, but one especially striking effect is to alter the patterns of interaction – political geography – of democratic institutions.

We could put things in this way: once upon a time, in the brief heyday of representative democracy, say immediately after the First World War, the thing called democracy had a rather simple political geography (Figure 2.1). Within the confines of any given state, from the point of view of citizens, democracy principally meant taking an interest in an election campaign and, on the great day of reckoning, turning out to vote for a party or independent candidate. He – it was almost always men – was someone local, a figure known to the community, a local shopkeeper or professional, or someone in business or a trade unionist, for instance. Their test was democracy's great ceremonial, the pause of deliberation, the calm of momentary reflection, the catharsis of ticking and crossing, before the storm of result. 'Universal peace is declared', was the sarcastic way the nineteenth-century English novelist George Eliot (1819–1880) put it, 'and the foxes have a sincere interest in prolonging the lives of the poultry.' Her American contemporary, Walt Whitman (1819–1892), spoke more positively of the pivotal function of polling day as the great 'choosing day', the 'powerfulest scene', a 'swordless conflict' mightier than Niagara Falls or the Mississippi River or the geysers of Yosemite, a 'still small voice vibrating', a time for 'the peaceful choice of all', a passing moment of suspended animation when 'the heart pants, life glows'.[8] If blessed with

---

[8] George Eliot, *Felix Holt: The Radical* (Edinburgh and London, 1866), ch. 5, p. 127; Walt Whitman, 'Election Day, November 1884', in *Leaves of Grass* (New York, 1891/2), p. 391.

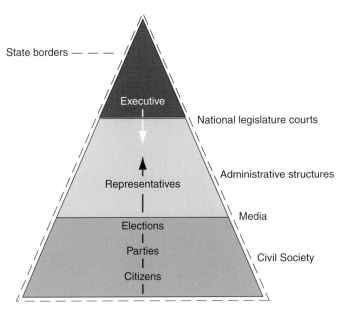

State borders — — —

Executive

National legislature courts

Representatives

Administrative structures

Elections

Media

Parties

Civil Society

Citizens

Figure **2.1** Territorially-bound representative democracy, by Giovanni Navarria.

enough votes, the local representative joined a privileged small circle of legislators, whose job was to stay in line with party policy, support or oppose a government that used its majority in the legislature, to pass laws and to scrutinise their implementation, hopefully with results that pleased as many of the represented as possible. At the end of a limited stint as legislator, buck-passing stopped. Foxes and poultry fell quiet. It was again time for the 'swordless conflict' of the great choosing day. The representative either stepped down, into retirement from political life, or faced the music of re-election.

This is obviously a simplified sketch of the role of elections, but it serves to highlight the different, much more complex political geography of monitory democracy (see Figure 2.2). There are historical continuities, of course. Just as modern representative democracies preserved the old custom of public assemblies of citizens, so monitory democracies keep alive and depend upon legislatures, political parties and elections, which continue to be bitterly fought, closely contested and consequential affairs. But such is the growing variety of interlaced, power-monitoring mechanisms that democrats from earlier times

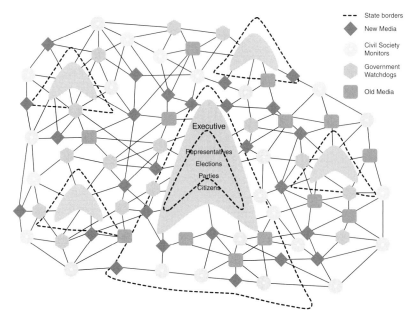

Figure 2.2 Monitory democracy, by Giovanni Navarria.

would, if catapulted into the new world of monitory democracy, find it hard to understand what is happening.

The new democracy demands a shift of perspective, a break with conventional thinking in order to understand its political geography. For this purpose, let us imagine for a moment, as if from a satellite orbiting our planet, the contours of the new democracy. We would spot that its power-scrutinising institutions are less centred on elections, parties and legislatures; they are no longer confined to the territorial state; and are spatially arranged in ways much messier than textbooks on democracy typically suppose. The vertical 'depth' and horizontal 'reach' of monitory institutions is striking. If the number of levels within any hierarchy of institutions is a measure of its 'depth', and if the number of units located within each of these levels is called its 'span' or 'width', then monitory democracy is the deepest and widest system of democracy ever known. The political geography of mechanisms like integrity commissions, citizens' assemblies, Web-based message systems, local action groups, regional parliaments, summits and global watchdog organisations defies simple-minded descriptions. So, too, does the political geography of the wider constellation of power-checking and power-disputing mechanisms in which they are embedded – bodies like human rights networks, citizen juries, audit and integrity commissions, and many other watchdog organisations set up to bring greater public accountability to business and other civil society bodies.

Possible misunderstandings

New ways of thinking about the political world inevitably produce confusions and misunderstandings. The theory of monitory democracy is no exception. While it is often said, for instance, that the struggle to bring greater public accountability to government and NGOs that wield power over others is in effect a struggle for 'grassroots democracy', or 'participatory democracy' or 'popular empowerment', the metaphors rest on a misunderstanding of contemporary trends. The age of monitory democracy is not heading backwards; it is not motivated by efforts to recapture the (imagined) spirit of assembly-based democracy – 'power to the people' – as some supporters of groups like Students for a Democratic Society (SDS) liked to chant at political demonstrations during the 1960s. Many contemporary champions of 'deep' or 'direct' democracy still speak as if they are Greeks, as if what really counts for a democracy is 'the commitment and capacities of ordinary people to make sensible decisions through reasoned deliberation and empowered because they attempt to tie action to discussion'.[9] The reality of monitory democracy is otherwise, in that all of the new power-scrutinising experiments in the name of 'the people' or citizens' empowerment rely inevitably on *representation*, that is, public claims about some or other matter made by some actors on behalf and in defence of others. These experiments often draw their legitimacy from the imagined, politically crafted body known as 'the people';[10] but they are not understandable

---

[9] Archon Fung and Erik Olin Wright, 'Thinking about Empowered Participatory Governance', in Archon Fung and Erik Olin Wright, *Deepening Democracy: Institutional Innovations in Empowered Participatory Governance* (London and New York, 2003), p. 5.

[10] To rephrase this paradoxical idea, if the principles of representative democracy turned 'the people' of assembly democracy into a more distant judge of how well representatives performed, then monitory democracy exposes the fiction of a unified 'sovereign people'. The dynamic structures of monitory democracy serve

as efforts to abolish the gap between representatives and the represented, as if citizens could live without others acting on their behalf, or find their true selves and express themselves as equals within a unified political community no longer burdened by miscommunication, or by mis-government.

Monitory democracy, in fact, thrives on representation, as the much-discussed example of citizen assemblies shows.[11] It thrives as well on elections, even though their changing status and significance prevents many people from spotting the novelty of monitory democracy. Since 1945, when there were only a dozen democracies left on the face of the earth, party-based democracy has made a big comeback, so much so that it tricked scholars like Francis Fukuyama and Samuel Huntington into thinking that nothing had changed, except for a large global leap in the number of representative democracies. Their mistake is understandable: following the widespread collapse and near extinction of democracy during the first half of the twentieth century, most parts of the world have since become familiar with the basic institutions of electoral democracy. Conventional party-centred forms of representation do not simply wither away. Millions of people have grown accustomed to competition among political parties, periodic elections, the limited-term holding of political office and the right of citizens to assemble in public to make their views known to their representatives in legislatures and executives that operate within the jurisdictional boundaries of territorial states. In contexts as different as Bangladesh, Nigeria,

---

as barriers against the uncontrolled worship of 'the people', or what might be dubbed demolatry. Monitory democracy demonstrates that the world is made up of many *demoi*, and that particular societies are made up of flesh-and-blood people who have different interests and who, therefore, do not necessarily see eye to eye. It could be said that monitory democracy democratises – publicly exposes – the whole principle of 'the sovereign people' as a pompous fiction; at best, it turns it into a handy reference device that most people know to be just that: a useful political fiction. There are, indeed, times when the fiction of 'the people' serves as a monitoring principle, as a former Justice of the Federal Constitutional Court in Germany, Dieter Grimm has explained: 'The circumstances are rare in which the fiction of "the demos" is needed as a reminder that those who make the laws are not the source of their ultimate legitimacy. Democracies need public power; but they need as well to place limits on the exercise of public power by invoking "the people" as a fictional subject to whom collectively binding powers are attributed: a "*Zurechnungssubjekt*" that is not itself capable of acting, but which serves as a democratic necessity because it makes accountability meaningful', interview, Berlin, 23 November 2006.

[11] Keane, *The Life and Death of Democracy*, pp. 699–701.

Trinidad and Tobago, Malta and Botswana, even among Tibetans living in exile, the mechanisms of electoral democracy have taken root for the first time. In other contexts, especially those where electoral democracy is well embedded, there are ongoing experiments to improve the rules of the electoral game, for instance, by keeping tabs on elected representatives via electoral literacy and parliament watchdog initiatives (examples include innovative Web platforms, such as Parliament Watch (Abgeordnetenwatch.de) in Germany and Vote Compass in Canada). Still other experiments include the introduction of primary elections into political parties; tightened restrictions on campaign fundraising and spending; improvements in voting facilities for disabled citizens; and the banning of elected representatives from party-hopping (a decision taken by the Brazilian Supreme Court in 2007).

For all these reasons, it seemed perfectly reasonable for Huntington and other scholars to speak of the spectacular rebirth and extension of representative forms of democracy in recent decades as a 'third wave of democratisation'. Enter monitory democracy: a brand new historical type of democracy that operates in radically different ways from textbook accounts of 'representative', or 'parliamentary' or 'liberal' democracy, as it is still most often called. In the age of monitory democracy, democracy is practised in new ways. Where monitory democracy exists, institutions like periodic elections, multi-party competition and the right of citizens to voice their public approval or disapproval of legislation remain familiar fixtures. To repeat: under conditions of monitory democracy, the whole issue of who is entitled to vote, and under which conditions, continues to attract public attention and to stir up troubles. Think of the legal and political controversies sparked by the question of who owns the software of unreliable electronic voting machines manufactured by companies such as Election Systems and Software. Or consider the disputes triggered by the withdrawal of votes for people such as felons; or by claims that groups such as diasporas, minority language speakers, the disabled and people with low literacy and numeracy skills are disadvantaged by the secret ballot; or the loud public complaints about how still other constituencies, such as women, young people and the biosphere, are either poorly represented or are not properly represented at all.

Struggles to open up and improve the quality of electoral and legislative representation are by no means finished. But slowly and surely, the whole architecture of democracy has begun to change fundamentally. So too has the meaning of democracy. No longer synonymous with self-government by an assembly of privileged male citizens (as in the Greek city-states), or with party-based government guided by the will of a legislative majority, democracy has come to mean a way of life and a mode of governing in which power is subject to checks and balances – at any time, in any place – such that nobody is entitled to rule arbitrarily, without the consent of the governed or their representatives. An important symptom of the redefinition of democracy is the advent of election monitoring. During the 1980s, for the first time in the history of democracy, founding elections in new or strife-torn polities began to be monitored systematically by outside teams of observers.[12] 'Fair and open' methods – the elimination of violence, intimidation, ballot-rigging and other forms of political tomfoolery – are now expected of all countries, including the most powerful democracy on the face of the Earth, the United States, where the Organization for Security and Co-operation in Europe (OSCE) observers played a role for the first time in the presidential elections of November 2004.

In the era of monitory democracy, the franchise struggles which once tore whole societies apart have nevertheless lost their centrality. As the culture of voting spreads, and as unelected representatives multiply in many different contexts, a brand new issue begins to surface. The old question that racked the age of representative democracy – *who* is entitled to vote and *when* – is compounded and complicated by a question for which there are still no easy answers: *where* are people entitled to vote, *for whom* and *through which representatives*?

The intense public concern with publicly scrutinising matters once thought to be non-political is unique to the age of monitory democracy. The era of representative democracy (as Tocqueville first spotted) certainly saw the rise of self-organised pressure groups and schemes for 'socialising' the power of government, for instance, through councils of soldiers, workers' control of industry and Guild Socialist proposals. Yet few of these schemes survived the violent upheavals of the first half of the twentieth century, which makes the contrast with monitory democracy all the more striking. The sea change in favour of extra-parliamentary monitors is evident in the unprecedented level of interest in the old eighteenth-century European term 'civil society'; for the first

---

[12] E. C. Bjornlund, *Beyond Free and Fair: Monitoring Elections and Building Democracy* (Baltimore, MD, 2004).

time in the history of democracy, these two words are now routinely used by democrats around the world.

The change is also manifest in the strong trend towards the independent public scrutiny of all areas of government policy, ranging from public concern about the maltreatment and legal rights of children, and bodily habits related to exercise and diet, through to the development of habitat protection plans and efforts to take democracy 'upstream' to ensure that the future development, for instance, of nanotechnology, alternative energy sources and genetically-modified food is governed publicly in the interests of the many, not the few. Experiments with fostering new forms of citizens' participation and elected representation have begun to penetrate markets; a notable early example, an invention of the mid-1940s, is the German system of co-determination, known as *Mitbestimmung*, in which employees in firms of a certain size are entitled to elect their own representatives onto the management boards of companies. More recent examples of efforts to constrain arbitrary power within markets include the struggles of the poor in such fields as land rights, food production and literacy. The 'guerrilla auditors' who made their presence felt during Paraguay's long transition to democracy are an interesting case in point: an activist movement that waged pitched legal battles in defence of Guaraní land and the right to literacy by winning public access to previously unobtainable written documents held in state archives.[13]

In the age of monitory democracy, there is also rising awareness of the possibility and desirability of exercising new rights of criticism and casting a vote in previously off-limits areas of health and social care design and patient choice. The experience of publicly voicing concerns and voting for representatives even extends into large-scale global organisations, such as the International Olympic Committee (IOC), which (thanks to its becoming a target of muckraking journalism in the 1980s) has been transformed from an exclusive private gentlemen's club into a global body where the rules of public scrutiny and representative government are applied to its inner workings, so that its co-opted governing members meet at least once a year in Session, an assembly open to journalists and charged with managing the common affairs of the IOC, including the recommendation of new IOC members,

---

[13] See Craig Hetherington, *Guerrilla Auditors: The Politics of Transparency in Neoliberal Paraguay* (Durham, NC, 2011).

monitoring the codes of conduct of existing members and overall performance of the IOC itself.

The vital role played by civil societies in the invention of power-monitoring mechanisms seems to confirm what might be called James Madison's Law of Free Government: no government can be considered free unless it is capable of governing a society that is itself capable of controlling the government. The rule (sketched in the *Federalist Papers*, No. 51) has tempted some people to conclude – mistakenly – that governments are quite incapable of scrutinising their own power. The truth is sometimes otherwise. In the era of monitory democracy, experience shows that governments, for the sake of their own efficiency and effectiveness, as well as for the good of their own citizens, can be encouraged to submit their own powers to independent public scrutiny.

Government 'watchdog' and 'integrity' or 'anti-corruption' institutions are a case in point. Their stated purpose is the public scrutiny of government by semi-independent government agencies (it is worth remembering that the word scrutiny originally meant 'to sort rubbish', from the Latin *scrutari*, meaning 'to search', and from *scruta*, 'rubbish'). Scrutiny mechanisms bring new eyes, ears and teeth to the public sector. In this way, they supplement the power-monitoring role of elected government representatives and judges, even though this is not always their avowed aim. While scrutiny mechanisms are often introduced and backed by the general authority of elected governments, for instance, through the mechanism of ministerial responsibility, in practice, things often turn out differently. Government scrutiny bodies tend to take on a life of their own, especially when they are protected by legislation, given adequate resources and managed well. Building on the much older precedents of royal commissions, public enquiries and independent auditors checking the financial probity of government agencies – inventions that had their roots in the age of representative democracy – the new scrutiny mechanisms add checks and balances to avoid possible abuses of power by elected representatives. The national policy conferences held periodically in Brazil are an example; so also are the offices of inspector general in all cabinet-level agencies and most major federal government agencies in the United States.[14] The trend is confirmed by more recent Web-based experiments, such as the Open Government

---

[14] Thamy Pogrebinschi, 'Participatory Policymaking and Political Experimentalism in Brazil', in Stefanie Kron *et al.* (eds), *Democracia y reconfiguraciones*

Platform (a joint initiative of the Indian and US governments) and Recovery.gov. These government-initiated scrutiny mechanisms are justified in terms of enhancing the capacity to govern, for instance (say their champions), through improved decision-making, which has the added advantage of raising the level of public trust in political institutions among citizens considered as 'stakeholders' entitled to keep track of state-sector spending. The whole process displays a double paradox. Not only are government scrutiny mechanisms often established by governments that subsequently fail to control the workings of these same mechanisms, for instance, in cases of fraud and corruption and the enforcement of legal standards. The new mechanisms also have democratic, power-checking effects, even though they are normally staffed by judges, professional experts and other unelected officials, who themselves operate at several arms' length from the rhythm of periodic elections.

It is worth noting, finally, that monitory democracy challenges the prejudices of those who are resistant to the whole idea of 'cross-border' or 'international' democracy. These prejudices have deep roots. They date from the era of territorially bound representative democracy, and, in consequence, almost all leading scholars of democracy today defend the supposed truth of such propositions as 'democracy requires statehood' and 'without a state there can be no democracy'. An interesting feature of monitory democracy is that it helps in practice to confront these prejudices head on. Agencies such as the Electoral Assistance Division of the United Nations, the Office for Democratic Institutions and Human Rights (part of the OSCE), as well as inventions such as global appeals through public occupations, cross-border parliaments, peer review panels, laws outlawing corporate bribery, regional and global courts and other latticed forms of power-monitoring effectively scramble the distinction between 'domestic' and 'foreign', the 'local' and the 'global'. Like other types of institutions, including businesses and universities, democracy too is caught up in complex processes of 'glocalisation'. This is another way of saying that its monitory mechanisms are dynamically interconnected, to the point where each monitor functions simultaneously as both part and whole of the overall system.

contemporáneas del derecho en America Latina (Frankfurt am Main and Madrid, 2012), pp. 111–36; Michael Schudson, 'Political Observatories, Databases and News in the Emerging Ecology of Public Information', *Daedalus* (Spring 2010): 100–9.

Innovations such as the US Foreign Corrupt Practices Act 1977 (the first
legislation anywhere to make bribery payments by corporations to
foreign government officials a criminal offence) and the follow-up
OECD Anti-Bribery Convention (1999) spotlight the point that public
resistance to arbitrary power is no longer 'housed' exclusively within
'sovereign' territorial states.[15] Under conditions of monitory democracy, parts (state-based monitors) and wholes (regional and global
monitors) do not exist in a strict or absolute sense. The units of monitory democracy are better described as sub-wholes – 'holons' is the term
famously coined by Arthur Koestler[16] – that function simultaneously as
self-regarding and self-asserting entities that publicly chasten power
without asking permission from higher authorities, and push and pull
each other in a multilateral system of monitoring in which all entities
play a role, sometimes to the point where the part and the whole are
blurred beyond recognition.

Why monitory democracy?

It is often said that the public business of power scrutiny changes very
little, that states and corporations are still the 'real' unchecked centres of
power in deciding not only who gets what in the world, but also when
and how. Evidence that this is not necessarily so is suggested by the fact
that all the big public issues that have erupted around the world since
1945, including civil rights for women and minorities, opposition to
nuclear weapons and American military intervention in Vietnam and
Iraq, poverty reduction and the greening of politics, have been generated not by political parties, elections, legislatures and governments, but
principally by power-monitoring networks that run parallel to – and are
often aligned against – the conventional mechanisms of party-based
parliamentary representation. These monitoring networks have played
a vital role in building and strengthening monitory democracy, but to
say this is to raise a difficult question: have there been other forces at
work in making monitory democracy possible? How can its unplanned
birth and development be explained?

---

[15] Frank Vogl, *Waging War on Corruption: Inside the Movement Fighting the
   Abuse of Power* (Lanham, MD, 2012).
[16] Arthur Koestler, *The Ghost in the Machine* (London, 1967), p. 48.

The query brings us back to the subject of communicative abundance, but not immediately. For the forces that resulted in the various power-scrutinising inventions described above are complicated; as in earlier phases of the history of democracy, generalisations concerning origins are as difficult as they are perilous. Yet two things can safely be said. More obviously, the new type of democracy has had both its causes and causers. Monitory democracy is not a monogenic matter – a living thing hatched from a single cell. It is, rather, the result of multiple pressures that have conspired over time to reshape the spirit, language and institutions of democracy as we know it today. The other thing about which we can be certain is that one word above all describes the most powerful early trigger of the new era of monitory democracy: war.

In the history of democracy, war and the pity and suffering of war have often been the midwife of new democratic institutions.[17] That rule certainly applied to the first half of the twentieth century, the most murderous recorded in human history. Two global wars plus terrible cruelties shattered old structures of security, sparked pushes and shoves and elbowing for power, as well as unleashing angry popular energies that fed major revolutionary upheavals, usually in the name of 'the people' against representative democracy. Bolshevism and Stalinism in Russia, fascism in Italy, Nazism in Germany and military imperialism in Japan were effectively twisted and perverted mutations of democracy, which was typically misunderstood within these regimes as a mere synonym for popular sovereignty. These were regimes whose leaders acknowledged that 'the people' were entitled to mount the stage of history – regimes whose hirelings then set about muzzling, maiming and murdering both opponents and supporters among flesh-and-blood people. Western democracy was denounced as parliamentary dithering and muddling, as liberal perplexity, bourgeois hypocrisy and military cowardice. A third of the way into the twentieth century, parliamentary democracy was on its knees. It seemed rudderless, spiritless, paralysed, doomed. By 1941, when President Roosevelt called for 'bravely shielding the great flame of democracy from the blackout of barbarism',[18]

---

[17] Keane, *The Life and Death of Democracy*; John Keane, 'Epilogue: Does Democracy have a Violent Heart?', in D. M. Pritchard (ed.), *War, Democracy and Culture in Classical Athens* (London and New York, 2010).

[18] President Roosevelt, Address to the White House Correspondents' Association Washington, 15 March 1941. The surviving electoral democracies included

when untold numbers of villains had drawn the contrary conclusion that dictatorship and totalitarianism were the future, only eleven electoral democracies remained on the face of the Earth.

The possibility of annihilation galvanised minds and gritted determinations to do something, both about the awful destruction produced by war, and the dictatorships and totalitarian regimes spawned by those wars. The great cataclysms that culminated in the Second World War demonstrated to many people the naiveté of the old formula that people should obey their governments because their rulers protected their lives and possessions. The devastating upheavals of the period proved that this protection–obedience formula was unworkable, that in various countries long-standing pacts between rulers and ruled had been so violated that rulers could no longer be trusted to rule. The problem, in other words, was no longer the mobocracy of 'the people', as critics of democracy had insisted from the time of Plato and Thucydides until well into the nineteenth century. The terrible events of the first half of the twentieth century proved that mobocracy had its true source in thuggish leaders (Theodor Adorno dubbed them 'glorified barkers') skilled at denouncing 'democracy' as decadence and calling on 'the people' to mount the stage of history, only to then muzzle, maim and murder flesh-and-blood people in their name, so destroying the plural freedoms and political equality (one person, one vote) for which electoral democracy had avowedly stood.[19] The problem, thus, was no longer the mob, and mob rule. Ruling – the arbitrary exercise of power by some over others – was, in fact, the problem.

The problem of ruling people from above stood at the centre of an important, though unfortunately little studied, batch of political reflections on democracy in the years just before and immediately after

Australia, Canada, Chile, Costa Rica, New Zealand, Sweden, Switzerland, the United Kingdom, the United States and Uruguay. Despite its use of an electoral college to choose a president under high-security, wartime conditions, Finland might also be included, as might Eire.

[19] A sustained fascist attack on 'democracy' was developed by Alfred Rosenberg, *Der Mythus des 20. Jahrhunderts., Eine Wertung der seelisch-geistigen Gestaltenkämpfe unserer Zeit* (Munich, 1934). Democracy is said to be based on 'abstract popular sovereignty'. It treats 'the people' as 'that part of the state which does not know what it wants'. It stifles 'folkish consciousness'; peddles 'faceless ideas of the state'; spawns 'parliamentary decomposition' and 'mass stagnation'. So-called democracy perpetuates 'mass swindling and exploitation' because in reality it is nothing more than 'a tool of capitalism and the moneyed classes'.

1945.[20] The intellectual roots of monitory democracy are traceable to this period, when the possible self-extinction of electoral democracy triggered a moment of 'dark energy': the universe of meaning of democracy underwent a dramatic expansion, in defiance of the cosmic gravity of contemporary events. The new energy is, for instance, evident in the contributions of literary, theological and intellectual figures otherwise as different as Albert Camus, John Dewey, Sidney Hook, Thomas Mann, Jacques Maritain, J. B. Priestley and, strikingly, in a work that soon became a classic, Reinhold Niebuhr's *The Children of Light and the Children of Darkness* (1945). Each of these authors voiced fears that the narrow escape of parliamentary democracy from the clutches of war and totalitarianism might just be a temporary reprieve. Several writers even asked whether the near-destruction of parliamentary democracy served as confirmation that global events were now pushing towards 'the end of the world' (Albert Camus). Thomas Mann gave voice to the trend when noting the need for 'democracy's deep and forceful recollection of itself, the renewal of its spiritual and moral self-consciousness'. Voicing puzzlement and shock at the way the electoral democracies of the 1920s and 1930s had spawned the growth of demagogues, most authors agreed that among the vital lessons provided by recent historical experience was the way the language and practice of majority-rule democracy could be utterly corrupted, to the point where the word democracy was not only wielded in 'a consciously dishonest way' (George Orwell), but its mechanisms were used and abused by the enemies of democracy in the name of the

[20] John Keane, 'The Origins of Monitory Democracy', available at: http://theconversation.edu.au/the-origins-of-monitory-democracy-9752, accessed 13 October 2012. The early years after the Second World War witnessed many new lines of thinking about the future of democracy, within a global context. See, for instance, Thomas Mann, *Goethe and Democracy* (Washington, DC, 1949); Carl J. Friedrich, *Constitutional Government and Democracy* (Boston, MA, 1941); Jacques Maritain, 'Christianity and Democracy', a typewritten manuscript prepared as an address at the annual meeting of the American Political Science Association, New York, 29 December 1949; Harold Laski *et al.*, *The Future of Democracy* (London, 1946); Albert Camus, *Neither Victims nor Executioners* (Chicago, 1972 (first published in the autumn 1946 issues of *Combat*)); Reinhold Niebuhr, *The Children of Light and the Children of Darkness: A Vindication of Democracy and a Critique of its Traditional Defenders* (London, 1945); Pope Pius XII, *Democracy and Peace* (London, 1945); Sidney Hook, 'What Exactly Do We Mean by "Democracy"?', *New York Times*, 16 March 1947, pp. 10 ff; A. D. Lindsay, *Democracy in the World Today* (London, 1945).

'sovereign people'. In quest of a new understanding of democracy, more than a few authors openly attacked metaphysical talk of 'the People' and their supposed 'Sovereignty'. 'Everything comes out of the people', said J. B. Priestley in a large-audience, night-time BBC broadcast, then asking exactly who are 'the people'. 'The people are real human beings', he answered. 'If you prick them, they bleed . . . They swing between fear and hope. They have strange dreams. They hunger for happiness. They all have names and faces. They are not some cross-section of abstract stuff.'[21]

Deeply troubled, more than a few authors called for fresh, untried remedies for the maladies of representative democracy. The abandonment of sentimental optimism was high on their list. Some political thinkers (Carl J. Friedrich) emphasised the need for constitutional restraints upon elected governments. Others called for the injection of religious principles into the ethos and institutions of democracy. Opinions were often divided, but all these writers of the 1940s restated their support for a new form of democracy, one whose spirit and institutions were infused with a robust commitment to rooting out the devils of arbitrary, publicly unaccountable power. The American theologian Niebuhr (1892–1971), who later won prominent admirers, including Martin Luther King Jr, provided one of the weightiest cases for renewing and transforming democracy along these lines. 'The perils of uncontrolled power are perennial reminders of the virtues of a democratic society', he wrote. 'But modern democracy requires a more realistic philosophical and religious basis, not only in order to anticipate and understand the perils to which it is exposed, but also to give it a more persuasive justification.' He concluded with words that became famous: 'Man's capacity for justice makes democracy possible; but man's inclination to injustice makes democracy necessary.'[22]

In perhaps the boldest move, still other thinkers argued for abandoning the presumption that the 'natural home' of democracy in representative form is the sovereign territorial state. So they pleaded for extending democratic principles across territorial borders. 'The history of the past twenty years', Friedrich wrote, 'has shown beyond a shadow of a doubt that constitutional democracy cannot function effectively on

[21] Later published as J. B. Priestley, *Out of the People* (London, 1941), pp. 111, 16–17.
[22] Niebuhr, *The Children of Light and the Children of Darkness*, p. vi.

a national plane.' Thomas Mann rubbished attempts to 'reduce the democratic idea to the idea of peace, and to assert that the right of a free people to determine its own destiny includes respect for the rights of foreign people and thus constitutes the best guarantee for the creation of a community of nations and for peace.' He added: 'We must reach higher and envisage the whole. We must define democracy as that form of government and of society which is inspired above every other with the feeling and consciousness of the dignity of man.'[23]

This way of thinking about the political dangers of arbitrary power undoubtedly helped to inspire one of the most remarkable features of monitory democracy: the marriage of democracy and human rights, and the subsequent worldwide growth of organisations, networks and campaigns committed to the defence of human rights. The intermarriage had roots extending back to the French Revolution, certainly, but its immediate inspiration was two major political declarations inspired by the horrors of the Second World War: the United Nations Charter (1945) and the Universal Declaration of Human Rights (1948). The second was arguably the more remarkable candle in the gloom bred by the death of 45 million people, terrible physical destruction and spiritual misery, and the escalating violence and mounting post-war tensions bound up with such political troubles as ethno-national cleansing in Europe, the bloody partition of Pakistan and India, the Berlin blockade and the unresolved future of Palestine. Drafted in 1947 and 1948, the Universal Declaration of Human Rights seemed to many at the time to be a mere sideshow of questionable importance. Its preamble spoke of 'the inherent dignity' and 'the equal and inalienable rights of all members of the human family'. It was in effect a call for civil societies and governments everywhere to speak and act as if human rights mattered; its practical effect was to help redefine democracy as monitory democracy. Today, networked organisations like Human Rights Watch, the Aga Khan Development Network, Amnesty International and tens of thousands of other non-governmental human rights organisations routinely deal with a wide range of rights matters including torture, child soldiers, the abuse of women and freedom of religious conviction. Their job is the advocacy of human rights through well-researched, skilfully publicised campaigns. They see themselves as goads to the conscience of

---

[23] Friedrich, *Constitutional Government and Democracy*, p. 34; Thomas Mann, *The Coming Victory of Democracy* (London, 1943), p. 22.

governments and citizens, and they solve a basic problem that had dogged representative democracy: who decides who are 'the people'? Most human rights organisations and networks answer: every human being is entitled to exercise their right to have rights, including the right to take advantage of communicative abundance by communicating freely with others, as equals.

Communicative abundance

The intermarriage of human rights and democracy and the many monitory institutions that have sprung into life since 1945 proved that democracy is not always cursed by war, and that there are times when terrible violence functions as a trigger for citizens and institution builders to take things into their own hands. But if the horrors of total war were the prime initial catalyst of the birth of monitory democracy, then more recently, without doubt, upheavals in the mode of communication media are proving to be a vital driver of its subsequent growth.

In the era of monitory democracy, all institutions in the business of scrutinising power rely heavily on these media innovations; if the new galaxy of communicative abundance suddenly imploded, monitory democracy would be finished. Monitory democracy and computerised media networks behave as if they are conjoined twins. To say this is not to fall into the trap of supposing that computer-linked communications networks prefigure a brand new utopian world, a carnival of 'virtual communities' homesteading on the electronic frontier, a 'cyber-revolution' that yields equal access of all citizens to all media, anywhere and at any time. The new age of communicative abundance, in fact, produces many contradictions and disappointments, for instance (as we have seen), in the widening power gaps between media rich and media poor, who themselves seem almost unneeded as communicators, or as consumers of media products, simply because they have no market-buying power. Communication poverty contradicts the basic principle of monitory democracy that all citizens equally are entitled to communicate their opinions, and periodically to give elected and unelected representatives a rough ride. Yet the fundamental point remains: when viewed from the standpoint of monitory democracy and its future, the advent of communicative abundance ought to be regarded as a most welcome development.

The combined effect of new information banks, the politicisation of private life, public muckraking and the appearance of new cross-border publics, some of them centred on unelected representatives, is to encourage people's suspicions of unaccountable power. Within message-saturated democracies citizens come to learn that they must keep an eye on power and its supposed representatives. They see that prevailing power relationships are not 'natural', but contingent, the resultant of political processes. One could go further. In the age of communicative abundance, or so it seems, bossy power can no longer hide comfortably behind private masks. Power relations everywhere are subjected to organised efforts by some, with the help of media, to tell others – publics of various sizes – about matters that had previously been hidden away, 'in private'. We live in times when private text messages and video footage rebound publicly, to reveal monkey business that forces the resignation of leading government officials. It is an age in which hand-held cameras are used by citizen reporters to upload materials featuring election candidates live, unplugged and unscripted; and this is the age in which mobile telephone pictures and leaked videos and cablegrams serve as evidence that soldiers in war zones commit war crimes. These and other acts of denaturing power are usually a messy business, and they often come wrapped in rumours and hype, certainly. But the unmasking of power resonates strongly with the power-scrutinising spirit of monitory democracy.

Helped along by red-blooded journalism that relies on styles of reporting concerned less with veracity than with 'breaking news' and blockbusting scoops, communicative abundance sometimes hacks into the power relations of government and civil society. It is easy to complain about the methods of muckraking journalism. It hunts in packs, its eyes on bad news, egged on by the newsroom saying that facts must never be allowed to get in the way of stories. It loves titillation, draws upon unattributed sources, fills news holes – in the era of monitory democracy news never sleeps – spins sensations, and concentrates too much on personalities, rather than time-bound contexts. The new journalism is formulaic and gets bored too quickly; and there are times (as we shall see) when it bows down to corporate power and government press briefings, sometimes even serving as a vehicle for the public circulation of organised lies. Such objections to muckraking journalism should be taken seriously; but they are only half the story. Simply put, red-blooded journalism, exemplified by the controversial efforts of

WikiLeaks to release and circulate cablegrams, keeps alive the old utopias of 'government in the sunshine', shedding light on power, 'freedom of information' and greater 'truth' and 'transparency' in the making and implementation of decisions. Given that unchecked power still weighs down hard on the heads of citizens, it is not surprising, thanks to a host of monitory mechanisms, muckraking journalism and easy access to cheap tools of communication, such as multi-purpose mobile phones, that public objections to wrongdoing and corruption are commonplace in the era of monitory democracy. Scandals seem to be a daily occurrence, sometimes to the point where, like earthquakes, breathtaking revelations rumble the foundations of even the most powerful or publicly respected institutions.

In the age of monitory democracy, some scandals have become legendary, like the public uproar in the United States caused by the inadvertent discovery of evidence of secret burglaries of the Democratic Party National Committee headquarters in the Watergate Hotel in Washington, DC, and by the subsequent snowballing of events that became the Watergate affair, which resulted in threats of impeachment and the eventual resignation of President Nixon in August 1974. On the other side of the Atlantic, 'classic' scandals have included the Filesa affair, the rumpus in the early 1990s within Spanish politics triggered by a government auditors' report that confirmed that senior Socialist Party officials had operated front companies, for which they were paid gigantic sums for consultancy services that were never rendered. Then there was the nationwide investigation by Italian police and judges of the extensive system of political corruption dubbed 'bribesville' (*Tangentopoli*), the so-called *mani pulite* ('clean hands') campaign that led to the disappearance of many political parties and the suicide of some politicians and industry leaders after their crimes were exposed. There was also the resignation of the French foreign minister and the admission by the French president on television that agents of the French secret service (DGSE) were responsible for the murder (in July 1985) of a Greenpeace activist and the bombing of their support vessel, the *Rainbow Warrior*, a boat that had been due to lead a flotilla of yachts to protest against French nuclear testing at Mururoa Atoll in the Pacific Ocean. And not to be forgotten is the bitter global controversy triggered by the whopping lies about 'weapons of mass destruction' spun by the defenders of the American-led military invasion of Iraq in the early years of the twenty-first century – an invasion, according to the most reliable estimates, that resulted in many hundreds of thousands of deaths, produced several million refugees and left behind many more traumatised children and orphans.

There is something utterly novel about the intensity and scale of these sagas. From its origins in the ancient assemblies of Syria-Mesopotamia, democracy has always cut through and 'de-natured' habit and prejudice and hierarchies of power. Democracy has always been a friend of contingency. It has stirred up the sense that people can shape and re-shape their lives as equals, and, not surprisingly, it has often brought commotion into the world. In the era of monitory democracy, the constant public scrutiny of power by many differently sized monitory bodies with footprints large and small makes it the most energetic, most dynamic form of democracy ever. The dynamics of monitory democracy are not describable using the simple spatial metaphors inherited from the age of representative democracy. Talk of the 'sovereignty' of parliament, or of 'local' versus 'central' government or of tussles between 'pressure groups', political parties and governments, is just too simple. In terms of political geometry, the system of monitory democracy is something other and different: a complex web of differently sized monitory bodies that have the effect, thanks to communicative abundance, of continuously stirring up questions about who gets what, when and how, as well as holding publicly responsible those who exercise power, wherever they are situated. Monitory democracy even contains bodies (the Democratic Audit network, the Democracy Barometer and Transparency International have already been mentioned) that specialise in providing public assessments of the quality of existing power-scrutinising mechanisms and the degree to which they fairly represent citizens' interests. Other bodies specialise in directing questions at governments on a wide range of matters, extending from their human rights records, their energy production plans to the quality of the drinking water of their cities. Private companies are grilled about their services and products, their investment plans, how they treat their employees and the size of their impact upon the biosphere. Various watchdogs and guide dogs and barking dogs are constantly on the job, pressing for greater public accountability of those who exercise power. The powerful consequently come to feel their constant pinch.

In the age of monitory democracy, bossy power can no longer hide comfortably behind private masks; in principle, and often in practice, power relations are subjected to organised efforts by some, with the help of media, to tell others publicly about matters that previously had been hidden away, 'in private', behind closed doors and curtains of secrecy. In the age of communicative abundance some people complain about its negative effects, such as 'information overload' and the tendency of media scrutiny to drag down the reputations of politicians and 'politics'. But, from the point of view of monitory democracy, it is at least arguable that communicative abundance has, on balance, positive consequences, or so it seems.

In spite of all its hype and spin, the new media galaxy makes possible the broadening of people's horizons. It produces wise citizens: experienced citizens who know that they do not know everything, and who suspect those who think that they do, especially when they try to camouflage their arrogant will to power over others. Communicative abundance does this by multiplying the genres of programming, information and storytelling that are available to audiences and publics. News, chat shows, political oratory, bitter legal spats, comedy, infotainment, drama, music, advertising, blogs – all of this, and much more, constantly clamour and jostle for public attention. Communicative abundance thus tutors people's sense of pluralism. It reminds them that 'truth' has many faces. Public awareness that 'truth' depends on context and perspective even prods (some) people into taking greater responsibility for how, when and why they communicate. Message-saturated democracies generate plenty of political dissimulation and lying, certainly;[24] but, partly for that reason as well, communicative abundance nurtures people's suspicions of media manipulation and arbitrary power. It tends to heighten awareness that democracy is an unending experiment in taming hazardous concentrations of power. All the king's horses and all the king's men are unlikely to reverse the trend – or so there are good reasons for thinking. The days of representative democracy and spectrum-scarcity broadcasting and mass entertainment are over. So, too, are the days when millions of people, huddled together as masses in the shadows of totalitarian power, found the skilfully orchestrated radio and film performances of demagogues fascinating, and existentially reassuring.

---

[24] See John Keane, 'Lying, Journalism, Democracy', Sydney, November 2010, available at: http://johnkeane.info/media/pdfs/lectures/jk-lectures-lying-media-and-democracy.pdf-revised.pdf; an audio version ('Alexandre Koyré: On the Political dangers of Telling Lies') can be found at: http://johnkeane.net/41/topics-of-interest/lying-journalism-democracy.

In the age of communicative abundance, (some) people are learning that they must keep an eye on power and its representatives, that they must make judgements and choose their own courses of action. These wise citizens understand that power monitoring can be ineffective, or counterproductive, and that it has no guaranteed outcomes. These citizens know that public scrutiny campaigns misfire or are poorly targeted. They note with frustration that public outcries sometimes leave everything as it is. They see that power wielders often cleverly find loopholes and ways of rebutting or simply ignoring their opponents. Sometimes wise citizens find the monitory strategies of organisations too timid, or confused or simply irrelevant to their lives as consumers, workers, parents, community residents and voters. Despite such weaknesses, which need to be addressed urgently both in theory and practice, the political dynamics and overall 'feel' of monitory democracies are very different from the era of representative democracy. Politics in the age of monitory democracy has a definite 'viral' quality about it. Think for a moment about any current public controversy that attracts widespread attention: news about its contours and commentaries and disputes about its significance are typically relayed by many power-monitoring organisations, large, medium and small. In the world of monitory democracy, that kind of latticed pattern – viral, networked – is typical, not exceptional. It helps to explain why citizens are being tempted to think for themselves; to see the same world in different ways, from different angles; and to sharpen their overall sense that prevailing power relationships are not 'natural', but contingent. Communicative abundance promotes something of a long-term mood swing in the perception of power. The metaphysical idea of an objective, out-there-at-a-distance 'reality' is weakened; so too is the presumption that stubborn 'factual truth' is superior to power.[25] The fabled distinction between what people can see with their eyes and what they are told about the emperor's new clothes breaks down.

Under media-saturated conditions marked by dynamism, pluralism and competing stories told about how the world works, 'information' ceases to be a fixed category with definite content. What counts as information is less and less understood by wise citizens as 'hard facts' or as chunks of 'reality' to be mined from television and radio programmes, or from newspapers or Internet blogs, and certainly not from

[25] See Gianni Vattimo, *A Farewell to Truth* (New York, 2011).

the mouths of people who think of themselves as authorities. The famous landscape photographer Ansel Adams (1902–1984) reportedly once remarked that while not everybody trusts the representational qualities of paintings, 'people believe photographs'.[26] Those who repeat the remark (usually out of context) seem so mid-twentieth century, for thanks to Photoshop techniques and the paparazzi many people have in fact come to understand that cameras do lie, that photographs should be looked at and looked into, and that every photograph minimally contains two people: the photographer and the viewer. In the age of communicative abundance, to put the point more sharply, 'reality', including the 'reality' promoted by the powerful, comes to be understood as always 'reported reality', as 'reality' produced by some for others, in other words, as messages that are shaped and re-shaped and re-shaped again in the process of transmission. Reality is multiple and mutable, a matter of re-description and interpretation – and of the power marshalled by wise citizens and their representatives to prevent particular interpretations of the world from being forced down others' throats.

[26] Ansel Adams, in Nathan Lyons (ed.), *Photographers on Photography: A Critical Anthology* (Englewood Cliffs, NJ, 1966), p. 32: 'To photograph truthfully and effectively is to see beneath the surfaces and record the qualities of nature and humanity which live or are latent in all things. Impression is not enough. Design, style, technique, – these, too, are not enough. Art must reach further than impression or self-revelation. Art, said Alfred Stieglitz, is the affirmation of life. And life, or its eternal evidence, is everywhere. Some photographers take reality as the sculptors take wood and stone and upon it impose the dominations of their own thought and spirit. Others come before reality more tenderly and a photograph to them is an instrument of love and elevation. A true photograph need not be explained, nor can be contained in words.'

3 | *Media decadence*

Given the positively self-reinforcing novelty of communicative abundance, it is unsurprising that more than a few journalists, media industry figures, politicians and citizens wax eloquent about the thrilling ways in which the new media revolution is fundamentally altering the landscape of our lives, and our politics, often for the better. Contemporary events – exemplified by the global occupation movements that spread from the media-fuelled uprisings against dictatorship in the Arab world during 2011 – are often cited as confirmation of the trend. The pundits have a point; they seem to have history on their side. Expanding information banks, public exposés of the corrupting effects of private and secretive power, enhanced political representation and expanding cross-border publics are important democratic facts of our time. Their technical basis and political originality, along with their power-chastening effects, should not be underestimated. But they should not be worshipped.

The opening phase of the new communications revolution, as we have seen, produced a giddy sense that freedom of communication and monitory democracy would win the world. Plenty of industry insiders remain utterly convinced that this is what is happening. Ponder the words of Pierre Omidyar, founder/chairman of the eBay auction site: 'We have technology, finally, that for the first time in human history allows people to really maintain rich connections with much larger numbers of people. It used to be, your connected group was really your immediate community, your neighborhood, your village, your tribe. The more we connect people, the more people know one another, the better the world will be.' Hear the prophecy of Bill Gates that 'the Internet is becoming the town square for the global village of tomorrow'. Or sample the spirit and substance of remarks by Micah L. Sifry, co-founder of the Personal Democracy Forum, who insists that 'we now live in an age of abundant public energies, in addition to abundant information' because 'abundant information, connectivity, and time are just the technical ingredients needed to foster an explosion of civic activity'.[1]

Lofty words, but five decades into the communications revolution trends on the ground are beginning to look quite different, and certainly more complicated. A change of mood is taking place. The presumption that everything is for the better in the age of communicative abundance is slowly but surely being questioned, seen at best as an inflated half-truth – even as a puffed-up dogma that serves to camouflage both the harsher and more complex realities and to stifle public awareness of the developing threats to open and equal communication, and its potentially democratic effects. Symptomatic is the way the old optimism has begun to attract a wide range of critics and censors, some of whom sharply attack what one of the best-known critics, Evgeny Morozov, dubs 'cyber-utopianism' and 'Internet-centrism'.[2] From his perspective, the communication technologies of our time have no determining power: 'the Internet' is a 'neutral' medium that 'provides nothing certain'. Its technical architecture, everything from packet switching and digital networks through to mobile phones and cloud computing, has no necessary shaping effects on social and political power relations, on the way people live their lives. Technologies of communication are neither intrinsically democratic nor intrinsically authoritarian. In their technical form, considered as ways of organising human communication in space and time, they are untainted by power and so can be used for an infinite variety of purposes, good and bad. The forces and relations of communication (to speak in Marxian terms) are not identical. Contexts marked by mediated power relations always trump technologies of communication. It follows, or so Morozov thinks, that 'it takes more than bytes to foster, install and consolidate a healthy democratic regime'. And since he thinks 'bytes' shape and structure nothing, that 'the Internet' is simply a tool in the hand of power, usable by any hand, it also follows that in contexts such as Iran, Saudi Arabia, Belarus, Turkmenistan and

---

[1] Pierre Omidyar, 'Connecting People', *Bloomberg Businessweek*, 20 June 2005; Bill Gates *Business @ the Speed of Thought: Using a Digital Nervous System* (New York, 1999); Micah L. Sifry, *WikiLeaks and the Age of Transparency* (New Haven, CT and London, 2011), p. 62.
[2] Evgeny Morozov, *The Net Delusion: The Dark Side of Internet Freedom* (New York, 2011), pp. xvi–xvii.

Venezuela the new galaxy of communications media actually 'empowers the strong and disempowers the weak'.

Morozov's warnings about the dark sides of communicative abundance should not be ignored, as we shall see. But his argument is as conceptually flawed as it is rhetorically powerful, initially because it dodges vital questions about the constitutive power of the technical architecture of communicative abundance. His unilateralism, his single-minded preoccupation with the ways the tools and techniques of communicative abundance are being used by dictators, is in fact a poor flipside parody of those for whom the same tools and techniques one-sidedly emit nothing but bright rays of sunshine. His 'realist' despair stands on the same continuum as those who cheer on the new media technologies as democracy's best friend. The trouble with both approaches is their lack of nuance. They fail to grasp the complicated 'medium is the message' dialectics of communicative abundance: the way media techniques and tools structure and shape the identities and activities of users, whose actions have various feedback effects on these same tools and techniques, which have hindering or enabling 'halo effects' on users as they go about their daily business within mediated circumstances they have not fully chosen.

Winners and losers

The Canadian scholar of television Marshall McLuhan liked to point out that societies have always been shaped more by the form of their media than the content of their communication. He exaggerated for effect, but his recommendation that we should simultaneously pay attention to the way 'the picture within the frame' is always fashioned by the frame itself is an important precept to bear in mind. It certainly applies to the media galaxy called communicative abundance, whose tools and techniques, products of human ingenuity, mould who we think we are, and how we act and interact with others. Techniques and tools of communication obviously have no self-consciousness or independent volition in the sense that humans talk about these qualities. Yet communications media are more than gadgets and machines; they always have 'inner effects' on their users. We are shaped and transformed by using the tools of communication others have invented for us. They alter both our sense of self and our connectedness with others.

They mould our thoughts, feelings and actions; even the moral decisions we make are mediated by techniques and tools of communication.[3]

The point that human agency depends upon modes of communication calls into question modern notions of 'free will'. It grates against the belief that self-conscious thinking individuals are the proximate cause or the key determining factor of our behaviour. To speak of technically mediated communication is to move beyond the familiar dualism of 'free will' and 'technological determinism'. It therefore refuses to indulge the view (famously expressed in Isaac Asimov's short story of a society so disordered by human mistakes that a supercomputer intervenes to restore order[4]) that we are (or are becoming) mere appendages of our own means of communication. The key point is that communications technologies are neither 'neutral' nor determinant; they help people who use these technologies to define themselves in unpredictable ways. The point brings us to the key provocation of this book: democracy does not feed automatically upon the untrammelled growth of communicative abundance. The doctrine that media opulence is good for democracy, and that together the two are coming of age, seems at best premature, if only because analysts of both democracy and media have so far paid scant attention to the troubling counter-trends, the *decadent* media developments that everywhere, in many global settings, encourage concentrations of cunning power without limit, so weakening the spirit and substance of public scrutiny and control of arbitrary power that is so vital for democracy. This book has already hinted at this decadence, for instance, in passing remarks on information poverty and crass commercialism. But these are just surface symptoms of a deeper and more troubling trend. The point that now needs to be explored is not just that communication is constantly the subject of dissembling, negotiation, compromise, power conflicts, in a phrase, a matter of political battling. The conjecture of this book is more controversial: the techniques and tools of media-saturated societies are being used by powerful forces in ways that are having harmful effects on democracy. In the pages that follow, careful attention is paid to these forces because communicative abundance does not automatically

---

[3] Peter-Paul Verbeek, *Moralizing Technology: Understanding and Designing the Morality of Things* (Chicago, 2011).
[4] Isaac Asimov, *The Life and Times of Multivac*, first published in the *New York Times Magazine*, 5 January 1975.

ensure the triumph of the spirit or institutions of monitory democracy. The diffusion of digitally networked media tools and techniques is a contradictory process. Within many settings around the world, its democratic potential is threatened by the troubling growth of *media decadence.*

Here a sense of historical perspective is important for understanding what is at stake when we speak about media decadence. As a rule, new historical forms or galaxies of media are never straightforward triumphs of human ingenuity, that is, uncomplicated enablers of people's ability to communicate with others as equals. Modes of communication are always structured by power relations; while their historically specific forms of communication shape people's sense of time and space and tender groups with new opportunities of acting in the world, a point famously made by Harold Innis,[5] modes of communication also enable some to take advantage of these forms in order to get their way, often at the expense of others. Whether, and to what extent, people are duped and disempowered by the media systems through which they live their lives always depends upon the multiple forces at work in any given context, including the chosen actions of citizens and their representatives. Politics always matters. The point is elementary but often forgotten, and so worth repeating and expanding: unless corrected democratically, modes of communication chronically produce unequal outcomes. They generate winners and losers, disappointments and silences, unjust patterns of communication that are potentially self-destructive of enhanced communication among citizens considered as equals.

The winners-and-losers rule, let us call it, was most definitely at work during previous communication revolutions. Think for a moment of the earliest stage of the development of the printing press. For the first time in human history, multiple copies of the same manuscript were printed and distributed across great distances, then placed into the hands of readers. Although those who were literate commonly read texts aloud to those with ears to hear, wide power gaps quickly opened up between the illiterate and the literate, who were disproportionately wealthy urban men. The divide persisted well into the nineteenth century; although there were exceptions, such as Sweden, the first country to promote universal literacy before the age of mass schooling, more than

[5] Harold Innis, *Bias of Communication* (Toronto, 1951).

half of the adult female and male population of the European region in the year 1800 was still unable to make sense of printed texts, including the all-important ability to read the Bible.[6] During the early phase of print culture there were strange sagas and violent political conflicts as well. Significant parts of the great book treasures of medieval Europe were lost as a consequence of the carelessness of monks. Books were buried or burned during peasant rebellions (as in Germany during the 1520s) or by champions of the Reformation; in England, fanatics intent on getting rid of works of 'evil' identified with the Church of Rome, and who presumed they had the printing press on their side, ransacked many monastery and church libraries, including the famous fourteenth-century library in Oxford, many of whose treasures were burned or sold off in 1550 by supporters of Edward VI. The early printing press certainly aroused great hopes, especially among the powerless. But among the powerful it often provoked great outbursts of political passion. An example is the way the new-fangled eighteenth-century 'fashion' of reading novels by women of the 'middling orders of society' was attacked as a 'great calamity'. Likened to 'poison instilled in the blood', reading was 'ruin'.[7] The tantrums against the spread of literacy

---

[6] See David Vincent, *The Rise of Mass Literacy: Reading and Writing in Modern Europe* (Cambridge, 2000), who points out (p. 18) that in the year 1886, Germany, the most literate society in Europe, with a population of 50 million, included some 20 million who could read the Bible, hymn books or almanacs; 30 million who could read a newspaper; 10 million who could manage 'demanding literary subjects'; around 2 million people who read the classics regularly and 1 million who 'followed literary developments'; Egil Johansson, 'Campaigns in Sweden', in Robert Arnove and Harvey J. Graff (eds), *National Literacy Campaigns: Historical and Comparative Perspectives* (New York, 1987), pp. 65–98; Daniel Lindmark, 'Reading Cultures, Christianization, and Secularization: Universalism and Particularism in the Swedish History of Literacy', *Interchange* 34(2/3) (2003): 197–217; Harvey J. Graff, *The Labyrinths of Literacy: Reflections on Literacy Past and Present* (London and New York, 1986); François Furet and Jacques Ozouf, *Lire et écrire. L'alphabétisation des français de Calvin à Jules Ferry*, 2 vols (Paris, 1977).

[7] Consider the typical anonymous polemic, 'Novel-Reading a Cause of Female Depravity', *New England Quarterly Magazine* 1 (April/June 1802): 173, which draws the conclusion that the spreading habit of reading novels guaranteed that 'woman is now but another name for infamy': 'A girl with her intellectual powers enervated by . . . reading falls an easy prey to the first *boy* who assumes the languishing lover. He has only to stuff a piece of dirty paper into the crevice of her window, full of *thous* and *thees* and *thys* and mel{li}fluous compounds, hieroglyphically spelled, perhaps, and Miss is not long in finding out that "many waters cannot quench love, neither can the floods drown it".'

were typically linked to deep fears that the printing press was turning out to be the engine of social implosion. The refrain survived well into the nineteenth century, when the printing press and its products, combined with the gradual spread of literacy and the advance of representative democracy, continued to be attacked savagely, sometimes even by democrats themselves, for tickling and twisting the fickle people's minds.[8]

Let us take just one other example of the winners-and-losers rule: during the course of the nineteenth century, the construction of a global network of electric telegraph cables meant that coded signals could be whizzed across continents and oceans, from, say, Shanghai to Cape Town, or from San Francisco to Auckland. The electrical telegraph was a revolutionary signalling system. It relied on an operator to make and break contact with a telegraph key so as to produce an audible 'clicking' signal, which was interpreted and transcribed at the other end by another telegraph operator. The new system of transmitting information to its destination before its usefulness expired had revolutionary effects. Regardless of time of day or weather, instant messaging across vast distances brought certain people closer together. Social bonds among telegraph operators (nicknamed boomers) were strengthened by chatting, jokes, swapped stories and playing chess. The telegraph was a medium of infatuation (Ella Cheever Thayer's novel *Wired Love* (1879) featured online romances), but it was above all a

---

[8] A striking example from this period is L. T. Hobhouse, *Democracy and Reaction* (London, 1904), pp. 74–5: 'That the people as a whole have learnt to read has no doubt had the result that a certain portion of them have read the literature that is worth reading. Another result has been that the output of literature that is not worth reading has vastly increased. Once again, to suit the man-in-the-street, everything must be chopped up into the smallest possible fragments to assist digestion; even the ordinary article of the old journalism has proved far too long and too heavy; it must be cut up into paragraphs, punctuated by frequent spaces, and spiced with epigrammatic absurdities to catch attention on the wing. It must be diversified with headlines and salted with sensationalism; if it is to sell, it must appeal to the uppermost prejudices of the moment. As to news, mere fidelity to fact ceases to be of moment when everything is forgotten within twenty-four hours, and when people do not really read in order that they may know, but in order that their attention may be momentarily diverted from the tedium of the train or the tramcar. Such a public may be swayed by pity, as by other obvious and easy emotions, provided no prejudice stands in the way of its humanity, but for the most part it takes its daily toll of bloodshed in the news paragraphs as a part of the diurnal repast, and if there were no real wars, murders or sudden deaths, would probably expect the enterprising journalist to invent them.'

great conqueror of the old tyranny of distance. Messages could now be sent from London to Bombay and a reply could be returned in a total of less than four minutes; or sent from London via Suez and Bombay to Sydney in just 7 hours (during the 1870s printed messages carried by fast clipper on average made the same journey in 60–80 days).[9] Pan-continental agencies (Reuters and Associated Press) brought news from afar to those who lived locally. Among the least expected consequences, thanks to the development of copper-wire grids, was the way the telegraph helped to lay the foundations of a much deeper electrification of communication within whole societies, through the use of telephones.

The Victorian Internet, as the electric telegraph has come to be called, had unprecedented bridging and bonding effects on the lives of millions of people. Some contemporary observers grew so excited that they predicted that the telegraph would hasten the end of nation-states and the coming of world peace by fixing the foundations of global banking and commerce. The 'rapidity of communication' fuelled by the telegraph, wrote Norman Angell in his best-seller *The Great Illusion* (1909), 'rendered the problems of modern international politics profoundly and essentially different from the ancient'. The telegraph made possible a global system of credit and the financial interdependence of governments; it thereby laid the foundations for peace based on 'the disappearance of State rivalries'.[10] Never mind that the first great global war was just around the corner; or that telegraph systems unleashed a swathe of winner–loser effects. Technical innovation and political impact were not the same things. Wire fraud was not uncommon, despite the efforts of telegraph network security experts. Fortunes were made and lost overnight by the corporate use of minute-by-minute reports from stock exchanges. Monopolies (such as Western Union) thrived; the Pony Express and other pigeon-carrying and horse-drawn carrier businesses, for instance, fell by the wayside in the United States, where from the 1860s onwards the telegraph proved to be superior in communicating bank transactions, money transfers, reports from Congress, police reports, news, election returns, death notices, ship departures and arrivals, and medical consultations.

---

[9] See C. A. Bayly, *Empire and Information: Intelligence Gathering and Social Communication in India, 1780–1870* (Cambridge, 1996).

[10] Norman Angell, *The Great Illusion: A Study of the Relation of Military Power in Nations to their Economic and Social Advantage* (London, 1909), pp. 229, 231, viii.

Figure 3.1 Planting the first pole on the 3,000-km overland telegraph linking Adelaide to Darwin, from a wood engraving by Samuel Calvert (1870).

The telegraph also gave powerful groups enhanced elbow room for deciding and determining things. In 1858, when the first transatlantic cable connected America and Europe, there were fireworks, hundred-gun salutes, torch-lit parades, church bells, sermons and much talk of mutual understanding, harmony and peace spreading throughout the world. The truth was that the telegraph functioned as a tool of political domination, sometimes imposed upon people by violent means. A case in point was the way (in central Australia) overland sections of the vast copper cable wrapped in latex passed through lands that belonged to Indigenous peoples (Figure 3.1).[11] Despite local objections, telegraph repeater stations were built on sacred sites. Colonisers and their cattle arrived, wielding guns; land was confiscated; Indigenous resistance was countered by punitive expeditions led by Europeans bent on inflicting mayhem and murder. The upshot was that the telegraph, the great potential liberator of human communication from the chains of time

---

[11] Peter Taylor, *An End to Silence: Building of the Overland Telegraph Line from Adelaide to Darwin* (Melbourne, 1980).

and space, bolstered forms of control whose administrative techniques and political symbolism had more than a passing resemblance to the later methods of apartheid.

Media decadence

Decadence was not confined to the age of the printing press or the telegraph. The history of shifting modes of communication shows that each induced bellyaches against its alleged decadent effects. Think of Plato's objection to the deluded speech of the Athenian assembly democracy. He called it theatrocracy (*theatrokratia*), a form of government whose citizens resembled rowdy theatregoers, posturing commoners drunk on the presumption that they were entitled to communicate publicly about all matters, in defiance of the immutable laws of philosophical knowledge.[12] Or consider, from the age of representative democracy that followed, Kierkegaard's charge that the printing press was heavily implicated in the rise of 'the public' ('a kind of gigantic something, an abstract and deserted void which is everything and nothing') and its ethos of mindless 'talkativeness', the 'mathematical equality' of 'silly gossiping people' who have 'hand-books for everything'.[13] Or consider John Stuart Mill's parallel attacks on the threats to liberty posed not by kings and tyrants, but by the burgeoning 'public opinion' nurtured by newspapers, pamphlets, books and petitions. 'At present individuals are lost in the crowd', wrote Mill. 'In politics it is almost a triviality to say that public opinion now rules the world.' He added:

Those whose opinions go by the name of public opinion, are not always the same sort of public: in America, they are the whole white population; in England, chiefly the middle class. But they are always a mass, that is to say, collective mediocrity. And what is still greater novelty, the mass do not now take their opinions from dignitaries in Church or State, from ostensible leaders, or from books. Their thinking is done for them by men much like themselves, addressing them or speaking in their name, on the spur of the moment, through the newspapers.[14]

[12] Plato, *Laws*, III, 700a–d.
[13] Søren Kierkegaard, *The Present Age* (London and New York, [1846] 1940), pp. 3–70.
[14] John Stuart Mill, 'On Individuality, as One of the Elements of Wellbeing', in *On Liberty* (London, 1859), ch. 3.

Our age of communicative abundance is similarly marked by claims about its decadent qualities. Some deserve serious attention, if only because we witness around our heads world-transforming media inventions accompanied by counter-trends that threaten to undermine the rich democratic potential of communicative abundance. Surprisingly, little attention has so far been paid within democratic theory to these negative developments. And so we need to ask: what is *media decadence*? And exactly which decadent trends are today threatening the growth of open communication under democratic conditions?

When this book speaks of media decadence it works with a special definition, one that is deliberately unconventional. It refers to the wide gaps that are opening up between the rosy ideals of free and fair public contestation and chastening of power, the unforced plurality of opinions and public commitment of representatives to the inclusion and treatment of all citizens as equals, even in cross-border settings – loosely speaking, the ideals of monitory democracy – and a rougher, wrinkled reality in which communication media are deeply implicated in the dirty business of promoting intolerance of opinions, stifling the public scrutiny of power and fostering the blind acceptance of the way things are heading.

Decadence is, of course, a tricky word with harshly negative connotations of luxurious self-indulgence. The different connotations of the term should be distinguished. It has often been used to describe the waning of a civilisation that once thrived on powerful taken-for-granted myths, whose hypnotic effects on the whole civilised order are now breaking down. Fascists in the 1920s and 1930s thought along those lines. So have many literary and political conservatives, for whom decadence sets in when civilised peoples, who once lived mostly by their instincts and prejudices, happily loving their existence, caring nothing for unstructured reflection on the contingency of their mode of living, suddenly begin to awaken from their hypnosis. When that happens, the cadence of the old order crumbles into de-cadence. Decline, deterioration and degeneracy take root. So does paralysis; the sense that paradise is possible disappears. The familiar world feels as though it is falling apart, but the accompanying restlessness produces no clear sense of advance. Age-old prejudices, once productive, are thrown into question. The reign of energetic doubt and dialogue commences; the spreading capacity for abstraction dissolves certainties. Yet frustration and fatigue get the upper hand. The old forms of life feel exhausted. Decadence is myth corrupted by blind doubt; it is pointless yearning for the end of the familiar world, or what the French call *vague à l'âme*.[15]

The conservative and politically right-wing understanding of decadence is rejected in what follows, simply because of its elitism, which stands squarely at odds with the egalitarian spirit, the strong public sense of contingency and illegitimacy of unequal power relations that monitory democracies are good at nurturing. In this book's account of communicative abundance and its negative effects, the category of decadence is deployed differently. Owing something to the spirit of Montesquieu's eighteenth-century study of the ruination of Roman citizenship by imperial expansion, *Considerations on the Causes of the Grandeur and Decadence of the Romans* (1734),[16] its purpose is to shock readers and stimulate 'wild thinking' by marking out a new field of enquiry about anti-democratic trends that should furrow the brows of every thinking democrat. In contrast to vernacular meanings of the term, for instance, the use of decadence as a loose synonym for

---

[15] Compare E. M. Cioran, *A Short History of Decay* (London, 1975), p. 116: 'Decadence is merely instinct gone impure under the action of consciousness.' Compare Jacques Barzun, *From Dawn to Decadence: 500 Years of Western Cultural Life, 1500 to the Present* (New York, 2000); C. E. M. Joad, *Decadence* (1948), who defines decadence as 'refusal to recognize "the object"', that is, 'a sign of man's tendency to misread his position in the universe, to take a view of his status and prospects more exalted than the facts warrant and to conduct his societies and to plan his future on the basis of this mis-reading. The mis-reading consists in a failure to acknowledge the non-human elements of value and deity ['the object'] to which the human is subject.'

[16] Charles de Secondat, Baron de Montesquieu, *Considérations sur les causes de la grandeur des Romains et de leur décadence* (Amsterdam, 1734), ch. IX ('Deux causes de la perte de Rome'), pp. 82–8. The vital role played by the concept of decadence within the modern European republican tradition deserves further investigation. Plenty can be learned from Matthew Potolsky, *The Decadent Republic of Letters: Taste, Politics, and Cosmopolitan Community from Baudelaire to Beardsley* (University Park, PA, 2012), an important reinterpretation of the late nineteenth-century group of European writers and artists known as the decadents (figures such as Charles Baudelaire, Aubrey Beardsley, Joris-Karl Huysmans and Oscar Wilde) as carriers of classical republican notions of beauty, understood as a form of civic virtue; and, more generally, see Gregory L. Schneider (ed.), *Equality, Decadence, and Modernity: The Collected Essays of Stephen J. Tonsor* (Wilmington, DE, 2005), where eighteenth-century conceptions of decadence are linked to post-Christian, desacralised interpretations of time, the engagement with the ancient Greek and Roman worlds and strong political criticisms of the blind belief in progress.

debauchery (consuming too much chocolate or some other lavish food, for instance), every effort is made in what follows to avoid crudely evaluative or flippant usages of the term. Decay amid abundance is what I have in mind; but in cutting the connections between the concept of decadence and conservative and fascist theories of declining civilisations, this book does not suppose that the contemporary manifestations of decline are permanent, or irreversible. In the pages to come, various remedies for media decadence are certainly suggested. Yet they are not detailed recommendations, simply because efforts to defend the democratic potential of communicative abundance perforce depend upon chosen courses of action within particular contexts, not on generally applicable formulae provided by how-to-do-it handbooks. This book emphasises the *contingency* and *reversibility* of media decadence. Fatalism, the belief that the world has its own ways, and that everything rises before falling into decay, is not what this book has in mind. Decadence is a process, a trend; and whether the decadent trends about to be summarised prove fatal for democratic energies around the world is treated as an open question. Answers to that question are ultimately political: they will be provided not just by time and circumstance and good fortune, but above all by the courage and intelligence of citizens and their elected and unelected representatives, combined with such forces as creative technical invention, new institution building, legal regulation and the behaviour of professional journalists and owners of media capital within market settings.

Everyday life: beehives and echo chambers

If decadence is understood as a relational term, as a word that marks out things that are opposed yet related to the best contemporary trends towards creative openness and equality in the field of abundant communications, then according to more than a few observers, among them scholars, journalists, bloggers and pundits, communicative abundance is most definitely blighted by corrupting trends. These critics have been especially quick to pounce on trends closest to home, within everyday life. They spotlight transformations in our ways of thinking and speaking and bodily interaction that they reckon are, on balance, negative. The complaint is serious, so let us consider their case carefully.

One influential line of criticism is fuelled by old-fashioned fears about the mob-like behaviour of citizens who are ill-informed about the world.[17] It typically begins by spotlighting the way 'endless communication' provides individual citizens with tools to filter what they access, so encouraging them to huddle in 'echo chambers' where only like-minded opinions reverberate. They flock like sheep to Fox News, or YouTube, Italy's Canale 5 or Japanese television's early evening Golden Time. Compared with times past – the time and place of the golden age is usually never specified by the critics – citizens are plunged into narcissistic narrow-mindedness. They end up communicating only with themselves. Communicative abundance, the supposed harbinger of diversity, hands out mirrors to citizens, who use them to preen themselves in the looking-glass of their blinkered choice.

The critics of echo chambers sometimes go further. Communicative abundance (here they switch metaphors) is synonymous with 'information cascades' that not only submerge citizens in their own and others' beliefs, in torrents of self-reinforcing cycles of mindlessness. Thoughtlessness flourishes as well. Political imagination and the creative individual voice give way to 'hive thinking'. Symbolised by Wikipedia, Facebook and Google searches, say the critics, everyday life is clogged with trivial and misleading 'mashups', online content comprising fragments without authors, materials whose source, point of view and spin factor are difficult or impossible to ascertain. Mashup culture is a 'meme': it has the effect of mass-producing mashed-up minds with mashed-up effects that very often go viral.

Why? Citizens, the critics say, may not in fact fully believe the clichés they are fed, but they nevertheless swallow them whole, partly because the mashed-up messages seem, on the face of things, to be plausible; partly because they are too busy to ponder or analyse them in detail; and partly because other busy people around them, the like-minded somnolent inhabitants of their own echo chamber, believe (or mouth) them. There are chain reactions. Fashion and fad and 'drive-by anonymity'

---

[17] The following section draws upon Cass Sunstein, *On Rumors: How Falsehoods Spread, Why We Believe Them, What Can be Done* (New York and London, 2009) and his *Republic.com 2.0* (Princeton, 2007); Andrew Keen, *The Cult of the Amateur* (New York, 2007); Jaron Lanier, *You Are Not a Gadget: A Manifesto* (New York and London, 2010). The 'hive mind' and 'beehive' analogy is an unfortunate anthropomorphism, the imaginary projection of human qualities onto the world of bees, who live rather differently, as suggested by the most recent research findings reported in Thomas D. Seeley, *Honeybee Democracy* (Princeton and Oxford, 2010).

gain ground. Citizens may even become unthinking proselytes of causes they do not properly understand, willing victims of slogans peddled by means of bigoted witch-hunts that amount to a kind of 'digital Maoism'. The result is worse than a Babel effect: millions of people communicate, yet very few people are able to communicate thoughtfully with one another. The critics sometimes quote James Madison (who was himself no democrat, it should be noted) on the importance of 'yielding and accommodating spirit' among citizens of a free republic. They reinforce their point by insisting that communicative abundance has more than fracturing, parochial and divisive effects. Suggestibility rooted in narrow-minded ignorance fuels the growth of unyielding, unaccommodating dogmatism. Popular belief in the 'wisdom of crowds' gains ground; the presumption that 'the collective is closer to the truth' flourishes. Mob rule looms. Indulging the online habit of gravitating towards websites and other mashed-up sources of information and entertainment that are mere extensions of themselves, citizens with damaged 'hive minds' live their lives anonymously in 'beehives' that are prone to swarm.

Objections to the growth of echo chambers, beehives, lynch mobs and online witch-hunts often meld with anxieties about solitude and solipsism, and their flipside – the fear that individuals indulged by the new tools of communication will lose their identity in the digital jungle. It is a curious paradox that the age of communicative abundance fuels bitter complaints about the socially isolating effects and political vulnerability produced by intensive online communication.

Some critics, often without knowing it, take their cue from the pioneering experiments conducted by Joseph Weizenbaum, the creator of the world's first banking computer and an early expert on artificial intelligence.[18] During the 1960s, working with his team on an IBM 7094 and MAC time-sharing system at MIT, Weizenbaum developed a natural language computer program written to simulate users' thoughts. He called his program ELIZA, after the character of Eliza Doolittle, in the George Bernard Shaw play *Pygmalion*, who, from her teacher Henry Higgins, learned to improve her communication through teaching methods based on parsing and substitution. Along the same lines, or so Weizenbaum reasoned, ELIZA was capable of picking up

---

[18] Joseph Weizenbaum, *Computer Power and Human Reason: From Judgment to Calculation* (San Francisco, 1976).

inputs of keywords and phrases, and could respond with clever questions, making it seem that the program was a benign teacher or a therapist.

Following tests of the program with his students, Weizenbaum grew worried. He was struck by their sensuous attraction to ELIZA's ability to respond in pre-programmed ways to their simple questions. It was as if these students had grown convinced that they could live *through* their computer, even that the computer was an extension of their own selves. If, for instance, they typed in the statement 'Men are all alike' then the computer replied: 'In what way?' An almost life-like exchange then followed: 'They're always bugging us about something.' 'Can you think of a specific example?' 'Well, my boyfriend made me come here.' 'Your boyfriend made you come here?' 'He says I'm depressed much of the time.' 'I'm sorry to hear you are depressed.' 'It's true.' And so on.

Weizenbaum underscored what was perhaps obvious at the time, but the point today often gets lost: ELIZA conversations were facilitated by clever programming techniques, not by a 'thinking' computer, and he went on to warn that computers were not 'mind-amplifying' universal machines (as some pundits were later to say[19]), but merely tools to assist humans in their everyday lives. They could enable decisions to be made by human beings, or even on behalf of human beings; but, according to Weizenbaum, decisions are merely forms of computational reasoning. They are not the same as choices, which are always shaped by judgements, which only humans equipped with prudence, compassion and thought can make. Fantasies about the merging and melding of humans and machines must be resisted, for the presumption in favour of

---

[19] Compare the prediction of Howard Rheingold, *Tools for Thought: The People and Ideas of the Next Computer Revolution* (New York, 1985), p. 13: 'Before today's first-graders graduate from high school, hundreds of millions of people around the world will join together to create new kinds of human communities, making use of a tool that a small number of thinkers and tinkerers dreamed into being over the past century. Nobody knows whether this will turn out to be the best or the worst thing the human race has done for itself, because the outcome of this empowerment will depend in large part on how we react to it and what we choose to do with it. The human mind is not going to be replaced by a machine, at least not in the foreseeable future, but there is little doubt that the worldwide availability of fantasy amplifiers, intellectual toolkits, and interactive electronic communities will change the way people think, learn, and communicate.'

computer reason necessarily involves lowering the standards for what counts as human intelligence.

Weizenbaum's defence of human judgement and warnings about its possible demise seemed to be lost on at least some of his laboratory users, who appeared bewitched by the 'intelligent' responses of their computers to their own questions; it was as if they had grown convinced that they were in a dialogic relationship with computers that functioned as extensions of themselves. Today's critics express corresponding worries about the same process of bewitchment: communicative abundance is accused of generating an everyday culture in which individuals so meld with laptops and other hand-held devices that they lose themselves in the workings of their machines. Their devices seem to take on a life of their own. We become like them. Communication tools are dumb, yet seemingly smart; lifeless, yet apparently interactive; devoid of feeling, but the object through which we store our memories, share our thoughts and feelings with ourselves, and with others, in that order. That is why we feel bereft without our communication machines; crashes and fatal 404 errors generate confusion, alarm, panics. While in the age of communicative abundance our networked contacts with the wider world undoubtedly flourish, or so runs the complaint, every moment of interaction, from shopping to socialising with friends, becomes bound up with buttons, keyboards and personalised screens. The world draws closer, feels ever present and instantly accessible, yet the paradox is that it comes to be experienced at one remove, mainly on our own terms, a mere illusion of interaction unhindered by life's disagreements, setbacks, personal complications, frank dramas and power plays. It is as if everything is a projection of the self: individuals become their own stored memories, their own interpretations of the present and projections of the future. They listen only to themselves. They decide where they have been, who they are and what they hope to become. Others no long really matter. The world fades away. It becomes a friendly screen, a scribbled SMS message, an ear piece, a download, a keyboard, a random thought.

Shouting nonsense

The complaint about mechanical solipsism is serious. The conjecture is that when individuals spend so many hours connected to the tools of their choice (the average is at least 5 hours a day for younger people in countries such as Japan, the United States and Germany) the world degenerates into their own self-projection. Everything is referred back to individuals who fall prey, unsurprisingly, to superciliousness. They become their own authorities, with indisputable weight, freed from contradiction by others. When confronted, they press the delete tab, or simply move to safer links, where they carry on confirming themselves, thanks to websites that offer them anonymous and risk-free interaction with others, whom they will never meet in their lives. On social networking sites, or within chat rooms, blogs and discussion threads they arrive tagged with cryptic names and addresses, or no name or address at all. Then they interact with others at a distance, saying whatever they like, with little or no consequences. They know the meaning of the oft-reprinted *New Yorker* cartoon that features a dog using a personal computer, with the caption: 'On the Internet, nobody knows you're a dog.'[20] Life comes to resemble chat roulette. Personal responsibility vanishes. Nothing seems to matter. There are no barriers to entry or exit. Unedited, unconstrained, the self appears to become an unlimited self.

The mechanical solipsism breeds at least two forms of decadence, or so the critics charge. For a start, big egos flourish. In the age of communicative abundance the cult of the amateur begins to prevail.[21] Peppered with provocative talk of 'long tails' and 'Web 2.0', everyday communication is overwhelmed by an avalanche of amateur, user-generated content that threatens to undermine professional newspapers, magazines, music and movies. Anyone and everybody with an opinion, however ill-informed, can post a video on YouTube, publish a blog or change an entry on Wikipedia. The arts of redaction disappear. The division between trained expert and uninformed amateur is blurred. Anonymous bloggers and videographers, unconstrained by professional standards or editorial filters, begin to alter patterns of public debate, and to manipulate public opinion. Truth becomes whimsical, a mere matter of opinion, a commodity to be bought, sold, packaged and reinvented. A coked-up 'cut-and-paste' online culture spoils quality. Copyright laws are repeatedly broken. The fruits of others' intellectual

---

[20] The cartoon, by Peter Steiner, appeared in the *New Yorker* on 5 July 1993, p. 61.
[21] Keen, *The Cult of the Amateur*.

labour are redistributed at random. Editors, producers, authors, journalists and musicians lose copyright protection and are robbed of their intellectual property rights. Everything in digital form is freely downloaded, uploaded, swapped, re-mashed and aggregated. Sources of advertising revenue are threatened. Digital piracy and file-sharing threaten the multibillion-dollar movie industry and music business; television networks feel the pinch of free user-generated programming on sites like YouTube; and the world of free classified ads flourish on sites like Craigslist.

According to the critics, public life is ruined by the culture of anonymity spawned by communicative abundance. The reliability of the information we receive from digital pirates and second-rate plagiarists is not only called into question. The freedom of individuals in 'cyberspace' to say anything they want, without checks or balances, makes them vulnerable to free-roaming predators and identity thieves. It also encourages unrestrained attacks on others whom they do not like, or with whom they just feel like taking issue, to let off steam, to vent their spleen, on a whim. The blogosphere, otherwise full of writers and readers who make independent contact and offer each other intelligent advice and serious commentary, also attracts (it is said) the Awkward Blog Squad: anonymous characters who are lightning-quick to react, never read what's been written, get things wrong and (of course) are nevertheless cocksure that they know everything about everything. Communicative abundance promotes big egos and meanness of spirit; sometimes it is dubbed 'snark' (after the imaginary elusive animal invented by Lewis Carroll in *The Hunting of the Snark* (1876); the word later resurfaced as an onomatopoeic verb, to mean 'snort' or 'snore', or to find fault with something or someone). Random shouting might be a better and more familiar phrase, for what passes as online communication is often nothing less than unqualified abuse of others. Contrary to those who worry about the advent of digital Maoism, random shouting might in the end be a good thing; just like public outpourings of hatred of foreigners, uncivil expressions of disrespect for others, although repugnant, may well have the unintended consequence of ruining their own aspirations to legitimacy. Whether or not that proves to be the case is for the future to decide. In the interim, or so the critics say, more than a few bloggers are more than just annoying. They hector, shout and scream, sometimes to the point of bullying, according to the decadent anti-political principle that the world must understand and bow down to the blogger, rather than the blogger understand and engage the world.[22]

This is not all, say the critics. For there is a negative flipside of the new mechanical solipsism: little egos. Communicative abundance is said to obstruct clear-headed thought and reality testing by way of deliberating publicly with others. Since online activity breeds ever more online activity, much of it repetitive, individuals' lives are sucked into a vortex of digital energy from which they cannot easily escape. They are always 'on', in wireless mode, glued to search engines, YouTube, Blackberries, iPads, Twitter and other tools. Solitude withers. Once upon a time, individuals put down newspapers or their favourite magazine or book, or switched off their stereo, radio or television; they went for a walk, or talked to a friend on the telephone, or made love or wrote a letter. Now they have no time for pondering the world. Always

---

[22] The practice of online shouting has prompted publishers such as the *Huffington Post* and the *New York Times* to regulate online free-for-all brawls by using a variety of moderating strategies: encouraging readers to flag objectionable comments for removal; ranking those who leave comments based on how well other readers know and trust their writing; requiring those who post comments to pre-register with the site and to provide some information about themselves that is subsequently not displayed; and conducting routine editorial checks and blocking comments from users who repeatedly violate a site's standards. Machine-based moderators are also used to deal with the growing volume of comments (the *Huffington Post* receives around 5 million comments each month, the equivalent of around eighteen times the lengthy novel *Moby-Dick; or, The Whale* (1851)). These editorial changes are driven in part by commercial instincts; advertisers do not much like to buy space next door to incendiary opinions. Whether the clampdowns will and should stick is another matter. Few question the advantages of generally enabling citizens to vent freely their opinions that would otherwise get them into trouble with, say, neighbours or at their place of work, but many doubt the legitimacy and/or effectiveness of the new methods. Policing online identities is labour-intensive, costly and (because of its censorial odour) off-putting for some readers; and even if all commentators were required to provide their real names for display online, there can be no guarantee that they will not tender false identities. The resistance is understandable. Anonymous warnings issued by rebellious subjects against monarchs (*lettres de cachet* from below) are an ancient practice (see Samuel McCormick, *Letters to Power: Public Advocacy without Public Intellectuals* (University Park, PA, 2012)). So, too, are literary doubles or pen names, *noms de plume*, pseudonyms used by authors to protect themselves from retribution, or to distinguish their names, or to disguise their gender or to distance themselves from their previous writings. These are well-practised arts in the medium of print, and especially in the age of communicative abundance they are not likely to disappear because some think others have gone too far.

communicating mindlessly with others, preoccupied only with themselves, these individuals fall victim to the fact that they have 'become so
unimportant for those in power and business that self-presentation is
the last resort'.[23]

It is unsurprising, or so say the critics, that communicative abundance adds to the general confusion among citizens about what to
believe and where to turn for information about what is going on in
the world. Citizens are drowned in democratic cacophony, the white
noise of sports results, traffic accidents and royal dresses.[24] News is
something that old people worry their heads about. That is why, from
this perspective, echo chambers and beehives and online shouting are
lesser problems. Much more worrying is the spread of thoughtless
gossip, or what Heidegger famously called *Das Gerede*: mere chatter
or 'passing on the word', talk for talk's sake, the habit of speaking
without knowing what is really being said, the experience of loquacity
that encourages individuals to suppose that 'things are so because one
has said so'.[25] The online age is said to produce sharp increases in
user-generated nonsense. In some quarters, the culture of communicative abundance and its cult of the amateur promote citizens' general
inattention to events. According to civics textbooks, they are expected
to keep their eyes on public affairs, to take an interest in the world
beyond their immediate household and neighbourhood, yet, say the
critics, there is plenty of evidence that more than a few citizens find it
ever harder to pay attention to the media's vast outpourings. Profusion
breeds confusion. Freedom thrives upon the elixirs of communicative
abundance, but one of its more perverse effects is to encourage individuals to escape the great complexity of the world by sticking their
heads into the sands of wilful ignorance. Trapped in the flotsam
and jetsam of fashion much loved by advertisers, they change their
minds, speak and act flippantly, embrace and celebrate opposites, bid

---

[23] From the interview with Friedrich Kittler by Andreas Rosenfelder, 'Wir haben nur
uns selber, um daraus zu schöpfen', *Welt am Sonntag*, Berlin, 30 January 2011.

[24] In Milan Kundera's novel *La lenteur* (*Slowness*; Paris, 1995), an exiled Czech
scientist finds it impossible to make sense of what he is watching on television in a
Western hotel. Raised under socialism, where information was apportioned,
carefully filtered before it reached the masses, he had been accustomed to
digesting information critically and pondering its wider political significance.
Catapulted into the multichannel information maze of the West, he loses his
bearings.

[25] Martin Heidegger, *Being and Time* (San Francisco, 1962), p. 211.

farewell to veracity, slip into the arms of what one of the best and most careful contemporary philosophers, Harry Frankfurt, calls 'bullshit'.

Bullshit: a technical term, with vernacular bite, is used to describe forms of communication emptied of all informative content, that is, phoney speech that dispenses with questions of truth and falsity, and so displays an 'indifference to how things really are'.[26] According to the critics, bullshit in this exact sense flourishes because communicative abundance requires people to speak about matters of which they are mostly ignorant. The widespread conviction that under democratic conditions responsible citizens must have opinions on every subject adds to the volume of 'truthiness'. So does the flourishing pseudo-culture of 'sincerity', the conviction that, since there is no such thing as Truth, we should listen to the call of our own true nature. The nonsense is manured by the 'spin' of public relations agencies and watered by floods of advertising, or so the critics insist. They hasten to refer to Rupert Murdoch's accurate summary of the trends: 'the Internet provides the opportunity for us to be more relevant to our advertisers', he once remarked, adding that digital networks allow media businesses 'to be more granular in our advertising, targeting potential consumers based on where they've surfed and what products they've bought'.[27]

Childhood

More than a few critics of communicative abundance insist that the most worrying thing about the media-powered bullshit of advertising is the way that it begins at the beginning, with young people, by clawing its way into their daily lives, helping to damage family life along the way. A recent British study exemplifies the tone.[28] It points out that on average under-18 year-olds spend over 5 hours daily in front of a screen, watching television, playing computer games or online. Each day, to be exact, they spend 2 hours, 36 minutes watching television; 1 hour, 18 minutes on the Internet; and 1 hour, 24 minutes on a games console.

---

[26] Harry Frankfurt, *On Bullshit* (Princeton, 2005), p. 34.

[27] Speech by Rupert Murdoch to the American Society of Newspaper Editors, 13 April 2005.

[28] There are many studies and many (conflicting) findings, but here particular use is made of a recent widely cited report by Ed Mayo and Agnes Nairn, *Consumer Kids: How Big Business is Grooming our Children for Profit* (London, 2009), especially chs 1–2 (from which all citations are drawn).

The total of 2,000 hours a year compares with 900 hours in a classroom and 1,270 hours with their parents. Ninety per cent of teens now have a personal television and so do almost 60 per cent of five- and six-year-olds. More than a third of all children have their own PC, while two-thirds own a games console. Almost 50 per cent of primary school girls (39 per cent of boys) and 98 per cent of senior school girls (90 per cent of boys) have their own mobile phone. 'The screen can no longer be classed as an electronic babysitter that keeps children occupied', says the report. 'It is a whole electronic world in which they are immersed and which is underpinned firmly and securely by a profit motive. The conventional paradigm of childhood as a stage that revolves around family and schools has had to change. It's the commercial world that dominates the time of today's children.'

The report emphasises that childhood is not yet doomed. Parents can still do much to protect their children by educating themselves and their offspring, and by pressurising government and other authorities to regulate advertising more effectively. The report arguably understates the benefits of communicative abundance for children, the ways in which it enables them to socialise with peers, explore the horizons of the world, experiment with identities and establish their own independence.[29] Yet the report rightly warns against efforts by parents to force their children back into idealised versions of their own childhoods. It insists that young people must not be treated 'in the same way the Victorian world treated women – as delicate, vulnerable and needing to be kept at home'. It recommends instead that children themselves must be given a 'leading role in the rules that are designed to protect and promote their interests'. How this is to be achieved remains unclear, for the report finds that many parents and guardians seem to be unaware of the scale and depth of the current trends. While alert to 'stranger danger' and threats posed by online sexual predators, they have a limited grasp of the ways in which business worms into the lives of children, for profit. Young people, says the report, find it hard to escape the clutches of big business advertisers. Many think they are grown up enough to understand the advertising that pays for the free websites

---

[29] See the contrasting report prepared for the American Academy of Pediatrics by Gwenn Schurgin O'Keeffe *et al.*, *The Impact of Social Media on Children, Adolescents, and Families* (2011), available at: http://pediatrics.aappublications. org/content/127/4/800.full.

they surf, interrupts the programmes they enjoy and pings their mobile phone screens. Ignoring their own see–want habits, young people frequently think themselves immune to the effects of their recruitment through enhanced membership schemes, or through special offers to promote toys and other products to their friends. They often find it hard, states the report, to distinguish the words 'gaming' and 'gambling', but they have no difficulty setting up company-sponsored wish lists which they email straight to their parents. They take for granted that their favourite websites are peppered with advertisements made to look like content. They know their personal information is routinely sought, often as a condition of getting access to a site. They are sure purchases boost their confidence; and that brands are a purchasable right that should be at the core of their sense of self-worth.

The scope and depth of stalking by commercial predators are astonishing, the critics emphasise in their report. Figures show that personal information is collected from around 85 per cent of children's favourite websites, a scale of harvesting made possible by the transformation of children's bedrooms into 'high-tech media bedsits' equipped with more gadgets than an entire family would have had a generation ago. Nearly all teenagers have a television in their bedroom. Two-thirds of five- and six-year-olds watch TV before school each day and a similar proportion watch it before bedtime. The report notes that the trend is shaped by class taste, so that, for instance, 98 per cent of 'tweens' from poor backgrounds have their own TV compared with 48 per cent from more affluent families. But what is really striking is the actual degree of overall business penetration of children's daily lives: a quarter of young people have access to the Internet in their bedroom. That makes it far easier for businesses to become 'child catchers', stalkers who obtain information and give children, including young children, a heavy sales pitch under the cover of entertainment. The report cites research that found that 85 per cent of children's favourite websites collect some sort of personal information, including email or home addresses, users' names, dates of birth, gender and age. Most of this requested information is 'compulsory', meaning that the child cannot use parts of the site without handing over these details; about 15 per cent of sites demand information from children even to get started, while another 35 per cent offer ring tones, wallpaper, newsletters and screensavers in exchange for users' personal details. Unsurprisingly, the report concludes, business is booming in childhood markets. In 2009, total sales volume in Britain stood at about £99 billion, up 33 per cent over the previous five years, £12 billion of which came from pocket money provided by unsuspecting parents.

Nostalgia

What are we to make of the torrent of complaints against communicative abundance and its damaging effects upon everyday life? Are the critics right to say that media-saturated democratic societies are choking public-spirited voices and undermining their own vital preconditions of equality and openness? Are the important democratising trends that belong to the age of communicative abundance turning out to be mere hollow promises? Are we entering a world in which citizens are being turned, slowly but surely, into narrow-minded, ignorant and suggestible subjects, cocooned creatures of fad and fashion, peddlers of snark who shout nonsense, thoughtlessly gossip and unwittingly spread mashed-up bullshit?

A pause is required, for it is hard to know how best to devise concise, fair-minded and plausible responses to such a wide range of objections. Aside from the obvious point that the critics stand incoherently at right angles to one another (for instance, some object to the active bigotry of citizens, while other critics dread their inactive cowardice), one thing is initially clear: the attacks on communicative abundance are typical of turbulent phases within communication revolutions, those choppy moments when commentators restlessly search for unorthodox inter-pretations to make sense of the unfamiliar phenomena swirling around their heads. Much might be learned from these attacks, but their own poor grasp of the measure of things is questionable. Rarely do they have any sense of the historicity of what they condemn; comparisons with the age of the printing press, or telegraph or radio and television go missing, or are presumed irrelevant. Since those who are ignorant of the past inevitably misunderstand the present, it should hardly be surprising that the critics of communicative abundance give little or no consideration to present-day counter-trends. Typical is the way blind eyes are turned to the means by which communicative abundance helps to nurture 'com-munities of practice' and other bonding and bridging patterns within everyday and institutional life.[30] Equally typical is the shortage of new

---

[30] The early work of Phil Agre is especially important on this subject, for instance, his 'Real-Time Politics: The Internet and the Political Process', *The Information Society* 18(5) (2002): 311–31: 'The Internet can connect anyone and anyone else,

concepts and innovative methods for capturing the viral quality of contested power relations. Especially striking is the way the subject of democracy is almost never broached. Topics such as the democratisation of access to information, the rapid growth of strong monitory mechanisms and their role as antidotes to solipsism and crowd 'mindlessness', their regular bombardment of citizens with many different and conflicting points of view, even in cross-border settings – all this is passed over in silence.

The rough summary provided above makes clear something else: although unafraid of making bold and brash generalisations, the critics typically rest their claims on methodologies that harbour weaknesses and probable errors of interpretation. Personal anecdotes abound. Simple extrapolations from single cases to general observations are commonplace. There are more than a few cases where claims are hyped in order to win headlines. Convincing reliable evidence is rarely adduced in support of the conclusions (the British study of children is a clear exception to this rule). There are even cases of suspected wilful ignorance, where evidence is set aside by best-selling authors in favour of sensationalist claims, for instance, that communicative abundance makes us 'fat, dumb, aggressive, lonely, sick and unhappy' and (horror) ensures that 'we already have digital dementia'.[31] To make matters worse, the perspectives are often heavily biased towards the Atlantic region, without justification or further explanation. Criticisms often rest upon highly selective examples, disproportionately drawn from experiences within the Atlantic region, especially the United States. Geographic variations, the different ways in which communicative

but the patterns of connection are not random. One pattern is that people exchange information with others with whom they have something in common. Choose any condition that people find important, and it is nearly certain that a far-flung community will have arisen of people who share that condition. These communities of practice include professions, interest groups, extended families, and people who live with the same illness or share a recreational interest. Most of the functioning online fora on the Internet are organized around these commonalities, but communities of practice should not be identified analytically with the technologies that support them. Few communities are strictly "virtual". Most communities employ several media, and most of them have some degree of formal organizational existence that is defined in technology-independent terms.'

[31] Manfred Spitzer, 'Digitale Demenz'. *Wie wir uns und unsere Kinder um den Verstand bringen* (Munich, 2012). Studies in geriatric psychiatry point to the opposite conclusion: senior citizens who regularly use digital media, for instance, are much less likely to develop symptoms of dementia, as is pointed out in Hilmar Schmundt, 'Generation Superhirn', *Der Spiegel*, 10 September 2012.

abundance take root in different societies with differing effects, are as uninteresting to the complainants as historical precedents and contemporary novelties that run wider than local, context-specific trends.

These methodological weaknesses often fuel nostalgia for the lost pleasures of the past, for the days (it is imagined) when the ruinous effects of communicative abundance had not yet set in. The melancholy of the critics is understandable. Communications revolutions always produce ruinous effects. By spreading new media tools and techniques, they smash settled ways of communicating, destroy age-old media habits and, consequently (in some circles) stir up yearnings for an imagined past innocence that never in fact existed. The resulting nostalgia recalls happier times, wraps arms around them, as if the present counted for little, or nothing. Desperate to escape the present, suffering nostalgia in the literal Greek sense of pain caused by the inability to return home, more than a few critics of communicative abundance sound reactionary. They are reactionary. They yearn for a golden past when (supposedly) patterns of communication were less sullied than those of today. Some of these reactionaries are rewarded handsomely: they discover that in the age of communicative abundance nostalgia can be a highly marketable commodity.

An example is the nostalgic modernism of those critics who lament the passing of an age (so they imagine) when books and reasonable discussion once occupied the centre of public life, or at least stood as its benchmark or lighthouse of hope.[32] Worrying about whether life on the Internet is making us stupid, sure that we click too much, read far too little, and remember even less, their nostalgic modernism is a spoiling affair.[33] It fears the consequences of information overload and mourns

[32] A highly influential example is the account of the replacement of the public sphere by mass opinion industries in Jürgen Habermas, *Strukturwandel der Offentlichkeit. Untersuchungen zu einer Kategorie der bürgerlichen Gesellschaft* (Neuwied and Berlin, 1962), pp. 172–216. See my commentary and early criticisms of Habermas' nostalgia in *Public Life and Late Capitalism* (Cambridge and New York, 1984) and *The Media and Democracy*.

[33] Nicholas Carr, 'Is Google Making Us Stupid?', *The Atlantic*, July/August 2008, is a prominent example: 'Over the past few years', writes Carr, 'I've had an uncomfortable sense that someone, or something, has been tinkering with my brain, remapping the neural circuitry, reprogramming the memory. My mind isn't going – so far as I can tell – but it's changing. I'm not thinking the way I used to think. I can feel it most strongly when I'm reading. Immersing myself in a book or a lengthy article used to be easy. My mind would get caught up in the narrative or the turns of the argument, and I'd spend hours strolling through long stretches

the death of quiet reflection, informed reason and rational deliberation. It blames the indigestion of viewers, listeners and readers on multimedia, the segmentation of audiences, low quality outputs. It supposes that communicative abundance eliminates any last resistance to the brainwashing that began with mass broadcasting media, especially television. Nostalgic modernism sometimes calls on governments to invent rescue schemes for reducing information ('TV turn-off days', for instance). It makes public appeals to citizens to turn their backs on information overload, in melancholic silence, book in hand. Some couch their case against communicative abundance in vaguely liberal terms, for instance, in ill-defined talk of the need for a 'new digital humanism' (Jaron Lanier) that honours and rewards creative individual expression. Others rest their case on the resurrection of fears of mass society and old-fashioned images of mindless crowds. Most often, the critics' political alternatives remain fuzzy or undisclosed, which has the effect of reinforcing the sense that everyday life really is going to the dogs.

Unhappy with the way things are heading, still other critics lash out in ways suggestive of a new cultural conservatism. They do not much like the age of communicative abundance: sometimes indulging old-fashioned imagery of brainless 'mobs', they pick on its adult mindlessness, its corruption of youth, its destructiveness of shared values based on family life, respect for authority and love of nation. Still others indulge their intellectualist prejudices – their rationalist belief in the virtues of rationalism – by turning against the supposed vulgarity circulated through the latest devices. There is plenty of shop-worn rhetoric about 'addiction' to 'the Internet'. It is accused of so distracting users that they neglect laundry and other basic household chores; ignore simple household courtesies, such as greeting and spending time with members of their household; and it is said that the Internet has the power to seduce users into a world of 'fantasy' that is at odds with 'reality'. There are flourishing anecdotes about wired insomniacs incapable of sleeping apart from their mobile phones, laptops and other portable devices. It is said that the addicts suffer attention deficits, sometimes in chronic form, as when a young person on Facebook

of prose. That's rarely the case anymore. Now my concentration often starts to drift after two or three pages. I get fidgety, lose the thread, begin looking for something else to do. I feel as if I'm always dragging my wayward brain back to the text. The deep reading that used to come naturally has become a struggle.'

spots a status update of song lyrics; Googles to find the name of the band; flits to Wikipedia to discover the name of the lead singer; looks at their Twitter; checks out their pictures on a multimedia blogging platform like Tumblr, before sampling their music on Grooveshark (a music search engine and streaming service); and, finally, rummaging through memes for photographs to upload and share with friends on Facebook.

The high-minded seriousness of some critics of communicative abundance judges these kinds of butterfly movements as flights of fancy that border on the pathological. The hanging judges ignore the democratic trends outlined in the first section of this book. They have little or no time for the supposedly outdated distinction between tools of communication and their users, or for the ways in which users engage creatively with the means of communication which otherwise shape them. Symptomatic is the way the critics turn a blind eye to the interesting fact that 'search' is both a leading metaphor of Internet culture and something that people do when they refuse to be sunk in the everydayness of their own daily lives. The hanging judges also downplay the equally pertinent fact that users often favour small talk, which is what flesh-and-blood people in all kinds of context have done since time immemorial. The chief magistrates of proper Internet use also pay little or no attention to the way the new tools of communication are tilling the soil of heterogeneity, above all by performing the function of circulating and re-circulating opinions – and doing so by holding a mirror to society, thereby revealing ourselves to ourselves, and to others, showing who we are, representing us at our best, our worst and everywhere in between.

The outbursts against the invention called Twitter are revealing of the purist prejudices of those nostalgic for times past. Despite its sizeable regular user base (75 million people worldwide by 2010), and its growing role in supplementing and enriching professional media outlets, Twitter is condemned as inane. It is said by its critics to resemble a freaks' show, a parade of neurotics, a medium that encourages gathered users to burp whatever is on their mind, to bring forth their inner selves, unprompted, in the form of banal reports about who they are, where they are, what they are thinking.[34] Twitter's prize is the re-tweeted *bon mot* born of an inner monologue. For all the fanfare accompanying its

---

[34] Examples of the offending banality are widespread, say the critics. Here's one: during September 2011, the London-based BBC website hosted a series of short

birth, say its critics, Twitter is trivial. It is not a public means of cleverly connecting people in difficult political circumstances, for instance, by circulating reports live, unfiltered by the sultans of spin, or by government censors. Worse still, Twitter is a friction-free medium of disinformation. It is said that crumbs of news of events often generate nonsense rumours whose tweeting ensure that they go viral, sometimes to the point where they morph from mere pitter-patter, water-cooler chatter into re-blogged and re-tweeted inaccuracies and outright falsehoods. For the critics, recycled information without edification produces falsification. The cut-and-paste carelessness, lack of questioning and non-editing of tweets is compounded by impatient fame-seeking fuelled by tweeters' desire to prove that they are the source of breaking news. The whole point, say the critics, is that tweeters are hooked on proving their own ability to attract substantial numbers of clicks and readers' eyeballs; some of them (like Gawker[35]) are interested in maximising clicks because they believe it will attract advertisers, build brand value and generate handsome profits.

Take just one randomly selected example of what the critics of Twitter have in mind, the moment (in early November 2010) of panic and confusion surrounding news of the mid-air explosion of a jet engine on a Qantas A380 bound for Sydney from Singapore. The event

advertisements for the telecommunications company Vodaphone, among them one that featured Australian cricket captain Michael Clarke speaking about the company's long-standing motto of the 'power' of new mobile phone networks. 'What's power to me?', asks Clarke. 'Staying connected. The main reason for me to be on Twitter is I guess to allow my fans and my followers to get a little closer to me. I was cutting onions and couldn't stop crying. I sent a tweet to say, how can you cut onions and stop crying? There was a million ideas. Wear sunglasses. Swimming goggles, maybe. Cut off one of the ends ... umm, but I'm not sure which end it is. The most popular idea was put the onions in the fridge. That seems to help.'

[35] See http://gawker.com. A taste of Gawker's style was provided by its incoming news editor A. J. Daulerio, who ordered his staff (February 2012) to conduct a pageview-chasing exercise designed to amplify the website anthem ('Today's gossip is tomorrow's news'). Each staff writer was assigned to what was called 'traffic-whoring duty', that is, a solid two-week trawl through the online world to find items that would attract the largest traffic. It resulted in 'the top nine videos of babies farting' and such items as 'little girl slaps mom with piece of pizza, saves life', and 'penguin shits on Senate floor'. It was not much of a change from dancing cat videos and Burger King bathroom fights, and the aim was consistent with standard Gawker goals: to attract as many 'eyeballs' as possible so as to keep or attract top-rated brand advertisers away from what the new editor called the 'snappy snarky snarking snark-snark shit' of 'gutter journalism'.

triggered a chaotic bluster of random tweets and other messages, unchecked and un-sourced, many of them wildly inaccurate. Speed dictated that even public service sources such as ABC News (@abcnews) compounded the bedlam with posts such as: 'Kyodo news wire is reporting a passenger plane thought bound for Singapore has crashed in Indonesia'. The ill-chosen words prompted a Qantas spokesperson to confess that Web-based reports fuelled by Twitter were 'wildly inaccurate'. By then the failed engine itself had chipped in with a tweet via @QF32_Engine_2: 'I've been a very, very bad engine'. The absurdity, say the critics, was well summarised by a tweet from Sydney journalist (@Jen_Bennett): 'I have an unconfirmed report that says your unconfirmed report is unconfirmed. More speculation as it breaks.'

It turned out during the dramatic minutes of mid-air tension that tweets sent by local users in the language of Bahasa Indonesia and received at company headquarters helped its officials to understand better what was actually going on, and what to do next.[36] The critics of Twitter arguably understate its importance in such moments of emergency. They overlook, once again, the fundamental point that, in spite of their interdependence, tools and users of tools of communication are not identical. Users of Twitter can, and do, regularly exercise discretion by hitting UNFOLLOW or BLOC to screen out unwanted tweets. Users of Twitter do political things, for instance, by gathering support for unelected representatives and by raising matters of public importance for public consideration. As would be expected in the age of monitory democracy, there are growing numbers of recorded cases where Twitter, which offers a friction-free route to an audience, has played a vital role in fomenting political resistance to sensed injustice, in protests ranging from objections to rigged election results (as in the 2009 anti-government protests in Iran) and calls for the removal of tyrants (the 2011 uprisings in Tunisia and Egypt), through to municipal struggles featuring public figures such as Margaret Atwood agitating in defence of the Toronto Public Library system.[37] Twitter critics will have

---

[36] From my interview with David Epstein, ex-head of the Qantas Government and Corporate Affairs division and Group Executive Committee member, Sydney, 2 December 2011.

[37] See Ghonim, *Revolution 2.0*; James Poniewozik, 'Iranians Protest Election, Tweets Protest CNN', *Time World*, 15 June 2009, available at http://entertainment.time.com/2009/06/15/iranians-protest-election-tweeps-protest-

none of this. They prefer to denounce it as a medium for producing and circulating unformed, thoughtless and unserious fluff. Deliberately uttered at the drop of a hat, or on a whim, tweets are condemned as meaningless beyond the context and the moment of their utterance. They do not really mean anything. They are merely a means of getting more and more into others' faces, of thrusting lips next to others' ears. Twitter is said to be a tool of frivolity, insouciance. It is a tool for twats whose quietest whispers sometimes come across as screams. They leave no room for silence, or privacy, or prudence or considered outrage. They are a new means of publicly amplifying private whims – tools of destruction of the unforced rational communication and public deliberation (so it is said) that democracy so desperately needs.

Hacking

Let us leave behind the unsubstantiated exaggerations about the destructive everyday effects of media abundance and turn instead to more measurable and more worrying signs of decadence within the emerging system of networked electronic communication. It turns out that Web-based communication can be immobilised by clever new forms of interference, ranging from the organised digital trespassing by crafty journalists into the personal lives of citizens to the tactic of infecting computers with viruses designed to capture banking and credit card data, as well as the shadowy sabotage tactic of cyberattack, immobilising government and corporate sites, plunging them into 'digital lockdown' for a time through 'flooding' or denial of service attacks (known in the trade as DDoS, they rely on infected computers called zombies that gain access to selected websites, all at once, for the purpose of overwhelming the sites with a surge of traffic that crashes the servers). Such forms of cyber-interference have major disruptive effects on social and political life. They should remind us of the bigger picture, the utter fragility of open media systems in the age of communicative abundance:

cnn, accessed 24 June 2009; and Margaret Atwood's account of the 2011 'war of the Toronto library system' in 'Deeper into the Twungle', *NYRblog*, 12 March 2012, available at http://www.nybooks.com/blogs/nyrblog/2012/mar/12/deeper-twungle-atwood-twitter, accessed 14 March 2012. A good survey of findings on the functions and effects of Twitter use is presented by Dhiraj Murthy, 'Twitter: Microphone for the Masses?', *Media, Culture & Society* 33(5) (2011): 779–89.

the ways in which complex systems are breakable in complex ways, their vulnerability to acts of unauthorised interference, popularly known as hacking.

The term should be handled with care. Its indiscriminate use blurs vital distinctions between the intended targets of interference, the digital methods used to disrupt the lives of people or whole institutions, and whether the tactics are aimed at, and perpetrated by, the powerful or the powerless.[38] The 'digital sit-ins' or electronic graffiti posted by the 'hacktivist' collective Anonymous on websites of the Syrian dictatorship of Bashar al-Assad are not to be confused with the retaliatory vigilantism of its electronic army; the malicious Trojan horse software unleashed on citizens' android phones by Russian cybercriminals in August 2010 drew upon different tactics and had different aims to those of the simultaneous hacking of Google by the government operatives, private security experts and Internet outlaws recruited by the Chinese government; and so on. What is nevertheless remarkable about these different cases is the way the revolution in favour of communicative abundance has powerfully amended the meaning of the word 'hack' and extended its use to cover so many different types of digital action. The word once referred to a second-rate writer producing dull and unoriginal work; a board on which a hawk's meat is laid out; and to a worn-out horse for hire, or a horse-drawn taxi; it also meant to pass one's time idly; to manage or to cope; to annoy someone; or to cut with a tool using rough or heavy blows. We still speak of having a hacking cough. But today the words 'hack' and 'hacking' are used primarily to refer to the act of gaining unauthorised access to computers. The semantic shift should be unsurprising, above all because multimedia-saturated societies dramatically multiply the chances of unwanted intrusions within distributed communication networks in ways that were not possible when the architecture of past media systems stood somewhere on the continuum between centralised and decentralised networks (see Figure 1.6).

What is the source of this vulnerability to sabotage? It is perhaps best explained by examining the internal logic of the lavish political economy claims that have been made in defence of communicative

---

[38] Gabriella Coleman, *Coding Freedom: The Aesthetics and the Ethics of Hacking* (Princeton, 2011).

abundance.[39] Its political economy defenders emphasise how the rich information environment associated with communicative abundance differs fundamentally from the 'industrial' information production system associated with large circulation mechanical presses, the telegraph, powerful radio and commercial mass-audience television transmitters, and early mainframe computers. Those centrally controlled, top-down systems were heavily capital-intensive. They erected high-wall entry barriers that served to restrict the production of information to elites, usually on a self-selected basis. Networked information production systems, which are built on cheap processors with high computation capabilities, interconnected through pervasive networks, radically alter this pattern in several ways, it is argued. The networked, distributed structures of the new information economy enhance individuals' capacity to do more for and by themselves. User-driven innovation (a phrase coined by Eric von Hippel) flourishes. The material means of communication among individuals are distributed much more widely than ever before. Individuals in consequence become much less dependent on the traditional mass-media model, where centralised ownership of the means of communication enabled owners (states or businesses) to select the information available to individuals, thereby shaping their lived identities. The new information economy is, however, not just a means of reinforcing individuation or selfishness. Peer production of information, knowledge and culture flourishes, as evidenced by cooperatively-produced encyclopaedias such as Wikipedia, free and open-source software initiatives (associated with figures such as Richard Stallman and Eben Moglen), local radio and news cooperatives and the flourishing of networked public spheres. The formation of Internet 'clusters', or communities of interest that engage in *de facto* peer reviewing and often link up with other communities of interest, so forming a vast web of interlinked clusters, is part of the same trend. By providing individuals with varied alternative platforms for communication, the new information economy provides individuals with many new opportunities to build bridges with others, to bond together in new

---

[39] The following draws upon the influential strident defence of 'liberalism' as the complement of a 'networked information economy' by Yochai Benkler, *The Wealth of Networks: How Social Production Transforms Markets and Freedom* (New Haven and London, 2006); Yochai Benkler, *The Penguin and the Leviathan: How Cooperation Triumphs over Self-Interest* (New York and London, 2011).

forms of commonality, with democratic effects. Finally, the new information economy, or so it is said, strengthens the capacity of individuals and groups to do more for themselves, not only within the heartlands of the capitalist economy (despite recent setbacks, Toyota's collaborative shop-floor, supply chain and management style is often seen as exemplary), but through formal organisations that operate well outside the sphere of markets.

The claim that the growth of a networked information economy is strengthening individuals' powers of choosing among different sources of information, often in non-market settings that defy the constraints of large-scale information providers, arguably contains more than a few grains of truth. The theme recurs through the pages of this book. The sluice gates that regulate the rivers of information have indeed been opened; traditional mass-media models are in trouble, and the horizons of political imagination of what is democratically feasible are being stretched by personal computers, networked connections and user-generated innovations. Champions of this line of thinking like to speak, as economists do, of 'coordinate effects': the large-scale enrichment of whole information environments thanks to the uncoordinated, not necessarily self-consciously cooperative actions of many millions of individuals. Sometimes these champions go further. Those of liberal persuasion say that the new information economy 'gives individuals a significantly greater role in authoring their own lives, by enabling them to perceive a broader range of possibilities, and by providing them a richer baseline against which to measure the choices they in fact make'.[40]

The trouble is that trends in the real world point in rather different directions, in part because certain individuals, usually organised in groups, take advantage of networked structures and flows of communication for their own private advantage. 'Individuals become less passive', it is said, without much reflection on the new ways in which these same individuals can do harm to others by throwing spanners in the works of information circuits. It turns out that these circuits were originally designed with security as an afterthought. The fact that an estimated 80 per cent of these circuits share the same operating system reduces their so-called 'cyber-resilience'.[41] Lacking multiple immune

---

[40] Benkler, *The Wealth of Networks*, p. 9.
[41] John Markoff, 'Killing the Computer to Save It', *New York Times*, 29 October 2012.

systems, they become highly vulnerable to design flaws such as 'buffer overflow', which permit an attacker to send files with a long string of characters that force a program to fail by overrunning a computer's memory, so making it possible for intruders to execute their own malicious programs.

A spicy example comes from France, whose political scene in the early years of the twenty-first century heaved with controversy about a legal investigation of an alleged large-scale case of hacking featuring the world's largest operator of nuclear power plants, Électricité de France (EDF). The rumpus had all the trappings of a breathtaking media event, with 'viral' qualities typical of the age of communicative abundance – a thrilling drama featuring a cast of extraordinary characters that included a disgraced testosterone-doped American cycling champion (Floyd Landis), laboratory officials, former French spies and military men operating in the shadows of corporate power, Greenpeace activists, the media and telecommunications conglomerate Vivendi, and a top judge (Thomas Cassuto) whose untiring investigations resembled an odyssey or (better) a textbook case of monitory democracy in action.

Cassuto's enquiry began after the Tour de France in 2006 in a sports doping laboratory.[42] Evidently, its records had been hacked by a Trojan horse program that enabled outsiders to download files of records remotely, which were then altered and passed to news media and other labs, apparently in support of the disgraced cyclist and with the aim of discrediting the original handling of test samples. The investigation quickly targeted a computer specialist, Alain Quiros, who was tracked down in Morocco by a special cybercrime unit of the French Interior Ministry. Monsieur Quiros confessed to having been paid a modest sum (up to €3,000) for hacking the lab; but he also revealed that a shadowy corporate intelligence company, Kargus Consultants, had spearheaded the attack. Really interesting stuff then happened. Things grew dramatic when the cybercrime police found on the computer of Quiros the hard drives of Yannick Jadot, the former campaign director of Greenpeace, and Frédérik-Karel Canoy, a French lawyer and shareholder rights activist seasoned by many campaigns against some of the largest French companies, including Vivendi and European Aeronautic Defence & Space Co. (EADS), the parent company of the aircraft

---

[42] The following draws in part on correspondence with Judge Thomas Cassuto (January 2010).

manufacturer Airbus. The corporate intelligence company Kargus Consultants subsequently alleged that it was employed by EDF to spy on anti-nuclear campaigners not only in France, but also in Spain, Belgium and Britain, where EDF had recently bought the largest nuclear power company, British Energy. EDF officials vehemently denied any wrongdoing. Vivendi, raided by cyberpolice on suspicion of conducting 'corporate intelligence' raids, also remained silent. Suspicion grew that Trojan horse attacks were becoming things of the past – that much more sophisticated, automated targeting of the 'cloud' of information that people and organisations generate through their online activities was quickly becoming the norm.

iPhones

France is not the only monitory democracy experiencing political difficulties with hacking. The days are over when we could comfortably suppose that we were safe from attacks if we kept away from the online porn circuit or never responded to messages from the widow of the governor of the central bank of the Central African Republic itching to transfer a few million dollars into our account. Every monitory democracy knows routine online disruptions: emblematic is the way that, in 2011, the password to the personal email account of a Twitter employee was guessed by an American hacker, who thus managed to extract their Google password and so gain access to a bundle of Twitter's corporate documents stored in 'the cloud'. Attacks of this kind are becoming common. Spam (from 'spiced ham', that wonderful neologism from the 1930s made famous by Monty Python) accounts for 80–90 per cent of all email around the world. There are constant reports of cyber-industrial espionage by corporations, organised criminal hacking and cyber-warfare launched by governments or intelligence services. A 2007 attack on Estonia reportedly forced it temporarily to shut down its Web-based links with the world. Some observers warn that the democratic potential of communicative abundance might well be wrecked by 'cyber-malfeasance' backed by states, corporations and criminals.[43] Websites testing positive for adware, spyware, spam, phishing, viruses and other noxious stuff are meanwhile multiplying. In 2010, Google

---

[43] Ronald J. Deibert, *Black Code: Inside the Battle for Cyberspace* (New York, 2013).

engineers noted that about 10 per cent of many millions of Web pages were engaged in 'drive-by downloads' of malware. The figure soon jumped (within a year) to 330,000 malicious websites, up from 150,000. The injection of malice into complex organisations and media systems and personal accounts is more than of news gossip value. For the plain fact is that it is driving another decadent trend: the rapid formation of security-protected online processes and products, even the formation of 'gated communities' that resemble private fiefdoms that have medieval effects by weakening the principle and fact of freedom of movement, 'open grazing' and universal access to the 'public commons' of communication with others.

An early scholarly diagnosis by Jonathan Zittrain correctly interpreted hacking as a form of attempted privatisation of the means of communication – as part of a much bigger struggle by the forces favouring market- and government security-driven enclosure against creative Web-based communication among citizens.[44] From the time of its launch in January 2007, the iPhone stood as an icon of the trend. A masterpiece of beauty, it is, Zittrain said, a brilliantly engineered device that combined three products into one: 'an iPod, with the highest-quality screen Apple had ever produced; a phone, with cleverly integrated functionality, such as voicemail that came wrapped as separately accessible messages; and a device to access the Internet, with a smart and elegant browser, and with built-in map, weather, stock, and email capabilities.' The trouble, argued Zittrain, was that the device was 'sterile'. It had limited 'generativity'. Unlike, say, Pledgebank, Wikipedia or Meetup, the iPhone was an iBrick. It did not invite or enable users to tinker with it, to improve upon it, to adapt it to their particular needs. Those who initially tried to tinker with its code, to enable the iPhone to support more or different applications, were threatened by Apple with legal action. 'Rather than a platform that invites innovation, the iPhone comes pre-programmed', Zittrain noted. 'You are not allowed to add programs to the all-in-one device … Its functionality is locked in, though Apple can change it through remote updates.'

[44] Jonathan Zittrain, *The Future of the Internet: And How to Stop It* (New Haven, 2008); see also the early contribution of Ronald J Deibert, 'Black Code: Censorship, Surveillance, and the Militarisation of Cyberspace', *Millennium: Journal of International Studies* 32(3) (December 2003): 501–30.

In matters of communication, it is a sign of our revolutionary times that Apple soon addressed this line of complaint by dramatically expanding the repertoire of user-generated 'applications' on its iPhone. Zittrain's analysis underestimated the technical dynamism of the product; and his approach suffered other weaknesses. Whether or not intended, it imbibed a generous draft of trust in an all-American 'can do' nativism, an early twenty-first-century version of nineteenth-century Ralph Waldo Emerson's faith in the ability of individuals to reach unfathomable places through moral force and creative intelligence, guided by the rule that the less government we have the better. Symptomatic was Zittrain's remark that 'the Net is quite literally what we make it' (the identity of the subject 'we' is unclear), and his defence of what he calls 'the procrastination principle' ('create an infrastructure that is both simple and generative, stand back, and see what happens, fixing most major substantive problems only as they arise, rather than anticipating them from the start'). This is to say that his work placed too much trust in competitive market forces; and too little emphasis on the political need to strengthen the public ownership of multimedia communications media, that is, to institutionalise, on an ambitious cross-border basis, a contemporary equivalent of last century's public service broadcasting principle that within any given political order the means of communication should be for public uplift, use and enjoyment. Yet – and it is a large caveat – Zittrain's key point should not be lost. Hacking, e-graffiti, identity theft, not to mention viruses, spam, crashes and other dysfunctions, are an unwelcome consequence of the freedom built into the generative PC. Zittrain put this well: 'Today's viruses and spyware are not merely annoyances to be ignored as one might tune out loud conversations at nearby tables in a restaurant', he wrote. 'They will not be fixed by some new round of patches to bug-filled PC operating systems, or by abandoning now-ubiquitous Windows for Mac. Rather, they pose a fundamental dilemma: as long as people control the code that runs on their machines, they can make mistakes and be tricked into running dangerous code.' As more people use Web-based media and become ever more accessible to the outside world through broadband connections, the value of corrupting these users' decisions rises. 'That value is derived from stealing people's attention, PC processing cycles, network bandwidth, or online preferences', he concluded. The clear implication was that 'a Web page can be and often is rendered on the fly by drawing upon hundreds of different sources scattered across the Net – a page may pull in content from its owner, advertisements from a syndicate, and links from various other feeds – means that bad code can infect huge swaths of the Web in a heartbeat.'

Gated communities

The vulnerability of operating codes to quick-time, malicious interference helps to explain another decadent effect of communicative abundance: the rapid growth of *gated online communities* organised and secured by big media firms. Talk of gated media communities may be unfamiliar, but it highlights the way in which the open-access architecture of media-saturated polities is compromised by its subdivision into no-entry zones that, in effect, prevent citizens from openly meandering and grazing the sites of their choice. Some early theorists of communicative abundance likened it to an infinitely tangled and dizzying enchanted garden of forking paths of space and time (the simile was drawn from Borges[45]), but many citizens now find everyday realities are trending in different directions. The garden of forking paths feels more like a conflict zone littered with digital no-fly spaces, checkpoints, sanitary cordons, land mines and unfinished battles. Citizens are aware that the choice to buy a particular notebook, e-reader or smart phone is not straightforward; the decision 'hooks' the user automatically into the *modus operandi* of the host platform and, hence, into competing but different functions, capabilities, services and advertised products.

We return here to Marshall McLuhan's 'law': tools and whole modes of communication lock their users into pre-determined patterns of usage and their corresponding effects. We could add: all tools of communication bind their users into pre-determined patterns of usage, but some tools do so more tightly than others, sometimes to the point where their primary function is to hitch users to the bandwagon strategies pre-decided by media firms in the marketplace.

The transformation of citizens into tool-using consumers is strongly evident in the field of hand-held gadgets designed for digital surfing. In the early days of the communications revolution, personal use of the

---

45 Jorge Luis Borges, 'The Garden of Forking Paths', in Donald A. Yates and James E. Irby (eds),*Labyrinths: Selected Stories and Other Writings* (New York, 1964), pp. 19–29.

Internet was regulated by open standards bodies such as W3C; now it is controlled by Apple, Blackberry, Samsung, Facebook and other platform vendors. As personal computers with standard-sized screens have been replaced or supplemented by various tools with large and small screens in both landscape and portrait formats, the permitted interactive applications have become different as well. When based on Java and Flash, for instance, they were once more open, in that they enabled users to graze through all websites; by contrast, applications nowadays increasingly depend upon privately-owned platforms and tailored passwords that determine who can and who cannot use the applications, and at what price.

In general, the shift taking place is towards the use of anytime-use devices structured by brand names and prices, site registration and personal profiles and passwords. Perhaps the term 'splinternet' is too strong for describing the shift, but it has the advantage of underscoring the movement away from the open access ideals of the Web, so that for growing numbers of people the experience of using smart phones, tablets, e-readers and other new gadgets to surf the Web is governed by platforms designed by media firms to corner and confine users within a corporate ecosystem of pre-determined gadgets, content and advertising. The whole trend is paradoxical. As walls to communication among people are torn down they are rebuilt, in many different shapes and sizes. It is unsurprising that the splinternet tendency and the corresponding battle among rival platforms is very much about money and, in particular, the struggle for advertising revenues and profit by market actors operating under conditions of intense market competition. The platform battle and the enclosure effects that result, in other words, are fuelled by risk- and profit-propelled corporate strategies, whose power to privatise the galaxy of communicative abundance potentially spells trouble for the democratic principles of open access and equality of opportunity for all citizens.

'But it's a free world, a free market economy', says the sceptic, 'and surely businesses have every right to take advantage of Web-based media and so improve the range and quality of people's communication with others? Business investment is vital for keeping people connected.' The sceptic raises a bundle of disparate points (including the contested meaning of freedom), but in this context easily the most pertinent is the growing power of private investors to shape the architecture of Web-based communication, in effect, to sideline a suitably twenty-first-century, more complex version of the public service broadcasting principle championed during the 1920s by Lord Reith and the BBC. The principle of public investment and ownership, use and enjoyment of multimedia systems of communication media today seems marginal, outflanked by the dynamic growth of gated communities, which are winning the battle for control over people's time and attention, arguably with counter-democratic effects. The erection of walled-off, locked-down and zipped-up areas where only the privileged can enter, wander and linger, points towards a neo-medieval topography of power. Unless citizens and governments act to reverse the trend, the future promises a hotchpotch growth of closed communities that are vertically arranged and definitely skewed in favour of those who can afford the access charges, have the Web cookies, know the password and pass the entrance test. The algorithms imposed for business reasons lead to 'mainstreaming' and the Matthew effect: 'To all those who have, more will be given.' Things from which profit can be made are strengthened by repetition and targeting versions of what works; things which are less popular, or unknown things or things that do not conform to trends are filtered out. Large corporations hunt profits and they therefore take aim at the biggest flocks; or, to switch metaphors, they prefer u-curves rather than long tails.[46]

The nether world of hyperlinks

The trend is potentially undermining of monitory democracy. Think of things this way: democracy is a form of self-government in which the means of deciding who gets what, when and how are in public hands. The privatisation of the means of making decisions is antithetical to its spirit and substance. A supplementary rule applies: since a democracy requires that citizens and representatives enjoy open access to the prevailing means of communication, their ownership and control by big businesses can have choking effects. A remarkable feature of communicative abundance is that its generative rules – analogous to the generative rules of a grammar that enables speakers to utter infinite numbers of different sentences – encourage the openness, dynamism,

---

[46] See the pithy remarks in support of social networks and the proliferation of tips, links, re-tweets, statements and comments by Jürgen Kuri in the *Frankfurter Allgemeine Zeitung*, 20 March 2010.

pluralism, experimentation and strong sense of the contingency of things upon which democracy thrives. As we saw earlier, their mutual affinity has tempted more than a few observers to conclude that the respective grammars of democracy and communicative abundance are mutually reinforcing, and that networked media are 'naturally' a force for democratic good.

Straightforward celebrations of the democratic inclusiveness of Web-based communication, its propensity to level hierarchies, create open public spaces and remove discriminations, are premature, at least when consideration is given to the detailed power manoeuvres of businesses to concentrate links, patterns of usage and online traffic in their favour. The galaxy of communicative abundance admittedly comprises millions of swirling interactions that take place daily, hourly, by the minute, second and microsecond. It is a wildly sprawling online landscape of linked spaces that organise our attention, and attention spans. These spaces suggest to us materials that are worthwhile, or imperative, or that satisfy what we are looking for or give us a competitive edge on others. The galaxy of communicative abundance appears to be a great liberation from Power. Structured by interlinked sites and spaces, sometimes called hyperlinks, it is the means by which people, who would otherwise go their separate and unequal ways, are connected with others, potentially on a global scale, as equals blessed with the capacity to disrupt the hierarchies of power that tend to accumulate within democratic societies.

The trouble is that corporate algorithms powerfully prefigure what citizens think, say and do. Communication giants like Google, AT&T, Nokia, Apple and British Telecom wield tremendous power not only as providers of trend-setting tools of communication, broadband access and video package deals. They also shape the 'hidden' plumbing of communicative abundance.[47] Just as early decisions about the location and specification of telegraph cables and operating equipment determined the patterns of use of telegraphed messages for decades to come, so choices now being made by corporate actors may result in immutable defining rules for future generations, for instance, through choices about which algorithms shape computerised systems of communication. The point cannot be underplayed: digital algorithms serve as the

---

[47] Eli Pariser, *The Filter Bubble: What the Internet is Hiding From You* (New York, 2011).

foot messengers, drum and smoke signals, semaphores and telegraphs within the galaxy of communicative abundance. They function, for the first time in human history, to draw together and communicate texts, sounds and images, more or less instantly, potentially on a global scale. Yet these algorithms do not exist in a social and political power vacuum; they are not untouched by the logic of power. Their design and implementation enable some individuals, groups, organisations and whole subnetworks to 'rig' the content of communications in their favour, for instance, by ensuring that their own visibility level on the Internet is much higher compared with other actors, who are pushed aside, some towards the shadowy margins of invisibility.

Think of algorithm-structured links as powerful maps that guide people's movements and perforce structure their sense of reality as they navigate or browse their way through digital landscapes. These links do more than anchor users to source materials. Links steer them towards targets, often through many-to-many links, which are, in turn, connected by background programs such as Web spiders or crawlers, which have the effect of gathering together many-to-many links under big tents. These big digital tents resemble a strange nether world of complex algorithms that most people either know nothing of, or that they simply take for granted. It is a labyrinthine space populated with strange neologisms like splogs, hot areas, WikiLinks, URLs, hyperlinks, link sources, link destinations, inline links and red links. It is also a world inhabited by powerful corporate actors.

Google's early efforts to pioneer an indexing system based on a secret probability-based algorithm called PageRank is a striking example. It did more than replace the existing clunky search methods (such as AltaVista) with a new definition of 'intelligent' ranking that assigned each and every page a rank according to how many other highly-ranked pages are linked to it. PageRank allowed Google Search to develop refined forms of what is called in the trade 'content-targeted advertising'. Google pioneered algorithms that provided users with information that is relevant, important and true, according to the principle of popularity rankings. It redefined information to mean attracting market-place consumers. Drawing on programs such as AdSense and AdWords, Google found ways of mapping users' interests and targeting advertisements so that they conformed, more or less accurately, to users and their context. The innovation created channels for advertisers to access several billion online users and untold numbers of audio-visual, film and text websites built by others. Google became more than a verb. Its customers became its products. Every act of searching for information was registered, instantly positioned within a global web of links and connected to advertisers hungry to harvest buyers and willing, through a combination of price bids and cost-per-click and cost-per-view, to pay Google to sell their wares. Information searching became synonymous with the bridging and bonding of attention givers (online users) and attention seekers (advertisers) through unsolicited targeted advertising, whose spirit and substance permeated many nooks and crannies of the Web.

Google

Among the strangest things about protests against the damaging effects of communicative abundance upon the daily lives of individuals is their frequent silence about the tremendous power of *media markets* and *media businesses* in shaping citizens' patterns of communication. The silence suggests more than the narrow 'cultural' focus of the critics. It reveals their underestimation of the vital ways in which the age of communicative abundance comprises much more than people doing unprecedented clever (and allegedly silly) things with new media tools. It is an age that features Walt Disney, Bertelsmann, News Corporation, AT&T, Vivendi and other giant global conglomerates energised by their pursuit of the massive profits that come with market leadership, and spurred on by their sensed ability to make history – their capacity to put their own thumbprints all over contemporary democracy and its media infrastructure.

It is essential to understand the contours of organised media business, because media firms do much more than invest capital and employ media workers who produce and circulate information, all for the sake of profit. Media conglomerates get under the skins of their clients. They shape and re-shape citizens' identities in the most intimate ways. They massage their language, their common sense, their fantasies; the results are variable, but invariably they do so from a position of formidable power, typically acquired through cut-throat battles waged against their opponents. Concentration of the means of communication in a few private hands is the normal resultant of unfettered markets, which rarely result in pure win–win outcomes; by definition, and in practice, competitors stumble, or are pushed, so that they fall behind and end up as losers. Oligopoly or monopoly proves to be the winner – until a new competitor equipped with formidable new strategies and tools emerges to challenge the dominant players.

Joseph Schumpeter was among those influential observers who reckoned that this competition/monopoly pattern was both inevitable and, on balance, desirable. For him, the market power of large firms certainly involves their ability to exploit workers and consumers, as well as competitors. But, or so he thought, big businesses are necessary for innovation, which is the core of effective competition. Capitalism is a dynamic system of permanent revolutionising of the means of production, which is why large media firms do everything to keep their production processes secret, protect their trademarks from infringement and to obtain patents. Corporate size delivers 'competition from the new commodity, the new technology, the new source of supply, the new type of organization', noted Schumpeter. It is the 'powerful lever that in the long run expands output and brings down prices'.[48]

In retrospect, Schumpeter underestimated the way monopoly retards innovation. Whether, or to what extent, innovation is the fruit of monopoly, or monopoly is instead the outcome of innovation, remained unclear within his analysis. More recent analysts have dubbed this innovation–monopoly nexus 'the cycle', by which they mean to underscore the way communications markets, through time, typically choke the channels of free communication by fostering market winners that try to protect their flanks by erecting barriers to innovation and entry, thereby restricting the range of choices available to communicating citizens.[49]

For the moment, we can suspend judgements about whether, and to what extent, media conglomerates have damaging effects on the spirit and substance of monitory democracy, and simply note the broad historical pattern of media concentration under conditions of market competition. Examples are easy to find: the age of eighteenth-century print culture saw the growth for the first time of large publishing houses dedicated to reducing market competition. It witnessed the first powerful press barons, eighteenth-century Rupert Murdoch-like figures such as Charles-Joseph Panckoucke, who aimed at monopolising the opinion

---

[48] Schumpeter, *Capitalism, Socialism, and Democracy*, pp. 84–5.
[49] Tim Wu, *The Master Switch: The Rise and Fall of Information Empires* (New York, 2010).

and reading markets by publishing books, periodicals and newspapers with a thoroughly 'modern' style.[50] There were subsequently many moments when the publishing trade resembled 'booty capitalism', a form of *brigandage* led by hucksters hungry for money and willing to take big risks. The same pattern shaped the era of electronic communications. In the United States, the heartland of radical innovations in the field of communications for a century and a half, corporate fights attended the race to design and sell a 'musical telegraph', a device capable of sending multiple messages simultaneously down a single copper line. In opposition to Western Union, the outfit that dominated the telegraph industry, Bell's telephone company proved to be the winning innovator, with system-disrupting effects.[51] The struggle for control of the telephone business was the harbinger of parallel conflicts within such fields as radio, film, aerial and cable television: each tool of communication became grist in the mill of highly integrated and centralised industrial organisations.

In the age of communicative abundance, the same trend towards oligopoly is palpable. For the case of the United States, the media researcher Ben Bagdikian has shown that in 1984, when the communications revolution was still young, some fifty large companies controlled the media industry. By 1987, the number had dropped to twenty-six; it then dropped further to around ten in 1996, so that by 2004 the lion's share of the media industry was controlled by a Big Five (Time Warner, Disney, Bertelsmann, News Corporation and Viacom). Although precise details of the market share of these giants are not made publicly available, the trend towards mergers, takeovers and concentrated ownership has strengthened, thanks to economies of scale and the general loosening of government regulatory controls. Similar trends are evident elsewhere, as in neighbouring Canada, where under pressure from media corporate mergers and takeovers the market share of independently owned newspapers declined from 17.3 per cent in 1990 to around 1 per cent in 2005, fuelling fears of declining standards of journalism, uncertainty about the mandate and role of public service media, and concerns about the absence of funding for Internet-based

---

[50] Suzanne Tucoo-Chala, *Charles-Joseph Panckoucke et la librairie française* (Paris, 1977); Robert Darnton, *The Business of Enlightenment: A Publishing History of the Encyclopédie* (Cambridge, MA, 1979); Keane, *The Media and Democracy*, esp. pp. 45–7.
[51] Herbert Newton Casson, *The History of the Telephone* (Chicago, 1910).

news media.[52] In the Czech Republic, German and Swiss big corporations own 80 per cent of newspapers and magazines. Big foreign capital, mostly German, Austrian, French and Scandinavian, dominates print media in the democracies of Bulgaria, Hungary, Poland and the Baltic states.[53] In Japan, despite the prominence of the public broadcaster NHK and laws that restrict cross-media ownership, four corporate conglomerates, including the Yomiuri Group, which owns *Yomiuri Shimbun*, the world's largest circulation newspaper, dominate the field of newspapers, affiliated television networks, advertising, book publishing, video production and direct marketing. Big business ownership of media enterprises is something of a tradition in India, stemming from the days when large-circulation newspapers like *The Indian Express* were controlled by the country's largest jute mill (owned by Ramnath Goenka, whose critics dubbed him the captain of the 'jute press' or '*jhoot* [or lies] press'). The concentration of business media power has accelerated in recent years, bringing to prominence corporate players such as the Rupert Murdoch-controlled STAR (Satellite Television Asia Region) group and Bennett, Coleman & Co. Ltd (BCCL), along with a discernible shift towards such products and practices as sexed-up 'breaking' news, paid content 'advertorials', private treaties (granting advertising space to companies in exchange for equity shares) and editorial coverage targeted at the three Cs for which middle-class Indians supposedly have a passion: crime, cricket and cinema.[54]

The grip of oligopoly has for some time been gathering pace in the field of the Internet, where 'hyper-giants' such as Apple, Microsoft, Facebook and Google's YouTube now generate and consume around one-third of all global traffic. Unless the trend is reversed, for instance, by tougher legal regulations and governments' and universities' support for not-for-profit Web platforms, it seems inevitable that further across-the-board

---

[52] Standing Senate Committee on Transport and Communications, Parliament of Canada, June 2006, *Final Report on the Canadian News Media*, available at: www.parl.gc.ca/39/1/parlbus/commbus/senate/Com-e/TRAN-E/rep-e/repfinjun06vol1-e.htm, accessed 19 February 2011.

[53] Commission of the European Communities, *Media Pluralism in the Member States of the European Union* (Brussels, 2007), pp. 9–10.

[54] See the (originally censored) study by the Press Council of India, *Report on Paid News*, 30 July 2010, Delhi, available at: www.outlookindia.com/article.aspx?266543, accessed 25 March 2012.

concentration of media ownership and control of the Internet will happen in virtually all the world's democracies.

The bitter battles that unfolded between Apple and Google in the early years of the twenty-first century illustrate what is at stake. Some observers reckon that their rivalry will shape 'the future of the world'.[55] At the beginning, it seemed as if the two companies were partners. Their mutual conviction that mergers and exclusive partnerships belonged to the past was striking; the synergies of layered networks, open protocols and joint cooperation would obviate the need for corporate mergers, or so they said. In times still dominated by central mainframe computers, Apple was the upstart outsider, champion of open computing and the first to put the principle into practice by giving it mass, practical appeal. Guided by its corporate motto, 'Think Different', and by talk (led by Steve Jobs) of wanting to sail with the pirates, not the navy, it built a small personal computer with an attached mouse and a graphic user interface of toolbars, icons and windows known as a 'desktop'. The invention, known as the Apple I or Apple-1, is today housed in the National Museum of American History, Washington, DC. Designed and hand-built by Steve Wozniak, some 200 units went on sale in July 1976 at a price of US$666.66, calculated to satisfy Wozniak's taste for 'repeating digits' and to include a one-third mark up on the $500 unit sold to a local shop. The wooden-box computer paved the way for Apple to achieve giant company status backed by enormous market power; in their skirmishes with the old established corporate navies, the underdog pirates made off with the gold.

Under the morally worthy banners of 'Don't be evil' and 'organize the world's information and make it universally accessible and useful', Google meanwhile launched a dot-com enterprise in the search business. Regarding itself as a flat organisation dedicated to collaborative work, initially with Stanford University, it made a copy of the entire World Wide Web, and, as we have seen above, pioneered, patented and deployed an indexing system based on an undisclosed probability-based algorithm called PageRank. Its core principle today seems obvious, although it wasn't at the time: replace the un-signposted chaos of the

---

[55] Tim Wu, *The Master Switch. The Rise and Fall of Information Empires* (New York, 2010), p. 273: 'If Huxley could say in 1927 that "the future of America is the future of the world," we can equally say that the future of Apple and Google will form the future of America and the world.'

Internet by re-organising online connections and content, not through conventional modes of cataloguing, such as alphabetical listing, but by assigning pages a 'popularity ranking' based on their numbers of links with other high-ranking pages.

The PageRank system had both a 'democratic' feel and took off commercially in a big way. The innovation seemed to confirm the company's stated commitment to the principle of network neutrality.[56] The innovation attracted venture capitalists and huge advertising revenues, and enabled Google to grow faster than any other large firm in the communications industry.[57] It launched a chain of products, triggered acquisitions and built business partnerships beyond its core Web search business. Emphasising a future in which easy access to information could become a reality for all users across fields as diverse as telephony, newspapers, video, film and television, Google developed Google Earth and YouTube. It offered traffic jam or coming meeting alerts through Google Now; launched a video chat facility called Google Hangouts; and promoted Google Glass, wearable spectacles connected to the Internet through Wi-Fi or Bluetooth. As we have seen above, it began to build an online library. It also pioneered Google Translate, a search enhancement tool called Google Instant, a capacious free-of-charge gmail service, an instant messaging application and the Android mobile operating system. The company set up Google News, a service that employed no editors, managing editors or executive editors. The company entered the mobile telephone business (with the acquisition of Motorola in August 2011), launched a satellite, invested in renewable energy projects and assembled a worldwide

---

[56] Says Google's guide to the neutrality of the Internet: 'Network neutrality is the principle that Internet users should be in control of what content they view and what applications they use on the Internet. The Internet has operated according to this neutrality principle since its earliest days ... Fundamentally, net neutrality is about equal access to the Internet. In our view, the broadband carriers should not be permitted to use their market power to discriminate against competing applications or content. Just as telephone companies are not permitted to tell consumers who they can call or what they can say, broadband carriers should not be allowed to use their market power to control activity online', 'Facts About our Network Neutrality Policy Proposal', 12 August 2010, available at: http://googlepublicpolicy.blogspot.com/search/label/Net%20Neutrality, accessed 19 August 2011.

[57] Steven Levy, *In the Plex: How Google Thinks, Works, and Shapes Our Lives* (London and New York, 2011); Siva Vaidhyanathan, *The Googlization of Everything (and Why We Should Worry)* (Berkeley, CA, 2011).

network of custom-built server farms, giant hangar-like information storage buildings equipped with power generators, cooling towers and thermal storage tanks.

Processing over 1 billion search requests and an estimated 25 petabytes of user-generated data each day, the company's market share of the online search business burgeoned. Within the US market, it quickly morphed into a monopoly (over 65 per cent by 2010), using pioneering methods of commercialising information seekers by way of a refined form of what is called in the trade 'content-targeted advertising'. Google not only pioneered algorithms that provided users with information that is relevant, important and reliable, according to the principle of popularity rankings, it also actually redefined information as a tool for commercially linking online users and advertisers. The strategy was clever. Even though the company owned no content or connections, it showed users the ads they might likely click on. In this way, by 2010, Google became an advertising machine that earned more money from search-based advertising than the entire newspaper business in the United States.

Its monopoly position in the search field sparked worries among anti-trust regulators about its general market dominance, as well as fierce public criticisms of its potentially decadent effects. Some analysts pointed out that the company's professed commitment to the democratic virtues of decentralised openness was contradicted by its corporate secrecy habits. Visitors to its California headquarters, for instance, found that if they refused to sign a non-disclosure agreement then their access was restricted. There is the well-known difficulty of using Google algorithms to extract independent information about the company itself, for instance, by googling Google to find out why it prohibits certain words within its instant search feature, or, say, to extract details of the methods and scope of its data-mining methods, or its political campaign spending patterns. In early 2013, Swedish users of Google even discovered that the company had reportedly lodged a formal complaint with the Swedish Language Council about the use of the Swedish word 'ogooglebar' (information that cannot be found on the Internet using a search engine). Others noted how Google's misadventure in China (from 2004) exposed its willingness to conform to government rules of arbitrary censorship for the sake of business. Bemused critics offer an example: the way that Google resolves the status of the land of dawn-lit mountains, Arunachal Pradesh, a disputed territory wedged between India and China, two major powers with nuclear weapons. If you live in India, Google Maps shows you that Arunachal Pradesh is part of India; but if you live in China, Google Maps shows you that Arunachal Pradesh is definitely part of China. Still other critics have attacked the company's bias towards advertising; its presumption that markets can do no evil has also come in for robust criticism. Triggered by moot public statements by Google senior executives, public alarms were raised about the threats posed to cherished notions of privacy and intellectual property rights by the company's information gathering and redistribution technologies.[58] The issue remains alive, even though the company was forced by the US Federal Trade Commission to strengthen its privacy disclosures to users, to obtain their consent for any data transfers to third parties, and to agree to public monitoring of the company's privacy policies for a twenty-year period.[59]

The Minot principle

By winning market power, big corporations like Google trigger a variety of complaints about their decadent behaviour. The crudest but perhaps best-known formulation is that they are conspirators in the 'manufacturing of consent'; the thesis that large corporations pull the wool over citizens' eyes, blinding them to the realities of their own

---

[58] Consider remarks by Eric Schmidt, Google's chief executive: 'I actually think most people don't want Google to answer their questions. They want Google to tell them what they should be doing next', 'Google and the Search for the Future', *Wall Street Journal*, 14 August 2010, available at: http://online.wsj.com/article/SB10001424052748704901104575423294099527212.html, accessed 19 August 2011; and in response to questions concerning policies such as Google's storage of 'cookies' with a lifespan of more than thirty years: 'If you have something that you don't want anyone to know, maybe you shouldn't be doing it in the first place. If you really need that kind of privacy', he told CNBC, 'the reality is that search engines – including Google – do retain this information for some time and it's important, for example, that we are all subject in the United States to the Patriot Act and it is possible that all information could be made available to the authorities', 'Only Miscreants Worry about Net Privacy', *The Register*, 7 December 2009, available at: www.theregister.co.uk/2009/12/07/schmidt_on_privacy, accessed 19 August 2011.

[59] See United States of America Federal Trade Commission, Agreement Containing Consent Order, File No. 102 3136, available at: http://www.ftc.gov/os/caselist/1023136/110330googlebuzzagreeorder.pdf, accessed 16 August 2011.

powerlessness.[60] The perspective correctly foregrounds the symbolic power of big media firms, their propensity to set public agendas, dominate the telling and diffusion of public stories, create public silences and even to shape and distort citizens' imaginations of who they are and who they could become. 'Only a handful of powerful, monopolistic corporations inundate the population day and night with news, images, publications, and sounds. It is a world into which every child is now born', says a seasoned observer of the trend, adding that big corporate money has become the mother's milk of contemporary politics. 'It pays for the expensive television political advertisements and mass mailings, and it is in the nature of wealth and politics that most of the money comes from conservative sources.'[61]

The insinuation is that corporate media are capturing and captivating public audiences. Some critics pelt corporations with the charge that their products and operating systems are rendering citizens 'stupid', or inducing 'digital dementia' caused by 'addictive' digital media that outsource human brain power, destroy brain and nerve cells, and result, in both young and old people, in such symptoms as reading and attention disorders, anxiety and apathy, insomnia and depression, obesity and violence.[62] Crudely un-ironic versions of the 'public mind management' thesis arguably rest upon shaky foundations. They suppose, without much further argument, that big firms are completely on top of the ongoing revolution of communicative abundance; that their media products are tightly tailored and free of contradictions; that the rivalry among competitors produces no free spaces for questioning the evils of oligopoly control; and that government regulation and judicial oversight always work unilaterally in favour of the new media fiefdoms. These are large, empirically questionable suppositions that fail to address the dynamics of communicative abundance examined so far in this book. Equally suspect is the faithless attitude towards citizens displayed by public mind management perspectives. Citizens are presumed to be dopes, victims of media manipulation of reception processes that allow them no room for self-development, perplexity or

---

[60] Edward S. Herman and Noam Chomsky, *Manufacturing Consent: A Propaganda Model* (New York, 1988).
[61] Ben H. Bagdikian, *The New Media Monopoly* (Boston, MA, 2004), pp. xiii–xiv.
[62] Carr, 'Is Google Making Us Stupid?'; Spitzer, 'Digitale Demenz'.

hermeneutic resistance, no political surprises and no unintended consequences.

The fault lines within mind management interpretations lend energy to more subtle criticisms of the oligopoly trend in media markets, among them the allegation that it violates the principle of the diversity of ownership, so jeopardising the variety of sources of information and range of contents that are essential for democracies to function. The pluralist objection usually draws on the norm of the 'informed citizen', doubts about which have already been raised, but it rightly raises the alarm about the political dangers of concentrated ownership of media. The trouble with unfettered market competition, according to the pluralist objection, is that it leads to the concentration of ownership, which in turn restricts the range of sources and contents that are available to citizens. 'Concentration of ownership', affirms a report prepared by the European Commission, 'may result in a skewed public discourse where certain viewpoints are excluded or under-represented.' It adds: 'because some viewpoints are represented while others are marginalized, abuse of political power can occur through the lobbying of powerful interest groups – whether these are political, commercial or other.'[63] The point can be rephrased: oligopoly results in the market censorship both of citizens' opinions and forms of communication that are deemed to be unprofitable or unfavourable to the big firm's perceived market interests. The more media firms trade in multiple 'product lines' that can be distributed throughout the various branches of the firm, so runs the reasoning of pluralists, the greater the opportunity to reap the benefits of the attendant economies of scale – with the result that 'unprofitable' and 'unmarketable' opinions and expressions are shoved aside, in accordance with what might be dubbed the Minot principle.[64]

---

[63] Commission of the European Communities, *Media Pluralism in the Member States of the European Union* (Brussels, 2007), p. 5.

[64] The Minot principle, the rule that large corporate media are more interested in economies of scale than in publishing unprofitable minority viewpoints, so named after a local disaster in the city of Minot, North Dakota in 2002, when a train freighting highly poisonous chemicals was derailed, causing one death and injuries to 1,600 people. None of the leading radio stations in the city reported the derailment and evacuation procedures, principally because at the time of the disaster they were broadcasting automated feeds from their owners, the ill-named Clear Channel Communications, whose corporate headquarters were located in San Antonio, Texas. More general treatments of the subject of market censorship include Keane, *The Media and Democracy*; Edwin C. Baker, *Media*

Media tycoons

There is a further concern, one that both overlaps and transcends the problem of the Minot principle. Evidence is mounting that media oligopoly breeds political arrogance, a brazen and insolent sense of being 'naturally' at the cutting edge of all things publicly important, the mind-set (to take just one example) displayed by News Corporation International's CEO Rupert Murdoch when unveiling (in February 2011) a new digital application newspaper called *The Daily*. 'New times demand new journalism', he said, explaining that the new multimedia publication, created specifically for the iPad tablet, would be free of charge for a short trial period, then available to readers by subscription only. 'The devices that modern engineering has put in our hands demand a new service, edited and designed specifically for them', he continued. His newspaper would allow journalists to 'completely re-imagine our craft' and to 'make the business of newsgathering and news editing viable again', he said. In the boldest prose, Murdoch summarised his company's intentions beyond the 'unthinkable innovations' offered by *The Daily* to the world of publishing. 'No paper, no presses, no trucks', he explained. 'We are very confident of the finances … We believe *The Daily* will be the model for how stories are told and consumed.' Murdoch underscored the 360-degree photographs, graphics that respond to the touch and 'other innovations that are unthinkable in print and television', before concluding with a short metric for the venture's success: 'When we are selling millions.'[65]

The words oozed chutzpah: the willingness to overstep accepted boundaries, gutsy presumption combined with gall, brazen nerve and arrogance, a conquistador attitude that wins friends and admirers, and most definitely spawns enemies, the embodiment of a spirit of adventure and innovation that has definite energising effects within the galaxy of communicative abundance. The move by News Corporation to establish *The Daily*, together with the earlier decision to charge online readers of its various other news sources, such as *The Times*, are small but

Concentration and Democracy: Why Ownership Matters (Cambridge and New York, 2006); David Croteau and William Hoynes, *The Business of Media: Corporate Media and the Public Interest* (Thousand Oaks, CA, and London, 2006).

[65] Ricardo Bilton, 'News Corp and Apple Unveil "The Daily"', *IBTIMES.com*, 2 February 2011.

telling symptoms of the 'gales of creative destruction' (Schumpeter) that from time to time sweep through market economies, uprooting old media habits and customary ways of communicating with others.[66] Corporate conquests are to be admired for their swashbuckling. They are also to be regarded with caution. All democrats should regard them with suspicion. To repeat, it is not only that private ownership of the means of communication by big firms serves to block citizen-generated innovations and reduce the pluralism of published opinions by driving out competitors and driving down employment standards for professional editors and journalists, who consequently find themselves under constant pressure to maximise audience size (to 'aim our guns where the ducks are thickest', as a CNN journalist once told me). The rapid growth of giant media firms has another decadent effect: it affords them opportunities to 'privatise' politics in their favour by bending, twisting and distorting the rules of representative government.

The distortion of parliamentary democracy by big media corporations is often seen through the prism of media barons. Analysts and critics picture them as proto-monarchs in the age of democracy, information bosses who enjoy 'power without responsibility',[67] to the point where their media propaganda and string-pulling make them influential political players capable of making and un-making governments. The imagery of the media tycoon (from Japanese *taikun* 'great lord') hails from the late nineteenth and early twentieth centuries. That was the moment when entrepreneurs such as the Anglo-Irish Viscount Northcliffe (1865–1922) minted the highly profitable art of buying and bundling together failing newspapers into big-circulation publications, such as the London-based *Daily Mail*, which was at the time the

---

[66] Schumpeter, *Capitalism, Socialism, and Democracy*, pp. 82–3: 'Capitalism ... is by nature a form or method of economic change' that 'never is but never can be stationary ... The fundamental impulse that sets and keeps the capitalist engine in motion comes from the new consumers' goods, the new methods of production or transportation, the new markets, the new forms of industrial organization that capitalist enterprise creates ... This process of Creative Destruction is the essential fact about capitalism'; cf. Manuel Castells, *The Rise of the Network Society*, 2nd edn (Oxford, 2000), p. 199: 'The "spirit of informationalism" is the culture of "creative destruction" accelerated to the speed of the optoelectronic circuits that process its signals. Schumpeter meets Weber in the cyberspace of the network enterprise.'

[67] James Curran and Jean Seaton, *Power Without Responsibility: The Press, Broadcasting, and New Media in Britain*, 6th edn (Abingdon and New York, 2003).

biggest in the world, the 'penny newspaper for one halfpenny'. At one point, Northcliffe directed the British Government's formal propaganda unit, which was perhaps a fitting symbol of the tremendous political influence of the new form of tabloid journalism that specialised in appeals to popular taste at exactly the moment when struggles to universalise the vote were coming to a head.

Measured in terms of thirst for political power, Rupert Murdoch (1931–) stands as Northcliffe's successor in the age of communicative abundance, at least in the eyes of critics who think of media decadence principally in terms of media tycoons. Murdoch is a media huckster with political clout. Although there have been moments of declared lack of interest in politics ('To hell with politicians! When are we going to find some to tell the truth in any country? Don't hold your breath', he tweeted in one outburst[68]), most observers rank him among the most powerful political figures on Earth. Many admire his business skills, especially his love of deals backed by ruthless drive and bold technical innovation. For some industry figures, Murdoch at his best is 'a man who has fought complacency, vested interests, status quo, incompetence and the belief that you can't change the world'.[69] Some of his closest friends use superlatives to praise him as a 'towering figure' who publishes 'first-class' newspapers and 'great' networked television.[70]

For six decades, Murdoch certainly mobilised his deal-making skills to transform a modest family asset, an afternoon newspaper in Adelaide and a small daily newspaper in the desert mining town of Broken Hill, into a global media octopus that includes Sky Italia, Fox News, Fox Movies, Dow Jones and the *Wall Street Journal* in the United States; several of the world's most infamous tabloid newspapers; metropolitan dailies; and many other media and entertainment assets around the world, including Star TV, which is among the largest broadcasters in the Asia and Pacific region. The acquisitions were the fruits of political calculation. In the early years of the communication revolution, Murdoch took on the political status quo. The old public service

---

[68] @rupertmurdoch, 15 February 2012, available at: https://twitter.com/#!/rupertmurdoch/statuses/169598517856321536, accessed 16 February 2012.

[69] The assessment of Richard Stott, former editor of the UK *Daily Mirror*, 'Murdoch's World', *The Guardian*, 11 October 2003.

[70] Former Australian Prime Minister John Howard, quoted in Andrew Clark, 'Adding up Murdoch's Ledger', *The Weekend Australian Financial Review*, 5/6 March 2011, p. 10.

model of broadcasting was among his prime targets. He presented himself as a champion of free markets and forcefully questioned the prevailing modes of state regulation. The strategy quickly captured the high ground of public debate by using terms like state censorship, individual choice, deregulation and market competition to criticise the prevailing mix of public and private communication systems operating within the boundaries of territorial states, whether democratic or not. Murdoch, the free market partisan, insisted that people 'want control over their media, instead of being controlled by it'; on this basis, Murdoch predicted an age of 'democratic revolution' and multi-channel communications structured by 'freedom and choice, rather than regulation and scarcity'.[71]

Scholars have pointed out that Murdoch's calculated defence of deregulation of media markets was from the outset only part of his story.[72] Behind the scenes, Murdoch operated according to other rules, with definite corrupting effects on the practice of democratic politics. The custom of politicians, presidents and prime ministers shuffling in his direction is long-established; if information is the political currency of electoral democracy, then Murdoch might be regarded as a mint where the currency is coined. Here was a media tycoon with an uncanny talent for simultaneously manipulating politicians and winning and holding the attention of large numbers of people.

The die was cast early in his career, in his native Australia, immediately following the mysterious disappearance in mid-December 1967 of Prime Minister Harold Holt.[73] Moments of political crisis are often revealing of the entanglements of big media business and government, and this moment was no exception. Holt's presumed death by drowning

---

[71] See the speech of Rupert Murdoch to the American Society of Newspaper Editors, 13 April 2005; and 'Freedom in Broadcasting', MacTaggart Lecture, Edinburgh International Television Festival, Edinburgh, 25 August 1989; cf. Keane, *The Media and Democracy*.

[72] David McKnight, 'Rupert Murdoch's News Corporation: A Media Institution with a Mission', *Historical Journal of Film, Radio & Television* 30 (September 2010): 303–16; David McKnight, *Rupert Murdoch: An Investigation of Political Power* (Sydney, 2012).

[73] The following section draws upon Alan Reid, *The Power Struggle* (Sydney, 1969), p. 67; G. J. Munster, *The Nation*, 20 January 1968, pp. 7–8; Patricia Clarke, 'On a Roller Coaster with Maxwell Newton Publications', Australian Media Traditions Conference, Canberra, 24–25 November 2005, available at: www.canberra.edu.au/faculties/comm-international/amt/PDFs/ AMT2005Clarke.pdf, accessed 10 January 2011.

triggered an intense struggle behind the scenes to determine his successor. It enabled Rupert Murdoch, still a young media empire builder, to enter the fray and to play a vital role in its resolution. Five days before the selection of a new leader, Murdoch agreed to meet in secret with the Acting Prime Minister, 'Black Jack' McEwen. For quite different reasons both favoured a candidate from the Senate named John Gorton (Murdoch did so because he judged, correctly, that he would be more pliable and sympathetic to allowing Murdoch to move capital out of Australia, in search of acquisitions in the United Kingdom). So together they decided that the best way of achieving their respective goals was to discredit Gorton's main rival, William McMahon, who happened to be a close associate of both the deceased prime minister and a former Murdoch journalist and powerful insider newsletter publisher named Max Newton. Murdoch targeted Newton, accusing him publicly of being a secret agent, in receipt of payments from JETRO, a Japanese trade organisation. Just days before the vital selection of the new prime minister, Murdoch's *Australian* carried a crude headline, 'FOREIGN AGENT IS THE MAN BETWEEN THE LEADERS', with the follow-up accusation that Newton was 'an active and paid representative of foreign interests'. Crudity worked. The allegation was heavily embellished, but within the governing parties it tipped the balance in favour of John Gorton, who was sworn in as prime minister three weeks after the disappearance of his predecessor.

Abu Dhabi

Contrary to those critics who indulge conspiracy thinking centred on the political effects of 'media barons', vulgar personal interference, as displayed in the Gorton election affair, is neither typical of how large media firms operate nor of Rupert Murdoch's behaviour when it comes to handling governments. Instead, they have a habit of using politicians and shaping governments from the near distance, rather than from close range. Big media firms are not much interested in governmental power for mischievous personal ends. Their chief concern is to secure existing investments and to consolidate their flanks by winning bigger and better deals. That is why, if they consider it to be in their interest, they will deal with any government and enter willingly into its arrangements, even when they fall far short of the standards of monitory democracy.

Far more worrying than the personalised rule of media tycoons, in other words, is the strong present-day tendency of corporate media and government to merge and meld, especially in contexts where constitutional and political resistance to the integration of organised media and political power is weak. The dalliance is driven by multiple forces. The policy efficiency and effectiveness of governments depend upon secure access to privately provided communication infrastructures. Big media firms generate employment and (limited) taxation revenues. Not to be underestimated is their role as fairy godmothers blessed with the power of sprinkling incumbent governments with the fairy dust of positive media coverage (or to hand out its opposite, crusades and bullying, shit-lists, character assassinations and other types of rough media treatment). Large media firms, meanwhile, depend upon the protective regulatory frameworks established by governments. They like tax breaks, safe havens, business parks and handouts in the form of government contracts. The combined effect of these forces is more than the blurring or dissolution of the division between 'the state' and the 'free market'. There are serious consequences for democracy: major matters to do with the ownership and control of both the means of communication and public decision-making cease to be matters of public debate and decision. In effect, they are removed from the public agenda, decided behind closed doors, privatised. A world beyond monitory democracy as we know it – for the sake of convenience, let us call it phantom democracy – becomes possible.

The thought that the revolution in favour of communicative abundance might have the unintended effect of combining government and corporate media in pseudo-democratic ways is sometimes interpreted as a regression to early twentieth-century 'fascism', but that is to miss the utter novelty of the trend. The mingling of government and corporate media, their corresponding efforts to control the ebbs and flows of communication, amid much talk of 'the people', is not a repeat of the 1920s and 1930s, when the world witnessed the crystallisation of the fascist and Bolshevik models of limited-spectrum, state-controlled broadcasting media geared to the top-down sacralisation of power. The advance of phantom democracy takes place under conditions of unlimited-spectrum communicative abundance. Business–government manipulations are more subtle, sophisticated and, hence, seemingly 'democratic' than the heavy-handed political methods of the early twentieth century. The days are over when millions of people, bubbling and huddling together as masses, were captivated by skilfully orchestrated newspaper, radio and film performances led by showbiz demagogues dressed alternatively in morning suits, military uniforms, muscular riding clothes and stripped to the waist helping sweating labourers gather harvests (Mussolini's specialty). Millions no longer celebrate in unity, marching in step, across a stage built from the glorification of heroes, cults of the fallen, national holidays, anniversaries, triumphs of the revolution, and electrifying performances of the Leader.[74] The pseudo-democratic trends within the age of communicative abundance require no political cults and no intense struggles for recognition and enfranchisement of the People. Today's leaders, Silvio Berlusconi among them, do indeed pay lip service to 'the people', but flesh-and-blood citizens are expected to stay quiet, locked down in circles of work, family life, consumption and other private forms of self-celebration.[75]

But what exactly does this drift towards phantom democracy entail? Consider the case of Abu Dhabi, a cosmopolitan metropolis that is both a potent symbol of the magnetic field of attraction between government and large corporate media and the scene of cutting-edge experiments in communicative abundance.[76] Capital city of the United Arab Emirates (UAE), the largest of its seven semi-autonomous city-states and currently ranked as the richest city in the world, Abu Dhabi, or at least its royal family rulers, have pulled out all the stops to transform its reputation from that of one of the world's largest oil producers into the new skyscraper Hollywood of the age of communicative abundance. Home to Etihad Airways, state-controlled mosques and nearly a million people, including a wealthy middle class and a large majority of non-unionised and often badly treated migrant workers, Abu Dhabi has become a haven for global media conglomerates. It aspires to be the king link in a global media production and supply chain that 'unites the world'. Huge oil and gas revenues and sovereign wealth funds (the world's largest) have been pumped into Abu Dhabi Media, the

---

[74] Emilio Gentile, *The Sacralization of Politics in Fascist Italy* (London, 1996).
[75] Paolo Mancini, *Between Commodification and Lifestyle Politics: Does Silvio Berlusconi Provide a New Model of Politics for the Twenty-first Century?* (Oxford, 2011).
[76] See the background details in Christopher M. Davidson, 'The United Arab Emirates: Economy First, Politics Second', in Joshua Teitelbaum (ed.), *Political Liberalization in the Persian Gulf* (New York and London, 2009), pp. 223–48.

state-owned group that owns and directs much of the domestic media, including the world's first fibre-to-home (FTTH) network, mobile phone services, newspapers, television and radio stations, including one that is devoted to readings from the Koran. Abu Dhabi Media has working partnerships with Fox International Channels, a unit of News International, and enjoys Arabic-language programming deals with such giants as National Geographic and Comedy Central. Abu Dhabi Media also hosts Imagenation, a body that underwrites the production of feature films. An office park free zone project called twofour54 (named after the city's geographical coordinates) houses foreign news agencies, including CNN, which produces a daily news show for its global channel. Twofour54 boasts state-of-the-art production facilities, as well as a venture capital arm to invest in promising Arabic-language media start-ups; and it hosts a world-class media training academy that offers short skills-based courses targeted at young and talented media workers.

For culture consumers, there is the government-controlled Abu Dhabi Exhibition Center; the Abu Dhabi Grand Prix; the Abu Dhabi Classical Music Society, which boasts a strong and visible following; and the Abu Dhabi Cultural Foundation, which works to preserve and publicise 'the art and culture of the city'. Of vital strategic importance to the ruling authorities is the government marketing and entertainment body called Flash Entertainment. 'Put simply, we make people happy' is its motto when advertising big-name acts like Beyoncé, Christina Aguilera, George Michael and Aerosmith. Vexed questions about whether, or to what extent, the citizens and non-citizens of the UAE are happy, what happiness means, or whether they or their journalist representatives might freely be able to remedy their unhappiness, remain unanswered. More than a few local expatriates simply do not care about answers.[77] The point is that Abu Dhabi is the new Hollywood without the old California. Governed by leading members of the ruling family, open public monitoring of power is abolished.

---

[77] A point captured in the lengthy report by Johann Hari, 'The Dark Side of Dubai', *The Independent*, 7 April 2009: 'When I ask the British expats how they feel to not be in a democracy, their reaction is always the same. First, they look bemused. Then they look affronted. "It's the Arab way!" an Essex boy shouts at me in response, as he tries to put a pair of comedy antlers on his head while pouring some beer into the mouth of his friend, who is lying on his back on the floor, gurning [pulling a grotesque face].'

Citizens are 'rentier' citizens, beneficiaries of state-guaranteed jobs, transfer payments and other forms of untaxed income and wealth. Free and fair elections are an ancient thing from yesteryear. Democracy makes no political sense say the local kingdom rulers privately. It causes unwanted social divisions, they add, hence the priority they give to blocking hundreds of websites considered to be publicly offensive and routinely cleansing local media infrastructures of pornography and other blasphemous commentaries on the God-given noble blood of the ruling royal family.

Mediacracy

The mediated oligarchy of Abu Dhabi is more than an oddity. There are similar examples from other parts of the world, among them authoritarian states with functioning markets, such as Iran, Singapore and Russia.[78] When handled carefully, with due respect for their separate histories and trajectories, these cases suggest that Abu Dhabi is not simply a one-off instance of how mediated governmental power can dispense with democracy in the age of communicative abundance. It stands as an emblem of political decadence, a warning sign of a 'softer' and more supple type of unchecked oligarchy that, for different reasons, has taken root within monitory democracies: a 'mediacracy', a mode of governing that draws strength from a tangle of arcane links with media companies, top-level journalists, lobbyists, consultants and public relations firms.

This new term 'mediacracy' is more than just a fun pun.[79] It delves critically into a hidden world not normally covered by journalists, or spoken about by politicians or seen naked with public eyes. The word spotlights the point that the age of organised political fabrication is

---

[78] See the accounts of the heavily mediated authoritarian politics of these states in Andrew Wilson, *Virtual Politics: Faking Democracy in the Post-Soviet World* (New Haven, 2005); Cherian George, *Singapore: The Air-conditioned Nation: Essays on the Politics of Comfort and Control, 1990–2000* (Singapore, 2000); Shai Raz, *Behind the Virtual Chador: Iran through Iranian Cyberspace* (Amsterdam, 2010).

[79] The neologism was coined by the American pundit and former Republican Party strategist Kevin Phillips, *Mediacracy: American Parties and Politics in the Communications Age* (New York, 1974). I am also relying upon Steven Schier, *By Invitation Only: The Rise of Exclusive Politics in the United States* (Pittsburgh, PA, 2000).

upon us, and that all popularly elected governments are today engaged in clever, cunning struggles to kidnap voters mentally through the manipulation of appearances, with the help of accredited journalists and other public relations curators. Mediacracy is a new form of political oligarchy, top-down power that is heavily mediated, especially through the press, radio and television, a new method of governing through invisible webs of back-channel contacts and closed information circuits. In Britain and the United States, as much as in the new democracies of central-eastern Europe, India and Japan, undercover media management skills and heavily manipulated, aggressively sensationalist and fast-changing publicity cycles in high-level politics have become routine. In each of these cases, governments from across the political spectrum daily strive to wrap themselves publicly in seamless symbolism, articulated to publics as bundles of messages that pretend to contain only logical truths, honest announcements, valid inferences and calculations designed to dampen controversy. The drift towards mediacracy is merely a political tendency; but there are signs that its grip is extending ever deeper into the nooks and crannies of everyday life. Utilising new media algorithms borrowed from the world of retail business and credit card companies, both governments and their opponents feed like parasites upon access to information about the personal lives of citizens.[80] Especially during election season, party campaigners purchase databanks from private companies (as happened during the 2012 US presidential campaign); harvest demographic data by planting software called cookies on voters' computers; and urge their supporters to provide access to their profiles on Facebook and other social networks. With the approach of election day, the data so acquired is used to track down potential voters using details such as shopping histories, levels of interest in sport or gambling, dating preferences and financial problems. Mobilising friends of friends, neighbours or long-lost work colleagues, party campaigners then plant messages, urging voters to pay attention to their candidate, and subtly prompting them to vote, for instance, by asking them whether they plan to drive or walk to the polls, what time of day they will vote and what they plan to do afterwards.

---

[80] David W. Nickerson, 'Is Voting Contagious? Evidence from Two Field Experiments', *American Political Science Review* 102 (2008): 49–57; Charles Duhigg, 'Campaigns Mine Personal Lives to Get Out Vote', *New York Times*, 13 October 2012.

It is true that the technologies and tactics of 'micro-persuasion' used by democratically elected governments always fall short of their Orwellian potential. The forces pushing media-saturated societies in the direction of mediacracy are just trends. Stuff happens, controversies simmer, voters behave unpredictably, dramatic scandals erupt, ministers and whole governments are forced to resign. There are plenty of counter-forces of the kind detailed in the first half of this book. The contested complexity and unfinished qualities of mediacracy are striking; but its inner connection with monitory democracy is equally impressive. Unlike the case of Abu Dhabi, where monitory democracy is absent, mediacracy, a new species of cunning power, resembles an auto-immune disease of flourishing monitory democracies. It is as if their dynamics unleash a new form of mediated oligarchy that mobilises the tools and methods of communicative abundance against communicative abundance. The whole process is not describable through the simplifying terms of 'spin' or 'propaganda', or the 'manipulation' of elected governments by 'big money' and 'big business'. The dynamics of mediacracy are more intricate: in power terms, it is the resultant of multidimensional forces operating both from within and outside government. For that reason alone, it demands new thinking and fresh frameworks of analysis.

Here we cross swords again with authorities for whom communicative abundance is, on balance, the driver and guardian of monitory democracy. 'As the Internet learns to wrap around obstacles, there will be more and more access to the Internet,' runs a version of the argument, this time defended by Evan Williams, wordsmith of the term 'blog', founder of several Internet companies, including Pyra Labs, and creator and CEO of Twitter. 'If you don't get it from your phone company, you'll get it from the sky, and it'll be harder and harder to block. It's inevitable to me.'[81] Media scholars often implicitly agree. Although their work understandably gives prominence to the structural biases of market-driven media – the privileging of advertising, packaged instant news, cheap sensationalist entertainment, celebrity views – far too much of their literature on democracy supposes that *organised media dissimulation by governments* does not exist, except in faraway 'autocracies', where media 'serve as an effective propaganda machine'

[81] *International Herald Tribune* (Paris), 17 December 2009.

and journalists 'see their primary responsibilities as "lapdogs," acting as loyal spokespersons for state authorities'.[82]

Trends on the ground look rather different. Using various instruments, blunt and sharp, governments are becoming skilled at hacking into the system of communicative abundance. Let us take the case of the British governments led for a decade (1997–2007) by Tony Blair. In his widely publicised farewell speech at Reuters, Blair used the metaphor of a 'feral beast' media to round on journalists for their aggression, for their degradation of public life.[83] He accused the media of hunting in packs, obliterating the vital distinction between 'opinion' and 'fact', sensationalising everything. Blair insisted that governments everywhere are now under siege from a media that is both 'overwhelming' and hungry for the kill. 'When I fought the 1997 election', said Blair, 'we took an issue a day. In 2005, we had to have one for the morning, another for the afternoon and by the evening the agenda had already moved on. You have to respond to stories also in real time.' He added: 'Frequently the problem is as much assembling the facts as giving them. Make a mistake and you quickly transfer from drama into crisis. In the 1960s the government would sometimes, on a serious issue, have a Cabinet lasting two days. It would be laughable to think you could do that now without the heavens falling in before lunch on the first day. Things harden within minutes. I mean, you can't let speculation stay out there for longer than an instant.' None of this is good for democracy, said Blair, and that is why, he concluded, governments have to don their armour: 'not to have a proper press operation nowadays is like asking a batsman to face bodyline bowling without pads or headgear'.[84]

Mr Blair undoubtedly had a point, for as we have seen earlier all major power players in the age of communicative abundance can expect rough media treatment. But one trouble with his diagnosis is its camouflage of the extent to which all democratically elected governments are

---

[82] Pippa Norris and Sina Odugbemi, 'Evaluating Media Performance', in Pippa Norris (ed.), *Public Sentinel: News Media and Governance Reform* (Washington, DC, 2010), p. 14. An alternative perspective is developed by W. Lance Bennett, Regina G. Lawrence and Steven Livingston, *When the Press Fails: Political Power and the News Media from Iraq to Katrina* (Chicago and London, 2008).

[83] 'Tony Blair's "Media" Speech: The Prime Minister's Reuters Speech on Public Life', *Political Quarterly* 78(4) (October/December 2007): 476–87.

[84] *Ibid.*, pp. 477–8.

today proactively involved in the business of protecting their flanks by relying on techniques of deception. Governments are not simply victims of communicative abundance, as Blair proposed. They are participants in media game playing, disinformation and deception, protagonists of the dark arts of colonising influential media, active contributors to 'the age of contrivance'.[85]

The point can be put differently: democratically elected governments are perpetrators of dissimulation. The word sounds harsh, but its force in contemporary politics should not be underestimated. It takes us back in time to Machiavelli, Guicciardini and other advisers to early modern European princes, to the age of state builders who were acutely aware of the constant need to camouflage their tracks, especially when dealing with suspicious opponents. For these advisers, dissimulation was the art of psychology, the knack of knowing others' minds as well as one's own, the ability to move freely between these two realms, ultimately the clever ability to be 'present' and 'absent' at the same time when engaging others, for instance, by convincing them in conversation that what is said is what is meant, even though the truth is the opposite.

Typical was Machiavelli's advice on 'the art of the state, the art of preserving and reinforcing the state *of* the prince'. He was sure that prudence and dissimulation were interchangeable arts. The secret of power is the ability to use power secretly. The cleverest rulers are those who know the arts of hiding their cleverness. True, rulers and their supporters should act as forceful lions, and they must do so openly, since the whole point of (threatened) violence is that it must be wielded openly, for maximum effect. But violence alone cannot guarantee the power of a state over its subjects and clients. Rulers must be foxes as well. The state must be a theatre of cunning (*astuzia*), with the prince as its charming principal player. 'He who best knows how to play the fox is best off', wrote Machiavelli, 'but this must be kept well hidden, and the prince must be a great simulator and dissimulator.' He added: 'people are so simple, and so concerned with present necessities, that whoever wishes to deceive will always find those who will let themselves be deceived'.[86]

---

[85] Daniel Boorstin, *The Image, Or, What Happened to the American Dream*; compare the account of the media efforts of the Clinton administration in Howard Kurtz, *Spin Cycle: Inside the Clinton Propaganda Machine* (New York, 1998).

[86] Niccolò Machiavelli, *Il Principe*, in *Le grandi opera politiche*, eds Gian Mario Anselmi and Carlo Varotti (Turin, 1992), vol. 1, pp. 102–3.

Although written five centuries ago, during times unsettled by deep religious conflict and savage political violence, Machiavelli's insight remains pertinent, a sober counterpoint to inflated hopes and expectations. The need for sobriety is suggested by the deepening involvement of democratic governments in the business of manipulation of appearances. Blair's autobiography contains telling examples of his governments' clever media management tactics. For instance, on the last night of the second millennium, when the British government's extravaganza spectacles were faring badly, Blair recalls with special horror his discovery that a pack of top journalists invited to attend the midnight Millennium Dome celebrations had been left stranded at a London underground station clogged with New Year's Eve revellers. Blair tells how he grabbed the lapels of the minister in charge, his old friend and flatmate Lord 'Charlie' Falconer, and said: 'Please, please, dear God, please tell me you didn't have the media coming here by tube from Stratford just like ordinary members of the public.' Lord Falconer replied: 'Well, we thought it would be more democratic that way.' Blair responded: 'Democratic? What fool thought that? They're the media, for Christ's sake. They write about the people, they don't want to be treated like them.' Falconer: 'Well, what did you want us to do, get them all a stretch limo?' Thundered Blair: 'Yes, Charlie, with the boy or girl of their choice and as much champagne as they can drink.'[87]

Champagne jollity was just one of a wide range of weapons in the arsenal of the Blair governments. They saw themselves as taking the arts of dissimulation to new heights. They contrived events, always for the purpose of winning headlines and positive press coverage. There were the conspiratorial whispered rehearsals about what (not) to say to waiting journalists; late-night and early-morning private telephone calls; breakfast powwows with funders, government friends and think-tank wonks; and invitations to celebrities to come on board the government cruise ship. Bad media coverage in the pipeline was turned off behind the scenes using persuasion, deals and threats. There was the tactic of feeding 'leaks' as exclusives ('you can have this, but only if you put it on page 1'). When embarrassing stories broke, they put out decoys. They tried to master the art of releasing bad news on busy

---

[87] Tony Blair, *A Journey* (London, 2010), p. 260. His governments' early obsession with image, style and novelty is described from the inside by Stephen Bayley, *Labour Camp: The Failure of Style over Substance* (London, 1998).

days (the media team called it 'throwing out the bodies'). The Blair governments denied. They told bald-faced lies (the biggest to do with the whereabouts of deadly weapons). In each case, several juicy recorded stories confirm that the Blair governments knew exactly what they were doing. Alastair Campbell, Blair's chief tactician, regularly practised the art of deception, and did so with cunning and finesse. His deputy (Lance Price) recalls that Campbell, testing the waters, deliberately told a *News of the World* journalist that Blair had stayed on the eighth floor of a hotel that in fact was only six storeys tall (the journalist never bothered to check); and that Campbell went to a Britney Spears concert and managed to be seen getting her autograph, then bet somebody £200 he could get the *Evening Standard* to splash a story that she supported Labour. He won the bet that very day.

These anecdotes are trivial, but they do reveal a bigger picture that naturally raises the question: how exactly do dissimulating governments manage to get their way in a world of communicative abundance? Conspiracy theories are unhelpful. Functionalist explanations are closer to the mark. Within any given representative democracy, so runs the explanation, politics officially takes place within a triangular relationship among citizens, elected representatives and journalists. The sets of players 'triangulate': they intersect and depend upon each other. Handbooks in the fields of journalism and public policy usually recommend that the consociation of professional media and elected politicians and governments should be no more than mutually necessary, courteous and subject to firm detachment. Yet the inconvenient truth is that each side functionally depends heavily upon the other.

Audiences of citizens require and expect journalists to get close to politicians and governing officials so that they can check their words against their deeds, to probe their bullshitting, to help judge their competence as leaders. Conversely, politicians need journalists to get their messages across to citizens. Politicians find it imperative to nurture 'the skills of media management' (a favourite phrase of Tony Blair's chief media spinner Alastair Campbell), minimally because journalists are vital translators and communicators of their words and deeds to audiences of citizens. Journalists attract and hold the attention of busy citizens, helping them to understand what politicians are saying and doing. They can, of course, do politicians a big favour by helping to convince citizens that their representatives are doing an excellent job, sometimes (as during political honeymoon periods) by singing lullabies to citizens who for a time politically sleepwalk their way through daily life. Politicians need to learn to work cooperatively with journalists for another reason: journalists have veto power. They can function as public early warning detectors, even as triggers of political scandals with the power to unseat individual representatives, or to bring whole governments crashing to the ground.

Elsewhere within the media–politics triangle, journalists, for reasons of reputation and career advancement, need direct access to politicians and governments. Scoops, breaking news and lead stories are a must in the curriculum vitae of every established or upwardly mobile journalist. But journalists need politicians and governing officials for other reasons, including the raw material that is constantly required to fill space and programming holes. The tactic of making constant 'announcements', preferably ones that reinforce the impression of getting on with the job of governing, without offending anybody who matters, becomes something of a governing imperative, a method (as an experienced ex-politician has pointed out[88]) that is usually much welcomed by news-hungry journalists because it fills voids, plugs gaps, provides copy that generates public attention.

For reasons well documented by experienced career journalists, the hunger for material can turn out to be a curse for their profession. It results in docile, petty, trivial journalism: who purportedly said what to whom, when and why. To understand the phenomenon requires ditching the image of a 'feral beast' media and talk of government 'spin'. They are equally misleading; neither captures the habitual docility of journalism, its 'bottom-up' connivance and entrapment within the trend towards government media management. *Flat Earth News*, by the respected English journalist Nick Davies, presents a compelling first-hand picture of the roots of this dynamic.[89] Davies is aware that in the age of communicative abundance there are widespread complaints about the way mainstream media, and professional journalists in particular, behave badly, objections that they have a reputation for hyping things and getting things wrong. He emphasises that there are many hard-working, honest and ethically open-minded professional journalists; yet he notes how many professional journalists are more trusted by publics who do not normally follow journalists. He admits another

---

[88] Lindsay Tanner, *Sideshow: Dumbing Down Democracy* (Camberwell, 2011).
[89] Nick Davies, *Flat Earth News* (London, 2008).

unpleasant truth: the percentage of journalists who have confidence in the ability of their citizens to make good decisions is markedly in decline (a polite way of saying that professional reporters and editors think their publics are stupid or gullible). The reasons for disrespect are unclear, although it might be interpreted as 'payback', an abreaction against the widespread bellyaching of citizens against the behaviour of professional journalists.

Such bellyaching can have positive effects for monitory democracy, for instance, by sharpening the wits of citizens and stoking a healthy scepticism about power, including the arbitrary power of professional journalists to define and interpret our world.[90] Bellyaching among citizens nevertheless has had damaging effects. Judging by their low popularity ratings, journalists are struggling to shore up their own reputations against politicians, real estate agents, car salesmen and bankers. Yet the problem is worse than this, Davies shows, for such complaints are in fact symptomatic of a deeper problem. For reasons to do with market pressures, job losses and top-down managerial control, he points out at length that journalists no longer work 'off diary'. Most have no time in which to venture out into the world and find their own stories or to check carefully the material they are handling. Their own experience teaches them that trying to be a first-rate journalist is virtually impossible (the American media critic and journalist Ben Bagdikian once remarked that trying to be a good journalist on the average American newspaper was as challenging as attempting to play Bach's St Matthew Passion on a Hawaiian stringed guitar, the ukulele). The consequence is that more than a few journalists grow complacent or downright lazy. They peddle prepackaged information supplied to them by governments, businesses and the public relations industry. Journalism produces 'churnalism'. Remember Rupert Murdoch's rosy description of contemporary trends, filtered through the lens of his News Corporation: 'More access to news; more visually entertaining news and advertising product; deeper and more penetrating coverage.'[91] Reality is different, or so Davies points out, in sympathy with his exploited profession. For rather like a human body lacking a

---

[90] Michael Schudson, *Why Democracies Need an Unlovable Press* (Cambridge and Malden, MA, 2008).
[91] Speech by Rupert Murdoch to the American Society of Newspaper Editors, 13 April 2005.

properly functioning immune system, professional journalism labouring under these difficult conditions produces a lot of distorted or pseudo-news, or pseudo-coverage about pseudo-events – lots of what he calls flat earth news. We could add: 'churnalism' also produces no earth news, might-have-been important stories, which journalists simply fail to take an interest in, or actually report. Such complicated subjects as the global surge in poverty, the arms trade and the shadow banking and credit sector go unreported, largely because their proper coverage requires professional patience and well-resourced, in-depth research.

Public opinion curators

There is, to repeat, no 'iron law' of mediacracy. The trends described here in functionalist terms must neither be misunderstood nor exaggerated. Whether and to what extent tight inner connections develop between top-level journalists and incumbent governments depends heavily upon situational dynamics, which (obviously) vary considerably from one setting to another. There are municipalities, regions and countries where the two sides are virtually one, as in the Japanese system of press clubs (*kisha kurabu*), an 800-strong countrywide network of associations of journalists who, as members of their exclusive clubs, enjoy privileged access not just to politicians but also to government ministries, political parties, businesses, the Tokyo Stock Exchange and even the imperial household.[92]

Dating from the 1890s, when the first press club was formed by journalists to gain access to parliament, these clubs have recently become the target of attempted reforms, understandably so since the *kisha* system is a powerful cartel-like arrangement, in effect a network of in-house public relations units nurtured by cosy links between

---

[92] See the works by Ofer Feldman, *Politics and the News Media in Japan* (Ann Arbor, MI, 1993); Ofer Feldman, *Talking Politics in Japan Today* (Brighton, 2005); Jochen Legewie *et al.*, *Japan's Media: Inside and Outside Powerbrokers* (Tokyo, 2010), esp. pp. 4–7; Ellis Krauss, *Broadcasting Politics in Japan: NHK and Television News* (Ithaca, NY, 2000), which examines how the peculiarities of Japan's democratic political system enabled the long-time ruling Liberal Democratic Party (LDP) to use many unofficial means of limiting journalistic freedoms.

government and business leaders and journalists, who are required to stay within the 'convoy' or 'pack'. But how does the cartel system work?

At the national level, *kisha* club membership is confined to accredited journalists from Japan's two news agencies, the business daily *Nikkei*, NHK and the five national commercial TV stations, and the country's four national and four regional newspapers. Each press club is housed within its hosting organisation, which provides members with working space, computer access and kitchen facilities, sometimes even beds for overnight stays. Journalists from other media, such as tabloid evening newspapers, specialty magazines, Internet sites, foreign press and freelancers, are excluded. Members of *kisha* clubs know they are highly privileged, and know they are expected by their hosts to behave themselves. Club members must avoid rash initiatives and ensure that what they publish contains no major discrepancies. The *kisha* customs of 'memo matching' (ironing out different interpretations of 'the facts') and 'black boarding' (listing stories that cannot be reported) are commonplace. Journalists who manage to pull off surprise scoops are cold-shouldered. Those who fail to report what the organisation wants officially to say are suspected of disloyalty. The palpable result is not necessarily 'accurate', 'speedy' and 'efficient' reporting of news, as its defenders like to claim. The clubs' system in fact tends to promote safe and sometimes spineless journalism whose debilitating effects were felt during the terrible earthquake and ecological disasters that beset Japan in the early months of 2011.[93]

Elsewhere, in other democratic settings, things are usually more fluid, more mixed, less settled. There are places and times when journalists and politicians and whole governments lock horns, like two stag deer fighting for territory during mating season. Fur flies and blood flows. No love is lost between them. There are even moments, though admittedly they seem rare, when politicians turn publicly against journalists by appealing to ethical principles, such as respect for personal privacy or professional standards. The possibility materialised during the Leveson Inquiry into Culture, Practices and Ethics of the Press in Britain,[94] and the whole theme is powerfully explored in Wolfgang Panzer's film

---

[93] John Keane, 'Silence and Catastrophe: New Reasons why Politics Matters in the Early Years of the Twenty-first Century', *Political Quarterly* 83(4) (October/ December 2012): 660–8.

[94] Evidence and other materials are located at: www.levesoninquiry.org.uk.

The Day of the Cat (*Der grosse Kater*; 2010), a political drama set in Switzerland, whose president, caught in a deep crisis within his own cabinet and suffering plummeting approval ratings, occupies the moral high ground by resigning from office after the local predatory paparazzi try to film his dying young son.

Principled stands of this kind are uncommon. When it comes to fundamental matters, open combat between journalists and politicians is far from typical. To the contrary, cursory acquaintance with the White House Press Corps in the United States or the so-called Westminster lobby in the United Kingdom suggests that patterns of close and quiet cooperation between governments and journalists are commonplace. Mediacracy is a democratic phenomenon, but the dalliance of journalists and high-level politics is always contingent. Synergy and symbiosis are not their 'natural' fate. Hard work and constant 'informal' priming from both sides is required. It takes various forms. Journalists and politicians drink and dine together. They bump into each other at gatherings, in shopping malls, airports and school grounds, and at formal functions. They frisk and frolic and keep in touch; sometimes they share beds. Their working habits coincide. They think about similar things and talk to the same people, often in tight circles of friends, sources, advisers, colleagues and former colleagues. When they do not already know each other they make approaches, for favours, usually under the cover of discretion and silence. Sweetheart deals are struck. Dissenting voices are excommunicated, pushed out through the revolving doors. Misfits and potential troublemakers are encouraged to understand that there are penalties, such as social and professional ostracism, for wandering too far from the cosy fold, off message.

The rest ought to be common knowledge, but rarely is. Public exposés of the back-channel contact and cooperation of journalists and politicians are not in the interests of either party; triangulation works best when citizens and independent journalism are marginalised. When that happens, the closed-circuit information flows produced by mediacracy flourish, especially because its beneficiaries understand that they have an interest in quietly preserving their own privileges. Hence, they do everything to hang on to their power, even if that means sacrificing personal integrity, in-depth investigative reporting and other standards of high-quality journalism. When the decadent dynamic gains traction, as happened in the global 'hacking scandal' that enveloped News

International in the United Kingdom,[95] journalists are at risk of undermining their own authority. Publics disbelieve them. Journalists are judged to be dissemblers, careless confabulators and liars. Politicians may suffer a similar fate. But when there is business as usual, none of this seems to matter to the respective partners. They enjoy their shadowy dalliance, egged on by a tangled variety of other causes and causers.

Public relations

Top-level journalists and politicians do 'inside baseball' (as Americans say) with an often bizarre assortment of players and teams. Consider the example of public relations organisations, which now play a vital role in shaping government policy agendas and outcomes.

The growing use of consultancy firms by governments and political parties reinforces the closed-system interactions among politicians, journalists and government officials. It adds grease to the revolving doors of the house of mediacracy, as can be seen from the example of Greenberg Quinlan Rosner, considered to be the leading political consultancy firm in the world.[96] With major clients on its list ranging from Coca-Cola and Tony Blair to Verizon and Nelson Mandela, the company brews its findings and recommendations by using a range of special techniques to gauge public perceptions of the 'brand, reputation, and image' of their clients, wherever they are on the planet. Greenberg Quinlan Rosner was among the pioneers of focus groups in election and issue campaign research. Its projects typically begin with what the company calls 'deep, open-ended listening' structured by professionally trained moderators of selected groups whose opinions are garnered through 'deep content analyses'. The company uses standard surveys and sampling techniques to measure representative samples of citizens' opinions gathered in 'raw' form from in-person interviews, Internet

---

[95] For summaries of the complex of events, see John Keane, 'Murdoch, Mediacracy and the Opportunity for a New Transparency' and 'Mediacracy: Rupert Murdoch's "Toxic Shadow State"', *The Conversation* (Melbourne), 16 July 2011 and 22 April 2012, available at: http://theconversation.edu.au/columns/john-keane-267; and Tom Watson and Martin Hickman, *Dial M for Murdoch: News Corporation and the Corruption of Britain* (London, 2012).

[96] See at: www.greenbergresearch.com, accessed 26 May 2011.

testing and telephone surveys based on live and automated interactive voice-recognition calling from voter lists.

The company boasts 'immediate turn-around' of results, including 'projective' data that explore people's likely reactions to possible policy moves. On other fronts, the company assists political parties and incumbent governments with campaign polling. It does so by using techniques such as benchmark and tracking surveys, segmentation modelling of the electorate and focus groups.[97] It uses 'dial meter testing' to measure the second-by-second, word-by-word reactions of target groups to advertising, news, speeches and debate performances. In the field of parties and governments, the company conducts staff training sessions, instructing them in such arts as messaging, media advertising, the recruitment of volunteers and focus group sessions. It samples staff attitudes, as well as recruiting 'key decision makers and power brokers', backed up by detailed survey data of their peers' attitudes. The company provides what it calls 'site-specific surveys' for clients in need of the opinions of citizens congregating at conferences, trade shows and festivals. It also specialises in 'model refreshing' techniques, ways of pinpointing, tracking and contacting undecided voters during campaigns, so enabling parties or candidates to 'redefine and optimize their targets throughout the election cycle'.

… and lobbying

There is another form of targeting of publics that reinforces the closed-system exchanges among politicians, journalists and public relations

---

[97] In this context, a focus group comprises a small circle of carefully selected members of the voting public whose views on matters of political interest are probed by a marketing person, who leads the discussion. Focus group members are recruited at random and paid a small honorarium for several hours' work. Sometimes observed by the client from behind a two-way mirror, the group participants are treated as if they represent the attitudes of uncommitted voters, typically those living in marginal seats. Much controversy surrounds the political utility and ethics of using focus group techniques. Their reliability is often questioned, for reasons summarised in pithy prose in the book drawn from the hugely successful British satire *The Thick of It*: 'The problem is focus groups are made up of members of the public and are therefore intrinsically unreliable/lopsided/racist/mental. And remember: People talk shit. They talk even more shit when they are asked to manufacture opinions on subjects they are totally ignorant of and/or couldn't give a gnat's anus about'; Armando Ianucci *et al.* (eds), *The Thick of It: The Missing DoSAC Files* (London, 2010), p. 61.

firms. Commonly called lobbying, it too plays a vital role in shaping government policy agendas and outcomes. The term lobbying covers many types of advocacy, from informal open consultations between legislators and tiny not-for-profit associations through to shadowy but well-organised links between regulators and giant global corporations. The particular aims of lobbyists can be 'good' or 'bad' (depending on the criteria of assessment), and at least some types of lobbying (defending citizens publicly against the injustice and corruption of the powerful, for instance) count as examples of monitory democracy in action.

However lobbying is viewed, and whatever forms it assumes, the practice itself has expanded dramatically in recent decades. Practically every democratically elected government nowadays resembles a beehive swarming with lobbyists busily engaged in linking outside interests with government policymakers. The trend has a cross-border dimension: for instance, around 15,000 trade associations, consultants, not-for-profit NGOs, international organisations, think tanks, regional organisations and other lobbyists currently operate in Brussels, where they seek to shape the legislation and regulations of the European Union. Many of these lobbyists operate simultaneously at the member state level, and that is why more than a few European observers note that if the regional lobbying trend continues then representative democracy in parliamentary form is fated to become a pale shadow of its former self.

Public defenders of the trend seem unworried. 'The practice of lobbying in order to influence political decisions is a legitimate and necessary part of the democratic process', notes a much-quoted parliamentary report. 'Individuals and organisations reasonably want to influence decisions that may affect them, those around them, and their environment. Government in turn needs access to the knowledge and views that lobbying can bring.'[98] Seen in this way, to pursue the simile of the beehive, lobbyists are vital pollinators and honey-makers, suppliers of information to government policymakers, who might otherwise be ignorant of the needs of stakeholders. Lobbyists line the nests and strengthen the cavity walls of democratic government with propolis. Lobbying is a source of campaign contributions. It provides jobs for

[98] House of Commons Public Administration Select Committee, 'Lobbying: Access and influence in Whitehall', HC 36-1, London, 5 January 2009, p. 9, available at: www.publications.parliament.uk/pa/cm200809/cmselect/cmpubadm/36/36i.pdf.

outgoing elected officials and their staffs; and it enriches the legislative process by providing it with outside expertise, with 'legislative sub-sidy'.[99] The honeycombed cells of representative government are popu-lated with propagators buzzing in multiple directions. While large corporations and even foreign governments are powerful lobbyists, individuals, groups and networks seeking to defend not-for-profit inter-ests and minority interests must also be included in the category. For all these reasons, say its defenders, lobbyists are a sweet source of legiti-macy to policymakers, who become better informed and potentially more understanding and responsive to the policy environments in which they operate.

The points are well taken. Lobbying is not simply a synonym for bribery, and there are indeed lobbyists who successfully strive to protect the weak, or who emphasise the importance of following such com-mandments as avoiding lies, misinformation and exaggerated promises, listening and working with policymakers and providing them with clear-headed proposals.[100] But there is more to the story than these claims. Especially when it draws on big money, lobbying (to extend the beehive simile) introduces poisonous toxins, strange diseases and dis-orders into the heartland nests of elected government. By strengthening the well-organised hand of the wealthy, it distorts election results and parliamentary democracy; and it feeds the drift towards mediacracy. To understand why this is so, we need to look carefully at the range of tasks performed by lobbyists.

What do they actually do? Partners within the busy hives of govern-mental power, lobbyists' brief is to set policy agendas, ultimately by persuading or dissuading legislators or regulators from taking a partic-ular course of action, especially when the issues are big and much is at stake in power terms. Moments of crisis are especially revealing of the political importance of lobbying. In the United States, where in Washington, DC alone an estimated 90,000 lobbyists ply their trade

---

[99] Richard L. Hall and Alan V. Deardorff, 'Lobbying as Legislative Subsidy', *American Political Science Review* 100 (2006): 69–84, where lobbying is pictured 'not as exchange (vote buying) or persuasion (informative signaling) but as a form of legislative subsidy – a matching grant of policy information, political intelligence, and legislative labor to the enterprises of strategically selected legislators'.

[100] Bruce C. Wolpe and Bertam J. Levine, *Lobbying Congress: How the System Works* (Washington, DC, 1996), pp. 13–19.

within a field dominated by large lobby firms such as Hill + Knowlton, the Duberstein Group and Patton Boggs, figures show that during the financial near-meltdown during the years 2007–2008, major banks minimally spent $56 million on intensive briefings and presentations to federal government representatives and officials; the data suggests that the failed mortgage lenders Fannie Mae and Freddie Mac had for some time been spending huge sums on lobbying to protect their flanks ($180 million over an eight-year period). During 2009, with talk of economic stimulus packages in the air and the American economy lurching towards stagnation, the Pharmaceutical Research and Manufacturers of America spent $6 million on lobbying; Monsanto paid out over $2 million; while military hardware and systems manufacturers spent over $17 million.[101] Striking (for the case of the United States) are the vigorous cross-border flows of funds. It is not just in Europe that lobbying knows no borders. More than 700 foreign companies, some of them (Daimler-Chrysler, GlaxoSmithKline and British Petroleum (BP) are the three largest) with extensive business operations in the country, employ Washington-based lobbyists to seek influence in federal legislation and agency regulations in fields ranging from pharmaceuticals, oil and gas production to environmental standards. The results are sometimes lucrative: between 1998 and 2004, for instance, just over a dozen foreign companies won military contracts worth more than $16.4 billion, over a third of that sum awarded without competition.[102]

Lobbyists typically spend their money, time and energy on a variety of tactics, which divide into two types: the 'inside' and the 'outside'. The more conventional 'inside' lobbying concentrates on striking close links with policymakers within and around official government circles.

---

[101] 'Corporate Lobbying and Democracy', *The Hindu* (Chennai), 29 September 2009. The following section draws upon Thomas Leif, 'Bestellte Wahrheiten – Lobby im Journalismus', *Neue Gesellschaft/Frankfurter Hefte* 7/8 (2010): 39–44; Robert G. Kaiser, *So Much Damn Money: The Triumph of Lobbying and the Corrosion of American Government* (New York, 2009); Lawrence Lessig, *Republic Lost: How Money Corrupts Congress – and a Plan to Stop It* (New York, 2012); Klemens Joos, *Lobbying in the New Europe: Successful Representation of Interests after the Treaty of Lisbon* (London, 2011).

[102] Julia DiLaura, 'Foreign Companies Pay to Influence US Policy', *The Center For Public Integrity*, 20 May 2005, available at: www.iwatchnews.org/2005/05/20/6561/foreign-companies-pay-influence-us-policy.

Influence is the name of the game, for instance, through the nurturing of regular personal contacts and friendly working relations with government officials for the purpose of promoting, or amending or blocking, legislation. Lobbyists organise campaign donations, good dinners, corporate boxes, complimentary holidays and media opportunities. Contrary to public perceptions, lobbying is not a synonym for bribery by sleazy parasites. Big money is very often involved, certainly; but it does not exchange hands in any straightforward sense of a 'cash economy'. Lobbying, rather, generates a media-intensive 'gift economy' of influential connections lubricated by cash flows. Within and around the institutions of government, the ultimate purpose of lobbying is to secure or strengthen the power of some interests against other, potentially opposing and conflicting interests, and to do so by building connections, regardless of the outcome of elections, or the composition of the existing government.

Lobbyists pressure governments from the outside as well, often using what are called grassroots tactics.[103] Lobbyists pay great attention to forming public opinion through perpetual media campaigning. That has the effect of abolishing the distinction between elections and in-between periods. In consequence, most democracies are now shaped by permanent media campaigning driven by lobbyists geared up to strike at their opponents. Negative imagery is among their specialties. The roadworthiness and reputation of individuals, groups, organisations and networks with whom they have disagreements are rigorously tested, sometimes through dirty tricks manoeuvres aimed at highlighting their alleged bias and corruption. Lobbyists do trade in positive imagery, through acts of orchestrated communication geared to anchoring positive themes and viewpoints in the minds of publics. Publicising the interests of membership organisations (professional and business associations, farmers' groups and trade unions, for instance) is a strategic priority. Lobbyists also work in defence of bodies without rank-and-file membership, such as large corporations, law firms and foreign governments.

Regardless of whether lobbyists target the 'inside' or the 'outside', communication with policymakers and publics matters. The whole point is to raise the salience level of an issue – regardless of the actual

---

[103] Ken Kollman, *Outside Lobbying: Public Opinion and Interest Group Strategies* (Princeton, 1998).

level of public support for it. Making contact with 'grassroots' supporters and sympathisers, or attempting to divine them into existence, is
certainly a specialty of lobbyists. Both narrowcasting (messages targeted at particular opinion leaders and selected prominent organisations and networked groups) and broadcasting to wider audiences of
potential sympathisers and active supporters are commonly used. The
aim in each case is to produce 'real' public messages that advance the
cause of particular interests by making them look not just salient, but
commanding 'real' support among a wider public. Epithets, slogans and
'flags' with the right pitch and positive connotations ('nuclear energy is
bridging technology' is a favourite of pro-nuclear lobbyists) are planted
within various media, including websites, blogs, online forums and
other social media platforms.

Encouragement is given to mass emails, petitions, phone calls, letters
written personally by prominent figures and meetings with outside
groups. Television and radio interviews with 'rent-a-mouth' experts
are booked. Newspaper op-ed pieces are arranged. Journalists and
government officials are supplied with 'commissioned research' in the
form of selective ('sexed-up') summaries of scientific reports, doctored
statistics, tailored opinion surveys, studies written by public relations
firms. Lobbyists offer journalists and officials 'exclusives' and 'scoops',
information that allegedly has a high need-to-know status. In return,
lobbyists expect to receive useful information from officials and journalists, according to the rule that within the protected and privileged
circuits of information near the pinnacles of power nobody should
bite the hand that feeds it.

The tight connections among elected representatives, government
officials and journalists, assisted by lobbyists and public relations
firms, adds to the mobile 'revolving door' system at the heart of the
trend towards mediacracy. The inside players try their hand at swap-
ping roles. Journalists become lobbyists. Lobbyists are sometimes fresh
from the fields of journalism; lobbyists morph into government officials,
or occasionally go into politics, or into think tanks, which (contrary to
their name) are not sites of cerebration, but temporary resting places for
former or wannabe politicians, journalists and consultants. Politicians,
meanwhile, move in all directions. Growing numbers of them have
backgrounds in journalism, or in public relations, or the lobbying
industry, or in all three. To cap things off, politicians also engage in
the strange practice that has been called 'reverse lobbying'. Instead of

receiving requests and fielding demands from the outside world, politicians, helped by government officials, work closely with selected lobbyists to pressure other representatives and government officials into accepting or dropping legislation. In the United States, to take one well-known early example, the Clinton administration harnessed the tactic of reverse lobbying by striking alliances with many dozens of health care reform groups. The aim was to use them to pressure Congress into accepting the proposed government package of health care reforms. The tactic ultimately failed; heavy resistance from other lobby groups prevailed. They spent in excess of $100 million, mainly defending existing health insurers, care providers, the pharmaceutical and tobacco industries and other groups, all of whom feared their interests would be badly compromised by the reforms.[104] Their success in killing the legislation drove home the pointed reminder that the closed-system consociations among politicians, journalists, public relations specialists and lobbyists are riddled with intrigue and uncertainty. For many of its players, contingency is part of its attraction: an exciting game where winner may lose everything, but can take all.

[104] See the well-documented study prepared by the Center for Public Integrity, *Well-Healed: Inside Lobbying for Health Care Reform* (Washington, DC, 1994).

4 | *Democracy's opponents*

The closed-system consociations among politicians, journalists, public relations specialists and lobbyists, the hidden power zones that this book has called mediacracy, sometimes assume scandalous proportions. The development of a bizarre 'toxic shadow state'[1] anchored in webs of exchanges among News International executives and journalists, police, snooping private detectives, celebrities, innocent citizens and politicians within the Westminster parliament is an example of what can happen in practice when the trend is left unchecked by toothy public scrutiny mechanisms. Other examples include the tendency of governing parties in the new democracies of central-eastern Europe to colonise state institutions with the help of 'friends' in the fields of journalism, business, lobbying and public relations; and the deep involvement of prominent journalists and political lobbyists in scandal-ridden efforts to broker deals between politicians and business leaders during the allocation of valuable parts of the second-generation (2G) mobile phone spectrum in India.[2] These episodes in the drift towards mediacracy bode ill for monitory democracy; for many observers, they reinforce its decadent 'feel'. Their sense of decay amid profusion is amplified by other trends. Communicative abundance (as we have seen) is deeply implicated in such phenomena as flat earth news and no earth news. It is bound up with cyberattacks; moves to restrict freedom of information through digital gatekeeping; and the proliferation of manipulative consumer marketing algorithms. Communicative abundance is linked to mushrooming media oligopolies and to claims (arguably exaggerated) that the growth of media-saturated societies damages everyday life, for instance, by amplifying the loneliness of citizens.[3]

---

[1] Watson and Hickman, *Dial M for Murdoch*.

[2] Paranjoy Guha Thakurta and Kalimekolan Sreenivas Reddy, *Paid News: How Corruption in the Indian Media is Undermining Democracy* (Delhi, 2011).

[3] Stephen Marche, 'Is Facebook Making Us Lonely?', *The Atlantic Magazine*, May 2012.

Looking back, looking forward

The various trends are, for the moment, not convergent, but their seriousness reminds us that monitory democracy has no historical guarantees – and that, in principle, this new historical form of handling power can suffer loss of traction and atrophy, perhaps even be snuffed out, as easily as a candle by puffs of wind.

Exactly this possibility is anticipated by critics of monitory democracy, for instance, ardent defenders of the primacy of electoral politics, for whom communicative abundance is, on balance, destructive of electoral integrity. Monitory democracy is adjudged a degenerate way of handling power, a defective political form that seduces voters, political parties and elected governments into pandering to piffle. Communicative abundance is adjudged bad for good government. It envelops governments in webs of public confusion, traps them into unnecessary media events and, hence, hinders political leaders from getting things done, efficiently and effectively. Some critics speak of a new 'tyranny of the time line', the pelting of governments with instant commentary and criticism by unlicensed 'information doers', who weaken the capacity of political authorities to 'function efficiently and with public confidence'.[4] This line of analysis lumps together monitory democracy, communicative abundance and media decadence. It pointedly stays silent about the organised media strategies of governments and this allows it to point backwards: suspicious of rough-and-tumble media coverage, it wants to disconnect parliamentary elections from the extra-parliamentary monitoring of power in order to grant parliamentary politics the respect that it once enjoyed. The perspective is tinged with nostalgia. In effect, it seeks to turn back the democratic clock, towards a supposed golden age of parliamentary representation and democratic politics that has since been victimised, especially by a dominant world view of politics dubbed the 'bad faith model of politics'.[5]

---

[4] Nik Gowing, *'Skyful of Lies' and Black Swans: The New Tyranny of Shifting Information Power in Crises* (Oxford, 2009).

[5] This and the following quotations are drawn from Matthew V. Flinders, 'The Demonisation of Politicians: Moral Panics, Folk Devils and MPs Expenses', *Contemporary Politics* 18 (March 2012): 1–17. A similar perspective is advanced by Thomas L. Friedman, *New York Times*, 15 November 2011: 'One wonders whether the Internet, blogging, Twitter, texting and microblogging ... have made

Defenders of electoral politics are understandably critical of the corrupting effects of cost- and profit-conscious red-blooded journalism, which, according to them, hunts in packs, its eyes on bad news, horned on by newsroom rules that include eye-catching titillation, reliance on official sources ('avoiding the electric fence'), 'if we can sell it, we'll tell it' stories, and, it is said, by the excessive concentration on personalities, rather than stories and analyses that are sensitive to time- and space-bound contexts. The critics of such journalism usually go further. They locate red-blooded journalism on the same continuum as other watch-dog mechanisms of monitory democracy, which is accused of cultivating a 'low-trust, high-blame' culture that disables the 'proper' democratic cycle of elections, parliament and political representation. Monitory democracy is interpreted as synonymous with the rise of unelected representatives, spirals of voter cynicism and political 'disenchantment', 'media malaise' and the general 'depoliticisation of functions away from elected politicians'.[6] Politicians and parliamentary politics suffer paralysis; they are drawn into a morass of conflicting accusations, insinuations and the general 'demonisation of politicians'. They become trapped (as Tony Blair complained) in 'the sheer force of a storm that is in an almost perpetual swirl of scandal and intrigue, breaking around their heads'.[7]

What are we to make of this bundle of complaints in support of old-fashioned parliamentary democracy against the decadent effects of communicative abundance and monitory democracy? The complainants are right to emphasise the continuing importance of free and fair elections and the vital role played by elected political representatives in the age of monitory democracy. They rightly note as well that 'politicians must be able to make decisions; governing capacity is therefore a requirement of any political system. Binding the hands of politicians by placing increased limits on their governing capacity, or subjecting their every decision to forensic analysis, and then attacking

---

participatory democracy and autocracy so participatory, and leaders so finely attuned to every nuance of public opinion, that they find it hard to make any big decision that requires sacrifice. They have too many voices in their heads other than their own.'

[6] The misinterpretation of monitory democracy as equivalent to the outsourcing or 'privatisation' of politics to administrative regulatory bodies draws upon Frank Vibert, *The Rise of the Unelected: Democracy and the New Separation of Powers* (Cambridge, 2007).

[7] Blair, *A Journey*, pp. 491–2.

them for failing to govern with conviction or take decisive action risks ensuring that democratic politics is always destined to disappoint.'[8] But this observation is prematurely judgemental. It serves merely to remind us (the point has been made earlier in this book) that the disappointment principle is intrinsic to democracy in representative form. The 'implicit distrust of elected politicians' is not unique to the age of communicative abundance and monitory democracy; it is a carry-over principle from the earlier age of representative democracy, a principle that still has practical bite. Whether or not opprobrium dogs elected politicians (as Tony Blair discovered to his cost) and hinders the future recruitment of competent representatives very much depends on the quality of their present-day actions, whether they tell lies or break promises, for instance, as well as on their learned ability to operate competently within the media-saturated environment of monitory democracy. This is the point: there is no necessary zero-sum relationship between electoral politics and the wider public monitoring of power. Positive synergies between the two processes are certainly possible, and desirable, but always and everywhere contingent upon circumstances.

Turn-back-the-clock efforts to defend the principle of parliamentary representation and elections as the supposed quintessence of democracy are one type of critical response to monitory democracy, communicative abundance and its decadent effects. A forward-looking version of the same insistence that good government is rendered unnecessarily difficult or impossible by the profusion of monitory mechanisms for openly scrutinising power has gained ground among believers in what in recent years has been called 'intelligent governance' or 'smart power'.

The stipulation that those who rule ought to radiate calm wisdom is an ancient principle to be found in many past civilisations. The actual phrase 'smart power' first surfaced in American foreign policy circles, in the aftermath of the bitterly contested 2003 invasion of Iraq, to mean a type of intelligent and cost-effective strategy that combines persuasion, diplomatic tools, capacity building and military force to achieve defined ends.[9] A stronger, extended version of the smart power thesis surfaced

---

[8] Flinders, 'The Demonisation of Politicians', p. 3; see also Matthew V. Flinders, *Defending Politics* (Oxford, 2012).
[9] Suzanne Nossel, 'Smart Power', *Foreign Policy* (March/April 2004), available at: www.foreignaffairs.com/articles/59716/suzanne-nossel/smart-power, accessed 30 June 2011; Ted Galen Carpenter, *Smart Power: Toward a Prudent Foreign Policy for America* (Washington, DC, 2008).

meanwhile in China, many of whose present rulers are perplexed by communicative abundance and have little or no political sympathy for democracy in monitory form. While they praise 'the people' as the foundation of their own form of self-government with putative 'Chinese' characteristics (a government 'White Paper' was even published on the subject[10]), they reject 'Western' democracy, which is treated as synonymous with the excessive public scrutiny and chastening of political power. Monitory democracy, a local version of which is manifested in the initiative called Charter 08, is accused of speaking in tongues.[11] It is said to produce far too many conflicting points of view that are in any case not of equal worth. 'Democracy allows citizens to go into the streets, hold assemblies and engage in actions that can fuel political instability', writes a leading Chinese intellectual. It makes simple matters 'overly complicated and frivolous', he continues, adding that democracy devours far too much time, reduces administrative efficiency and affords opportunities for 'certain sweet-talking politicians to mislead the people'.[12] The key problem with monitory democracy, say others, is that open public scrutiny of the Party and the state breeds short-term thinking, confusion, dissension and disorder. It breeds unnecessary resistance, potential chaos and 'counter-revolution'. Monitory democracy violates the principles of the Harmonious Society. It threatens the proven ability of the state to raise standards of material well being, and so hinders the overall improvement of people's lives. Social harmony is said to require 'a people's democracy [*minzhu* or *minch'uan*] under the leadership of the Communist Party of China'. That implies the need to recognise that the Chinese people are not quite ready for democracy because their '*suzhi*' (a Chinese term that includes everything from manners to educational level) still needs improvement. It further requires long-term thinking, forceful leadership and smart power unconstrained by the vices of party competition, useless

---

[10] State Council Information Office, *Building Political Democracy in China* (Beijing, 19 October 2005).

[11] The full text of Charter 08 was published on the 60th anniversary of the UN Declaration of Human Rights, 10 December 2008, and is available at: www.charter08.eu/2.html.

[12] Yu Keping, *Democracy is a Good Thing: Essays on Politics, Society, and Culture in Contemporary China* (Washington, DC, 2009), p. 3. On the attempted revival of past wisdom for the purposes of governing, see Daniel Bell Jr, *Ancient Chinese Philosophy, Modern Chinese Power* (Princeton, 2010).

parliaments and querulous civil society organisations that represent nobody save their own interests or the designs of 'foreign' powers. Another way is possible, and desirable: 'intelligent governance' that harnesses such techniques as the promotion of meritocratic leadership, extensive and frequent public opinion surveys and top-down efforts to combat 'corruption and mistrust between the population and the government'.[13]

The China labyrinth

Behind this reasoning lurk presumptions about freedom *from* communicative abundance and vigorous public scrutiny of power as necessary requirements of governing others well. The presumptions matter. The People's Republic of China is not just an emerging superpower and possible challenger and successor of the United States on the global stage. It is more than the second largest economy, the greatest carbon polluter, the centre of the world's telecommunications industry. China also represents a frontal challenge to most of our preconceived understandings of the communication revolution of our times (Figure 4.1). China – remember that 'China' is neither a political monolith nor an uncontested word – resembles a giant political laboratory in which many crafty techniques are being developed to structure and control the patterns of communicative abundance – to harness the Web-structured media usage of citizens to the dynamics of a resilient 'post-democratic' authoritarian regime.

The phrases 'resilient authoritarianism' and 'authoritarian state capitalism' roll easily from the tongues of many China analysts, but, in practice, state censorship and control in that country is not a straightforward matter. In contrast to the period of Maoist totalitarianism, the new Chinese authoritarianism does not demand total submission from its subjects. In such matters as what they wear, where they work and which social company they keep, most citizens are left alone by the authorities. Belief in communism is no longer compulsory; few people now believe its tenets and the ruling Party (as a popular joke has it)

---

[13] Eric X. Li, 'The Life of the Party: The Post-Democratic Future Begins in China', *Foreign Affairs* 92(1) (January/February 2013): 34–46; Nicholas Berggruen and Nathan Gardels, *Intelligent Governance for the 21st Century: A Middle Way Between West and East* (Cambridge, 2012).

Figure 4.1 China Carnival No. 1: Tiananmen (detail; 2007), by Chen Zhou and Huang Keyi.

comes dressed in Nike trainers and a polo shirt topped with a Marxist hat. The regime officially welcomes intellectuals, foreign-trained professionals and private entrepreneurs (once denounced and banned as 'capitalist roaders') into its upper ranks. The Party is everywhere. It prides itself on its active recruitment strategy and its organisations are rooted in all key business enterprises, including foreign companies. The methods of governing are clever. Ruling by means of generalised in-depth controls, or through widespread violence and fear, mostly belong to the past. While the authorities reject both independent public monitoring of its power and free and fair general elections, they actively solicit the support of their subjects. Protestors are crushed, but also bribed and consulted. Obsessive controls from above are matched by stated commitments to rooting out corruption and the rule of law. There is much talk of democracy. Top-down bossing and bullying are measured. The regime seems calculating, flexible, dynamic, constantly willing to change its ways in order to remain the dominant guiding power.

It is as if the ruling authorities are determined to prove wrong the claim (famously put by James Madison) that a 'popular Government, without popular information, or the means of acquiring it, is but a

Prologue to a Farce or a Tragedy; or, perhaps both'.[14] Whether they will succeed is an open question, but China is for the moment the world's largest exception to this rule. Its rulers claim their authority is rooted within a new and higher form of popular government, which promotes social harmony by delivering material goods and services, and by rooting out 'harmful behaviour' using information control methods that are complex and crafty. Their point is to deny farce and to stop tragedy in its tracks. True, China consistently performs badly on global media freedom rankings. Reporters Without Borders has singled out the Chinese Government for the sorry distinction of being the leading jailer of journalists and the 'world's largest netizen prison'.[15] But things are often not what they seem. While journalists are locked up that does not prevent thousands of them from testing and evading the rules and generally playing cat and mouse with the authorities. Growing commercial pressures on media, following the partial withdrawal of state subsidies, adds to the complexity.[16] Many media outlets, in order to avoid bankruptcy and to attract audiences from potential competitors, plump for lurid and often trashy reportage (called *dofu* or 'bean curd' stories) that sometimes turns edgy, especially when the spotlight turns to a local or even high-ranking official corrupted by favours, lust, money and power.

The topography of direct government controls mirrors the overall complexity of the regime. The Party-state in China feeds upon a labyrinthine system of unusually well-coordinated dos and don'ts, backed up by sanctions ranging from a cup of tea with the censors, sharp reprimands by editors, and sideways promotion, to physical attacks by unidentified thugs, disappearances and imprisonment, sometimes in 'black jails' operated by outsourced mafia gangs employed by the authorities. Tight-fisted controls are most evident in the field of television, where over a billion Chinese people access country-wide and local stations. The rapid, top-down 'televisualisation' of the population

---

[14] Letter from James Madison to W. T. Barry, 4 August 1822, in Saul K. Padover (ed.), *The Forging of American Federalism: Selected Writings of James Madison* (New York, 1953), p. 337.

[15] Reporters sans Frontières, 'Web 2.0 versus Control 2.0', 18 March 2010, available at: http://en.rsf.org/web-2-0-versus-control-2-0-18-03-2010,36697, accessed 16 January 2012.

[16] Daniela Stockmann, *Media Commercialization and Authoritarian Rule in China* (Cambridge and New York, 2012).

during the past three decades has been a striking feature of China's recent transformation. Foreign satellite channels such as CNN are not widely available and are subject to periodic shutdown. Audiences for provincial and metropolitan channels are large. Programmes are not necessarily dreary. Sometimes they arouse great audience interest and controversy, as happened during the years 2004–2006 with the singing contest series known as *Super Girl*. Produced by provincial government-owned Hunan Satellite Television (HSB), the blockbuster series attracted a huge audience (nearly 300 million in a concluding episode), as well as widespread media coverage, rather in the fashion of an American-style presidential campaign, with 'audience judges' and audience voting by telephone and text messages. The official multi-channel China Central Television (whose unfortunate English-language acronym is CCTV) denounced the series as 'vulgar and manipulative', no doubt in part because it operates the only country-wide network and is the sole purchaser of overseas programmes. Staffed by state appointees, the operations and programme content of CCTV are subject to strict dual controls operated by the Propaganda Department and the State Administration of Radio, Film, and Television. Those bodies regularly intervene in matters of programme content throughout the country, for instance, by ordering channels to limit the length and frequency of entertainment shows, to carry state-approved news items and, in tricky situations, to disregard audience ratings when deciding programme schedules.

Controls on the content of radio programming are similarly strict, certainly stricter than in the field of newspapers, where a combination of regional and linguistic differences and commercial pressures often results in significant variations and the evasion of controls. The avoidance game is played hard in the exceptions. The labyrinthine structures of Party-state control within the world of newspapers are difficult to grasp, even for insiders, in part because in recent years their variety and numbers have blossomed under the pressures of commercialisation. The likes and dislikes of readers have grown more important; as a consequence, plenty of in-depth investigative journalism happens.[17] Whereas in 1968 there were forty-two newspapers, today there are an estimated 2,200 daily and weekly newspapers, whose circulation is in excess of

[17] David Bandurski and Martin Hala, *Investigative Journalism in China* (Hong Kong, 2010).

400 million copies (the exact figures are unknown, in part because publishers avoid taxes by deliberately understating the figures and also because newspapers frequently use their own distribution networks). Most newspapers function as content engines for other media – what they report gets recycled again and again within other newspapers and other media.

Re-posted on China's major news portals, such as Sina.com and QQ. com, stories circulate rapidly, well beyond their local point of origin. That makes them the target of ongoing strict controls, especially when they enjoy a reputation for daring journalism (*Southern Weekly* in Guangzhou is an example, a bold counterpoint to much tamer organs such as the *People's Daily* and *Liberation Daily*). Although the authorities sometimes practise the art of 'control by media' (*yulun jiandu*) by giving their backing to the release of critical information, for instance, damning reports of poor quality food products, official regulation of sensitive news from the outside world is particularly tight in the print journalism sector. The Party-state authorities understand well that information comprises 'any difference which makes a difference in some later event' (Gregory Bateson's well-known definition of information[18]). That is why – the reports are typically unconfirmed, though the evidence from various sources is mounting – the authorities are actively engaged in the dirty business of coordinating campaigns of computer sabotage at a distance. The sabotage is carried out by government officials, private surveillance experts and Internet outlaws recruited and sponsored by the Party authorities, who target figures such as Tibet's exiled spiritual leader, the Dalai Lama, and the governments of the United States and its allies.[19] The information-as-difference effect is also a major reason why, from 2007, Xinhua News Agency operated as the gatekeeper of foreign news, the principal provider of edited reports, and often heavily censored and reinterpreted versions of material garnered by the BBC and other foreign news services. It is also why the Chinese authorities have for some time been manipulating information flows from the outside world by providing staff and buying into

---

[18] Gregory Bateson, *Steps to an Ecology of Mind: Collected Essays in Anthropology, Psychiatry, Evolution and Epistemology* (London, 1972), p. 381.

[19] See the reports, taken from a variety of global sources, listed on China Digital Times, at: http://chinadigitaltimes.net; and the report in the John L. Thornton China Center Monograph Series by Kenneth Lieberthal and Wang Jisi, *Addressing US–China Strategic Distrust*, 4 (Washington, DC, March 2012).

Chinese-language media (such as the *Sing Tao Daily* and television and radio stations) in the United States and other countries, leveraging advertising revenues and offering free, ready-to-go media content that provides more 'favourable' assessments of the Chinese government.[20]

On the domestic front, potentially bad, or embarrassing or confidential news is filtered through the so-called neican system of internal reference reports (*nèibù cānkǎo zīliào*). These are provided on a strictly limited basis to high-ranking government officials by trustworthy official Party journalists from organs such as the *People's Daily* and *Xinhua News Agency*. The reporting system is in effect an elaborate surveillance mechanism operated for Party members by Party members. Resembling the *tipao* palace gazettes and bulletins used by central and local Chinese governments during the Tang Dynasty (618–907 CE), the neican messages function as early warnings, as confidential investigative reports covering such matters as corruption, natural disasters and public unrest, which are seen as potentially threatening to the image and power of the Party-state authorities.[21]

Reports of monopoly gatekeeping or 'firewalling' of this particular type need to be handled with care. Firewalling is a misleading metaphor when used to understand the overall functioning of Chinese media. An interesting feature of censorship in China is that it has no handbook of guidelines, rules and regulations. Journalists are left to second-guess and third-guess what is officially required of them, and to make their own mistakes. The forces of self-censorship are naturally powerful, for every journalist knows that putting a foot wrong can prove to be costly. The diffuse sanctions are mirrored and reinforced by controls diffused throughout the political order.

China, to restate the point, is a novel type of resilient authoritarianism, a form of phantom democracy, a one-party state that resembles a body with one head, many mouths and multiple hands, many of them concealed in velvet gloves. Many things are permitted: finance, housing markets, sports and light entertainment inoffensive to the Party leadership's morals. Other subjects are less straightforward and more ticklish;

[20] Mei Duzhe, 'How China's Government is Attempting to Control Chinese Media in America', *China Brief* 1(10) (November 2001).

[21] Irving Fang, *A History of Mass Communication: Six Information Revolutions* (Boston and Oxford, 1997), p. 30; Cho Li-Fung, 'The Emergence, Influence and Limitations of Watchdog Journalism in Post-1992 China: A Case Study of *Southern Weekend*', PhD thesis, University of Hong Kong, 2007.

the time–space context can be an important determinant of controls, as, for instance, during the sixteenth Asian Games hosted by the city of Guangzhou (in mid-November 2010), when, under the official banner of 'Thrilling Games, Harmonious Asia', journalists were warned that 'accidents and mishaps' should not be reported on television and radio, or in the newspapers.[22] Blanket bans are meanwhile permanently in place when it comes to highly sensitive issues. Criticisms of the leading role of the Party and its leading figures are never permitted; the boot can be sunk into the backsides of comrades only when they have already been disgraced. The subject of American-style free and fair elections is taboo; so, too, is the open analysis of 'sensitive' regions such as Tibet and Xinjiang; or of 'sensitive' topics, such as religion, a subject which is said, usually behind closed doors, to stir up trouble and spread infections through the body politic. Especially sensitive is the matter of past crimes committed by the Party, above all the worst catastrophe in Chinese history, the Great Famine of 1958–1962, which recent evidence suggests claimed the lives of perhaps at least 45 million people, many of them forced by the Party to commit terrible atrocities against their own families, friends and neighbours.[23]

Grass-mud horse

Resistance to the Party-state is most pronounced within the world of online communications. China first hitched itself to the Web in 1994. The country now has an estimated 500 million users, twice as many as in the United States; two-thirds of them are under the age of thirty. The Chinese Academy of Sciences reports that in 2008/9 alone, 90 million Chinese citizens connected to the Internet for the first time. The overall size of Internet traffic is expected to double every 5.32 years.[24] What is not officially reported is that the sphere of text messages, blogs and other digital systems nurture the spirit of monitory democracy, with remarkable vigour. The range and depth of resistance to unaccountable power are often astonishing. The regime comes wrapped in propaganda, but counter-publics flourish. Helped by sophisticated proxies

---

[22] Interview with Guangzhou journalists, 12 December 2010.
[23] Frank Dikötter, *Mao's Great Famine: The History of China's Most Devastating Catastrophe, 1958–62* (London, 2010).
[24] Guo-qing Zhang *et al.*, 'Evolution of the Internet and its Cores', *New Journal of Physics* (Chinese Academy of Sciences, Beijing), 10 (2008): 1–11.

Figure 4.2 The Grass-mud Horse and the River Crab, linocut by Jessi Wong (2010). The river crab says: 'I will harmonise you'; the grass-mud horse replies: 'F*** your mother'.

and other methods of avoiding censorship, salacious tales of official malfeasance circulate fast, and in huge numbers, fuelled by online jokes, songs, satire, mockery and code words (an early sensational example was the 'grass-mud horse' mascot) that develop meme-like qualities and function as attacks on government talk of 'harmony' (Figure 4.2).[25]

[25] The mythical grass-mud horse, which began as an online video, soon featured in catchy songs, fake nature documentaries, cartoons and everyday speech. It was originally created as an in-joke way of poking fun at government censorship of so-called 'vulgar content'. Sounding nearly the same in Chinese as 'f*** your mother' (*cáo nǐ mā*), it featured in a smash-hit online video depicting the grass-mud horse defending its habitat (successfully) against a 'river crab' (*hé xiè*), a homonym for 'harmony', a favourite propaganda catchword of the regime. In verbal form, river crab can be used to mean that something has been censored or 'harmonised', that it has been 'river-crabbed'. A 'crab' also refers in Chinese to someone who is a 'bully'. Since the Communist Party, the supposed guarantor of harmony, is often described officially as 'the mother of the people', the phrase grass-mud horse or 'f*** your mother' thus implies the need to 'f*** the Party'. It

From the outset, online publics were countered by government censorship methods traceable to the Bolshevik strategy of Party-directed control from above. A system drawing on router technology was used to block undesirable chunks of information from the outside world; effectively, parts of the Internet became tools of the Party governing apparatus. The system became known as the 'Great Firewall of China', and its heavy-handed methods are today still used frequently to suppress points of view that diverge from the dominant positions formulated by the information office of the state council (the cabinet) and the propaganda departments of the ruling Party.

Examples of the mechanics of the firewalling process are not hard to find. When inside China, for instance, visitors' efforts to use Mozilla Firefox or Internet Explorer to key in English words such as 'media china people's republic' on Wikipedia are greeted with the luckless report: 'The connection to the server was reset while the page was loading . . . Try again'. Users need not bother, for server cuts are applied rigorously, from above, to all matters deemed sensitive by the authorities. Chinese citizens who regularly use Baidu, the country's most popular search engine, to access the Internet are greeted with a similar message: 'In accordance with local laws, regulations, and policies, some search results are not shown.' The instruction is part of a bigger, often highly confused, country-wide pattern, which includes the configuration of Internet gateway infrastructures; the surveillance of Wi-Fi users in cybercafes and hotels; efforts to 'phish' for social network usernames and passwords, to ban 'illegal or unhealthy' keywords from text messaging; and the foiled attempt to constrain public criticism of the Green Dam Youth Escort, a content-control software that the government had ordered to be installed on all new computers for the sake of rooting out 'harmful' content. The pattern includes slowing down Internet connections, so making it difficult or impossible to send or receive photos or videos; sudden Internet blackouts; and cuts to mobile phone services, as in July 2009 during violent demonstrations in the province of Xinjiang. It extends to the re-direction of users to sites containing malicious software and ongoing interference with online discussions of the 4 June 1989 events, whose twentieth anniversary was celebrated by the government with week-long shutdowns of Twitter, Hotmail and other

was not long before a grass-mud horse also came to mean a Web savvy opponent of regime censorship.

applications. The opposition of Google, in 2010, to allegedly organised attacks on its Google.cn information infrastructure, including the gmail service used by human-rights activists, forms part of the same picture. When all else fails, the authorities resort to pre-digital methods, including the intimidation of witnesses; after-hours swoops by plain-clothes police known as 'interceptors'; house arrests and 'fake releases' (the methods used to deal with the blogger Hu Jia and cyber-dissident Hada, who campaigns for the rights of Mongolian citizens); illegal detentions; beatings and disappearances.

Similar patterns exist elsewhere in the Asia and Pacific region; in recent years, the governments of Vietnam, Singapore, Thailand and other countries have set up computer research departments devoted to creating Internet surveillance software and have pioneered Web-based censorship of pornography, 'terrorism', hate speech, online gambling and spam (all are broadly lumped in with the 'propagation of damaging information', 'mail-bombing' and other public protest campaigns).[26] The strikingly decadent thing about current Chinese developments is the resort to much more sophisticated Internet control methods whose aim is the productive channelling of dissent into government control mechanisms. The novel feature of these methods is that information flows in China are not simply blocked, firewalled or censored. The authorities instead treat unfettered online citizen communication as an early warning device, even as a virtual steam valve for venting grievances in their favour.

There are certainly plenty of banana skins and semantic 'slippage' within the existing system of control. Things can quickly get out of hand, and when they do they trigger widespread discussion, as recent events show. One well-known example is the so-called XP Incident in 2007, an Internet firestorm that was sparked by the proposed plans of a Taiwanese company to construct a chemical plant in Xiamen. Although official local media and local government refrained from reporting the issue, thousands of local citizens began to send emails and text messages through cell phones to alert others to their environmental concerns about the proposed plant. Without organised leadership, a 'Let's go for a walk on a certain day at a certain time' campaign quickly developed. The chemical plant plans were soon dropped. The style of

---

[26] James Gomez *et al.* (eds), *Asian Cyberactivism: Freedom of Expression and Media Censorship* (Hong Kong, 2008).

protest – sudden 'strolls' led by middle-class office workers, company managers, young families and the elderly, carefully organised initiatives using new media that enable citizens to speak and act anonymously for fear of retribution by government officials in a country that stifles dissent – showed signs of spreading, for instance, in the 2008 anti-maglev trains protests in Shanghai and the country-wide resistance to local garbage incineration plants. What is interesting about these citizens' initiatives is their heavy reliance upon networked media, the projection of very specific and local goals by people who do not challenge the state's legitimacy as such, but simply call on the government to live up to its promises of 'harmony' and responsiveness to the people by listening to their concerns about the material and spiritual well being of citizens.[27]

Such challenges can be infectious, in part because in China, as in many other countries, what happens online at a computer terminal or on a mobile phone can have 'swarm' effects, simply because users find themselves ever more tightly interconnected with other communication media, such as television and radio. One consequence is the weakening of the old rule (studied by Yongshun Cai and others) that local Party authorities typically ignore or suppress small-scale protests.[28] In many local contexts, communicative abundance has helped to alter the balance of power by enabling protests involving a small number of people, or even just a lone individual, to attract wide attention, creating the same effect as a huge street crowd demonstration. In the past, Chinese people were often compared (unflatteringly) to a 'dish of sand', but digital media usage by otherwise physically isolated individuals now enables them to act as citizens who retain their sense of self, with their own sets of values, while periodically acting together for a particular purpose, with others whom they do not personally know, without 'common leaders, sometimes not even a common political goal'.[29]

The growing popularity among citizens of Twitter-like microblogs (called weibos) is a potent example of this trend. Foreign social networks such as Facebook and Twitter are blocked in China, but their local counterparts thrive. Although the Communist Party organ

---

[27] Jeffrey Wasserstrom, 'NIMBY comes to China', *The Nation*, 4 February 2008.

[28] Yongshun Cai, *Collective Resistance in China: Why Popular Protests Succeed or Fail* (Stanford, 2010).

[29] See the comments by Ai Weiwei in 'Spiegel-Gespräch: Ich sollte mich schämen', *Der Spiegel*, 21 November 2011.

People's Daily maintains a weibo, the field is dominated by two officially licensed companies (Sina and Tencent), which, in early 2012,
jointly claimed to have over 350 million subscribers. Like their foreign
counterparts, weibo users are restricted to 140 characters, but since
many Chinese characters are themselves words, much more can be said
within that limit. Local users commonly re-tweet their posts (a practice
nicknamed 'knitting', the word for which sounds like 'weibo') and
comment on others, so that messages are easily turned into conversations, illustrated with pictures and other files. If the authorities try to
block posts, then users typically have time and technology on their side;
instantly forwarded posts tend to keep ahead of the censors, whose
efforts at removing posts are countered by re-tweeted screenshots. The
aggregate effect is that conversations easily go viral, as happened (to
take a well-known example) when a citizen nicknamed 'Brother banner', a software engineer in Wuxi, was catapulted into online celebrity
status overnight after holding a banner that read 'Not Serving the
People' outside the gate of a local labour relations office. In desperation,
he had been protesting its failure to intervene in his pay dispute with his
former employer. The banner turned the Party's slogan 'Serving the
People' on its head, and proved to be most effective in embarrassing the
department officials after a one-person protest gained national prominence through the Internet and, eventually, coverage in the official
media.[30]

The digital storms often happen suddenly, especially when they
assume the form of demands that government officials should do a
better job of listening, and make good on their own stated goals of
improving the material well being and quality of life of the Chinese
population. Take another example: the great public controversy suddenly aroused by a morning report (dated 17 June 2009) broadcast by
the radio station Voice of China. In the village of Xi Gang in Zhengzhou
province, the programme reported, a serious conflict had been triggered
by the decision of the local municipal authorities to scrap a plan to build
housing for the poor – in favour of a project that involved using local
land as the site of an up-market complex of a dozen villas and several
luxury apartments. When a journalist questioned the head of the City
Planning Office, Dai Jun, about the reasons for the decision, he replied

---

[30] Lu Yiyi, 'Chinese Protest in the Age of the Internet', *Wall Street Journal*, 14
December 2010.

by asking the journalist: 'Who are you speaking for? The Party, or the people?' His ill-chosen words triggered an avalanche of Internet protests. Many tens of thousands of netizens hurled complaints that the official had violated a foundational principle of the Communist Party of China, that the interests of the people and the Party are one and indivisible. Many netizens accused Dai Jun of pushing the Party and its citizens into a contradictory relationship, and many went on to say plainly that the official and his City Planning Office were acting loyally on behalf of the Party and its interests, at the expense of citizens. Dai Jun did not last long; his superiors in the City Planning Office kicked him downstairs.

Balancing on a slippery egg

In the face of such protests, the Chinese authorities have gradually changed tactics. Their counter-strategies confirm the paradoxical rule that the governments of authoritarian regimes are much more sensitive to popular resistance than those of democratic regimes. The Internet is not just firewalled or treated as a tool of repression and control. Unfettered online communication by citizens is treated as an instrument for improving the ability to govern. Some sympathetic observers liken the Chinese authorities to skilled doctors equipped with surveillance equipment and various tools for the 'continuous tuning' (*tiao*) of the body politic;[31] the critics of these methods of 'harnessing' media for the purposes of top-down control liken them to 'giving toys to dogs to stop them barking'.[32]

The divided opinions suggest that the official repressive tolerance of communication is a dangerous tiger to ride, but here is how things happen. An important feature of the whole system is that the means of top-down surveillance and political control are distributed in labyrinthine ways, high and low, through government departments stretching from the propaganda ministry and state council information office down through provincial, county and city government administrations

---

[31] George Yeo and Eric X. Li, 'China's Parallel Universe', *New Perspectives Quarterly* 29(2) (Spring 2012), available at: www.digitalnpq.org/articles/global/572/01-20-2012/george_yeo_and_eric_x._li, accessed 10 February 2012, and my reply, 'The China Labyrinth', *New York Times*, 14 February 2012.

[32] Interview with a prominent Chinese author and scholar of communications, Shanghai, 25 July 2009.

and deep into the offices of managers and employees of Internet companies, both domestic and foreign. The Party-state is constantly on the lookout for new and improved ways of governing its population, for instance, by means of an elaborate system of government websites designed to interact with their subjects. Experiments (as in Guangdong province) with virtual petition offices, online webcast forums where citizens can raise complaints and watch and hear officials handle them, are an innovative case in point. All central government and provincial-level government departments have their own websites, and so do most prefectures and county-level governments. More than a few of these official websites are left idle by government officials, who still think that they are a waste of money and time. Still other officials are reluctant to let ordinary people express their views on government websites and so have shut down their bulletin boards. And so, from time to time, there are top-level Party instructions issued in support of using the Internet to track swings of opinion. 'There has never been such a convenient channel as the Internet for a government to view and collect public opinion', it is noted, sometimes in a tone of admonition. 'The Internet has made it possible for anyone to express their views on anything. This should have made it much easier for governments to interact with residents and thus improve their governance.'[33]

The operative words here are 'interact with residents' and their 'governance', and their use is revealing of the will of government to use the Internet to control the Internet. The establishment of a Chinese intranet is a basic component of the whole strategy, which is driven by many causes and causers. Of critical importance has been the Internet adoption of Chinese characters and domain names ending in '.cn'. This means that whenever users rely on ideogram-based domain names ending '.com.cn' they are redirected to the Chinese version of their chosen website; in consequence, they disconnect themselves from the World Wide Web and confine themselves to the strongly regimented intranet. Confinement within '.cn' means subjection to other disciplinary tactics, such as saturation online postings from the authorities by means of highly regulated state media digital platforms, including China Central Television and Xinhuanet. A well-organised Internet police force is also considered strategically vital. According to some

---

[33] The quotations are drawn from the newspaper editorial 'Public Opinion via Internet', *China Daily* (Hong Kong), 16 December 2010, p. 8.

sources, it is currently 40,000 strong and operates through the ministry of public security, which operates on the front lines, at all key points within the labyrinth. Their guidelines are not made public, but operations are typically conducted 24 hours a day. The tactics include the use of sophisticated 'data-mining' software that scrutinises the largest blog platforms and tracks down keywords on search engines such as Baidu, and the follow-up notification of Web hosts to block, erase or amend postings considered to be subversive. A combination of URL filtering with the blanking of keywords labelled as 'harmful' is also a common strategy in blocking tens of thousands of websites.

Government departments watch online reactions to their policies. Signs of brewing unrest or angry reactions to their own officials are noted. Sometimes reports are passed to the local information offices and propaganda department, which then decide whether or not local action is required. State media can be instructed to take a certain line on any particular issue; and news websites can be told whether or how they should cover the matter, including keeping the coverage short, so as to bury it down deep memory holes. Calls for 'discipline' and 'self-regulation' are commonplace. Official talk is sometimes more sinister because it is more far-reaching, as when demands and moves are made for the real-name identification of micro-bloggers. So-called 'rumour refutation' departments staffed by censors also pitch in. They scan posts for forbidden topics and issue knock-down rebuttals, as happened during the student-led disturbances that shook Inner Mongolia after a protesting herder was knocked down and killed by a Chinese coal truck driver.[34] A pivotal role is played by licensed Internet companies. Subjected to periodic reminders that safety valves can turn into explosive devices, they regularly use filtering techniques to delete, amend or infect 'sensitive' content. Proposals meanwhile circulate within official circles to establish 'situation centres', early warning systems to handle problems before they get out of hand.

Among the cleverest tactics used by the authorities is the recruitment of netizens, whose numbers are growing fast (by the end of 2008, there were already an estimated 162 million). The cutting-edge tactic is to

[34] The government responded with this widely distributed online message: 'Dear students and friends, it was just a road accident. Some people with an ulterior motive have interpreted it as an ethnic conflict, or linked it to oil and gas. The government is taking the case very seriously ... We hope that students will not believe the rumours ...'

draw them into a cat's cradle of suspicion, surveillance, denunciation, praise and control, for instance, by encouraging citizens to report anti-government conversations to the authorities, or by recruiting hirelings known as '50-cent bloggers' (so named after the price that was initially paid by the authorities to entice them to sign up to bulletin boards and chat rooms in defence of the government). The heavily-used Twitter-like micro-blogging site Sina Weibo operates an experimental points-based system, dubbed 'Weibo credit', which rewards points to users (maximum 80; minimum 60) who shame other users by reporting them for circulating 'untrue information', or for engaging in 'personal attacks, plagiarised content, the assuming of others' identities, harassment of others, etc.'.[35] Appeals by the Internet surveillance authorities for netizens to sign on as 'Internet debaters' are meanwhile becoming routine. So, too, is the use of e-consultation exercises, such as Q&A sessions, 'chats' between the authorities and citizens, e-petitions and discussion forums, such as 'Strengthening the Nation Forum' operated by *People's Net*. These methods – 'authoritarian deliberation' is the phrase used by some scholars – come packaged in official references to the need to avoid 'incorrect depictions of the Chinese people', to encourage 'transparency', to 'balance' online opinions for the sake of 'guiding public opinion' (*yulung daoxiang*) and creating the 'harmonious society'. In using these phrases, the ruling authorities know well that they are engaged in a tricky political game tempered by rules that are not altogether clear, in consequence of which outcomes are often indeterminate. They find themselves engaged in a constant tug-of-war between their will to control, negotiated change and unresolved confusion. They learn that power is harder to use, and easier to lose. Hence, their familiarity with a new Chinese proverb: 'ruling used to be like hammering a nail into wood, now it is much more like balancing on a slippery egg'. Armed with such wisdom, the authorities believe that they will prevail over the spirit of monitory democracy. 'The Internet is a platform where anyone can express their opinion', commented a deputy propaganda chief of Yunnan province. 'Whenever opinion leans totally

---

[35] See Josh Chin, 'Censorship 3.0? Sina Weibo's New 'User Credit' Points System', *Wall Street Journal*, 29 May 2012, available at: http://blogs.wsj.com/chinarealtime/2012/05/29/censorship-3-0-sina-weibos-new-user-credit-points-system, accessed 29 October 2012.

to one side we will indeed put some different voices out there to allow the public to make their own judgement independently.'[36] Whether the doctrine of harmonisation will prevail in practice, so proving James Madison wrong, is among the global political questions of our time, but it is for the future to tell.

[36] Cited in Kathrin Hille, 'How China Polices the internet', *Financial Times*, 18 July 2009.

5 | *Why freedom of public communication?*

Plenty of voices, not just in China, but in many places elsewhere on our planet, think they already know the (positive) answer to this question. They are certain that the 'liberal', or 'Western' or 'bourgeois' principle of freedom of expression is passing out of fashion, or a sham, in that positive talk of communicative abundance is a mask for ugly realities, or a mere diversion from more important political aims and tasks. The critics, whether or not they realise, are supported in their convictions by the various decadent trends now working against communicative abundance. The effects of media decadence speak louder than words. In the early years of the twenty-first century, this decadence sounds the alarm that freedom of communication and its twin, monitory democracy, are neither inevitable nor a necessary and desirable feature of complex political orders. The dialectics of communicative abundance and media decadence prompt discomposing questions: when measured in terms of its positive contributions to monitory democracy and, by contrast, the damaging and disruptive effects of media decadence, does the age of communicative abundance, on balance, proffer more risk than promise for the lives of citizens and their representatives? Since the extent to which people are duped and disempowered by media systems always depends upon many forces, including the chosen actions of citizens and their representatives, are there developing parallels with the early twentieth century, when print journalism and radio and film broadcasting hastened the widespread collapse of parliamentary democracy? Is the media decadence of our age the harbinger of profoundly authoritarian trends that might ultimately result in the birth of phantom democracy, that is, polities in which businesses are publicly unaccountable and governments claim to represent majorities that are artefacts of media, money, manipulation and force of arms? If that happened, what, if anything, would be lost? What exactly is so good about the power of citizens and their representatives to express themselves openly within a variety of institutional settings? In plain words: why should anybody care about media decadence?

Remembrance of things past?

The questions should remind us that there have been circumstances in the past when the normative principle of unrestricted communication was conspicuous by its absence. We know, for instance, that with the military and political defeat of ancient democracies, the classical Greek principle of *parrhēsia* (it roughly translates as bold, frank speech) died an untimely death as a working principle of political life;[1] and that later, in the societies of medieval Europe, the principle of 'freedom of communication' was unknown. There was much talk of the need for silence and respect, or for confession and speaking in awe and reverence of God, but there were no public champions of 'freedom of expression' and its concomitant faith in the capacity of flesh-and-blood people to speak intelligently for themselves as public equals. When strange-sounding terms, such as liberty of the press and unlicensed expression, eventually appeared on the scene they were not uncontroversial. Born of bloody political controversies, they met with fierce resistance that left permanent marks on their definition and justification. As we shall see shortly, for reasons of philosophical weakness, loss of context and/or political rejection, many of these originally European justifications, such as the insistence that freedom of communication can nurture the 'reason' of individuals in human affairs, are now highly questionable or plain antiquated, even if they continue to be used as political tropes by journalists, politicians, lawyers and others. What subsequently came to be called freedom of communication is an even more recent invention (as John Durham Peters has shown[2]). The whole principle that hearts and minds can be opened so that uninhibited expression results in transparent mutual understanding is an invention of the late nineteenth century. It is only from that time that the grand belief in communication as 'communion, a sharing of inner experience'[3] gives rise to terms such

---

[1] Michel Foucault, *Fearless Speech* (Los Angeles, 2001).

[2] John Durham Peters, *Speaking into the Air: A History of the Idea of Communication* (Chicago and London, 1999).

[3] Leo Lowenthal, 'Communication and Humanitas', in Floyd W. Matson and Ashley Montagu (eds), *The Human Dialogue: Perspectives on Communication* (New York, 1967), p. 336.

as 'mass media' and notions of communication as the mediated exchange of information, as well as their opposite: distorted communication, propaganda and communication breakdown.

The terms media decadence and communicative abundance undoubtedly belong to this older tradition of regarding freedom of communication as an important principle of political order. The prominence of the principle has been given a big boost by the unfinished media revolution of our time, sometimes to the point where it is regarded as an unqualified good. Even when wild tempers are unleashed among disputants convinced that their opponents are plain wrong, and therefore should be muzzled, freedom of communication and what is often called 'press freedom' have become twin public goods. The phrases are used interchangeably; tremendous lip service is paid to their desirability. 'Freedom of expression, understood in a broad sense, is required for civic, social and political life, and indispensable for democracy', is the way things are typically put, with more than a touch of tautology. 'Without it, communication with and among citizens will be limited in ways that may leave some or many unable to understand, to assess or to participate in their own public and political culture.'[4] Within most analyses of the media and democracy, the principle of 'media freedom' and 'free public communication' is typically taken for granted. It is sometimes even used as a convenient cliché, as can be seen, for instance, within the work of analysts of the 'quality of democracy', for whom the criterion of 'freedom of communication' is a measurable good using supposedly uncontroversial criteria.[5]

---

[4] Onora O'Neill, 'News of this World', *Financial Times Weekend*, 19–20 November 2011, p. 1.

[5] See the criterion of 'freedom of communication' in the European Democracy Barometer survey, in which, by virtue of its automatic inclusion as a defining variable, the criterion is not only taken for granted, but is also defined through rather blunt instruments. The Democracy Barometer claims to be a new index of democracy. Its stated aim is 'to overcome the conceptual and methodological shortcomings of existing measures, in order to measure the subtle differences in the quality of established democracies' (see at: www.democracybarometer.org). Admitting that 'democracy' is 'a complex phenomenon and a minimalist measurement cannot do justice to it', the Democracy Barometer understands it as a political system that establishes 'a good balance between the normative, interdependent values of freedom and equality', and thus seeks to place controls on the exercise of governmental power. Among the key 'democratic functions' to be measured is what it calls the 'public sphere'. For its purposes, this vital function is

A more measured approach to the subject of free communication would see that the principle, which originated in early modern Europe, has a variety of conflicting justifications, and that, consistent with its propensity to upset prevailing certainties, the principle of freedom of communication has stirred up bitter controversies about its own veracity and geographic scope. The vital point is that the norm has a history, heavily contested from many directions since the seventeenth century. What is striking is the way political imaginations in the age of monitory democracy are still heavily under the influence of a small handful of justifications of unrestricted public communication that have been inherited from the age of the printing press. We are going to see that these ways of thinking about freedom of communication are less credible than they once seemed; that their metaphors are outdated, lines of reasoning flawed or that they feel 'dead' in the much-changed circumstances of the twenty-first century.[6] Yet they manage to live on.

Let us start with the case of John Milton and other *theological* champions of an unfettered printing press and freedom of speech. They regarded public censorship as repugnant because it stifled the exercise of individuals' freedom to think, to exercise discretion and to

disaggregated into two components, each of which is supposedly measured by several 'subcomponents' and 'indicators'. Striking in this connection is the bluntness of its indicators – at least when compared with the type of detailed and nuanced analysis called for in this book. The Democracy Barometer approach notes that democracy involves 'taking part with others in expressing opinions and seeking to persuade and mobilize support' and 'communication about politics and moral norms' within 'a vital civil society and a vivid public sphere'. Note how its 'subcomponents' and 'indicators' scramble together different practices. Freedom of association (component 1) comprises written constitutional guarantees of freedom of association and a high density of membership of trade unions, professional associations, and 'humanitarian' and 'environmental/animal rights' organisations. The modes and means of communication used by these organisations are glossed over. The other criterion (component 2) of open communication in a democracy is 'freedom of opinion'. This is said to comprise constitutional guarantees of freedom of speech and of the press. Since in 'modern, representative democracies, public communication primarily takes place via mass media', the Democracy Barometer relies on a strange mix of criteria, including the importation of newspapers measured against GDP, the 'number of daily newspapers per 1 million inhabitants' and the 'political neutrality of the press system', measured in terms of its 'ideological balance' and market share of 'neutral/independent newspapers'. As this book has tried to show at length, these are blunt-pencil and outdated measures of a much more complex dynamic that must draw upon fresh concepts, a different historical sensibility and quite different methods.

[6] See my previous discussion in *The Media and Democracy*, pp. 10–21.

choose a Christian life. They thought that the keys to free communication are given from heaven to earthly individuals, so that they might cultivate their reason, their capacity to read and to choose, according to the precepts of conscience, between evil and good. Others plumped for freedom of public communication on the ground that each individual has a *natural right* or *human right* to express and publish their opinions freely against governments, for the sake of good government under the rule of law. Still others, among them Jeremy Bentham, defended a *utilitarian* case for freedom of expression as a means of presenting despotic government by making and applying parliamentary laws supportive of the greatest happiness of the greatest number of citizens. Some critics of this utilitarian defence of freedom of communication complained that since utility is itself a matter of opinion, the veracity of an opinion is more fundamental. Believers in the principle of attaining Truth through unrestricted public discussion among citizens – John Stuart Mill was its most famous champion – insisted that only a free press can guarantee that citizens are supplied with 'the facts' and arguments about 'the facts', so enabling them to question and correct false opinions and ensure the victory of Truth over falsehood.

Strong traces of these early modern, originally European, arguments are today still detectable in the way many people think and talk about 'the media'. Think of the way some politicians speak in theological terms about constitutional protections of God-given 'freedom of expression'; or the way professional journalists and editors describe their job in terms of 'speaking truth to power'. In spite of their obvious conceptual incommensurability, the combined effect of these different arguments has been to endow the principle of 'freedom of communication' with kaleidoscopic power. The fact that it means quite different things to many different people, in a wide variety of times and settings, has been a secret of its great global influence. Considered separately, and with hindsight, each argument for freedom of communication nevertheless looks unconvincing.

Philosophically speaking, each perspective on freedom of communication indulged a superiority complex by supposing itself to be incontrovertible and applicable universally. Bearing more than a passing resemblance to a tyrant bent on ruling over unlimited territory, each thought of itself as 'right', as invulnerable to contradiction, questioning or rejection by others through counter-argument. Seen in retrospect, each approach suffered other unresolved difficulties lurking inside its

core argument. It soon became clear, for instance, that Christian theological justifications of 'liberty of the press' could not square with the
views on the same subject expressed by Buddhists, Muslims, Hindus, as
well as non-religious others. Talk of 'natural rights' or 'human rights'
begged questions about their allegedly 'natural' or 'human' status, why
they were supposedly immune from variation of definition in different
spatial and temporal settings, how and why 'unnatural' or 'inhuman'
violations of these rights happen, and whether the 'non-human' world is
entitled to having a say in human affairs.[7] The insistence that freedom of
communication was essentially about minimising pain and maximising
happiness side-stepped prickly questions about the contested meanings
of pain and pleasure, and about the bias towards a definition of happiness rooted in private property and the accumulation of wealth
(strongly evident in Bentham's version of utilitarianism). The defence
of free communication as the guarantor of Truth drew on the dis-
credited metaphysical idea of an objective, out-there-at-a-distance 'reality' that could be summarised as 'factual truth',[8] and so on.

The strangely old-fashioned feel of these justifications stems as well
from their anti-democratic prejudices. Born of a bygone era, when
democracy in representative form had barely taken root, each was
convinced that the noisy, mindless hot-headed pack known as 'the
people' was threatening of civilised order. David Hume's much-cited
defence of 'liberty of the press', which he saw as a vital precondition of
restricted or constitutional monarchy, well illustrates this deep ambivalence about democracy. Insisting that the free press ideal is an historical invention (he was right about that), Hume thought of freedom of
communication in proto-republican terms. 'The spirit of the people
must frequently be roused in order to curb the ambition of the court',
he wrote, 'and the dread of rousing this spirit must be employed to
prevent that ambition.' Hume's proto-republicanism paid lip service to
popular spirit, yet the metaphors he mobilised in support of liberty of
the press harboured deep doubts and fears about the fickleness of the
people. Liberty of the press is 'the common right of mankind' because it
discharges the potentially subversive force of 'murmurs' and 'secret

---

[7] See Robyn Eckersley, 'Representing Nature', in Sonia Alonso, Wolfgang Merkel
    and John Keane (eds), *The Future of Representative Democracy* (Cambridge and
    New York, 2011), pp. 236–57.
[8] See Gianni Vattimo, *A Farewell to Truth* (New York, 2011).

discontents' by making them public to lawmakers, thus giving them time to remedy bad laws. 'The liberty of the press, therefore, however abused, can scarce ever excite popular tumults or rebellion.' Press freedom is in fact a cure for the 'harangues of the popular demagogues' that plagued the ancient democracy of Athens. Against the harum-scarum of democracy, it encourages men to be reasonable, to ponder things, to think things through, to read in peace and quiet, to pause before acting. Liberty of the press is a powerful corrective to impetuosity. 'A man reads a book or pamphlet alone and coolly', Hume concluded. 'There is none present from whom he can catch the passion by contagion. He is not hurried away by the force and energy of action.'[9]

Arbitrary power

The coming of universal franchise representative democracy, in stormy circumstances, often bitterly resisted by powerful elites, ensured that strong traces of Hume's way of thinking survived. They are still with us, as can be seen, for instance, in claims about the elevating effects of education upon the character of impetuous young people, accusations that the unemployed poor are prone to the disorderliness of the mob, and idealised defences of the early twentieth-century BBC model of broadcasting as the best means of countering crass commercialism and the free-wheeling clash of unbalanced opinions through the non-market principles of impartiality, probity and public service. The spirit of Hume's call for curbing and balancing the ambitions of both the powerful and the powerless nevertheless remains important. It finds expression within a viewpoint that is today arguably the strongest available justification of freedom of public communication: the view that it serves in principle and in practice to frustrate and prevent the arbitrary exercise of power.

According to this approach, whenever people act arbitrarily they do so in accordance with the *arbitrium*, that is, they decide things without

---

[9] David Hume, 'Of the Liberty of the Press', in *Essays Moral, Political, and Literary* (London [1742] 1889), essay 2. During the same generation, using similar language, Sweden's path-breaking Freedom of the Printing Press Act 1766 was anticipated by Peter Forsskål, *Thoughts on Civil Liberty (Tanka om Borgerliga Friheten)* (Stockholm, 1759), section 9: 'A wise government will ... let the people express their discontent with pens than with other guns, which enlightens on the one hand, appeases and prevents uprising and disorder on the other.'

reference to, or respect for, what others think or say or do.[10] Those who exercise arbitrary power act as if they are authorised by a higher being to do so.[11] That is why they do not care what others may say they want. Fine self-justifications and alibis aside, they treat others with disrespect. They put themselves on a pedestal and, by doing that, they shove aside the dignity principle, the precept that people should be regarded as beings who are worthy of respect because they are capable of explaining themselves and their actions to others in public. The merchants of arbitrary power try to rig things in their own favour. They restrict or ban outright opportunities for others to call into question or actively refuse their own power. Sometimes they resort to eliminating their opponents, through torture, imprisonment, disappearance or death.

This line of thinking about arbitrary power urges that freedom of communication is a trumping principle, in that it enables citizens and their representatives to speak against arbitrary exercises of power. Their ability to express their own concerns freely in public is said to be an antidote to *fear* generated by arbitrary power. When some people, for instance, employers, government officials or groups of armed gunmen, act without restraint or consultation they inject uncertainty and anxiety into their subjects' lives, sometimes to the point where they so fear for their lives that their actions are paralysed. Arbitrary power is unpredictable power; its unconstrained quality means that it can act spitefully, according to whim, changing direction at will, exacting revenge on its victims. Free communication with others, the gathering of the afraid, can serve to dissolve these fears; it can also send signals to the practitioners of arbitrary power that fear is a public problem, that it can ruin people's lives, and that it will therefore not be tolerated.

---

[10] The following section draws upon Martin Krygier, 'The Rule of Law', in Michel Rosenfeld and András Sajó (eds), *Oxford Handbook of Comparative Constitutional Law* (Oxford, 2011), pp. 233–49; and Martin Krygier, 'The Rule of Law: Legality, Teleology, Sociology', in Gianluigi Palombella and Neil Walker (eds), *Relocating the Rule of Law* (Oxford, 2009), pp. 45–69.

[11] Early modern objections to arbitrary power typically cited resistance to God as the key reason for its illegitimacy. Traces of this view persisted well into the nineteenth century, as can be seen in the remark by Alexis de Tocqueville, 'Tyranny of the Majority', in *Democracy in America* (New York, 1945), vol. 1, ch. 15, p. 270: 'Unlimited power is in itself a bad and dangerous thing. Human beings are not competent to exercise it with discretion. God alone can be omnipotent, because his wisdom and his justice are always equal to his power. There is no power on earth so worthy of honor in itself or clothed with rights so sacred that I admit its uncontrolled and all-predominant authority.'

Yet freedom of communication is not just a weapon for preventing harm to others. Its defensive function has constructive implications; it serves the more positive cause of reminding others of the importance of fostering the *dignity* of citizens. Free communication is a form of action. It rejects the view that people are fit only for bowing and scraping in the presence of masters. Grovelling is not its thing. Freedom of communication supposes that citizens are capable of defining life's projects for themselves. It therefore anticipates and requires an end to the practice of people being treated as objects of others' wills. This is another way of saying that freedom of communication is the ally of the *liberty* of citizens, their capacities to live their lives in the expectation that they will not be bossed and bullied by arbitrary power. When citizens enjoy the liberty to express themselves, to say their piece, then freedom of communication serves another important positive purpose: it enables citizens to make sense of the multiple choices and decisions that are the result of their liberty. Freedom of communication enables the *nonviolent coordination and resolution* of their potentially conflicting views on who should get what, when and how. Communication without restraint implies that *democratic politics* can flourish. It points to a world in which power is no longer subject to the rule of the wealthier, or the stronger, or the capricious, where fraud, mendacity, lawlessness and violence are not respected, a world where those who exercise power are required to give account of their actions and to be held publicly responsible for their actions.

Hidden power

Those who exercise power arbitrarily do so typically by camouflaging their *modus operandi*. The logic of concealment was spelled out in many works on the subject by the leading Italian analyst of democracy of the past generation, Norberto Bobbio (1909–2004). He consistently warned against the damaging anti-democratic effects of publicly unaccountable power, which he saw as a threat rising from several directions. 'Democracy is an attempt to make power visible to everyone', he wrote. 'It is or at least it should be "power in public" ... a form of government in which the sphere of invisible power is reduced to its absolute minimum.' He liked to reinforce the point by quoting a famous passage from Kant: 'All actions affecting the rights of other human beings are wrong if their maxim is not compatible with their being made public.' Visibility of power is the core principle of democracy, but in practice, Bobbio argued, today's democracies are plagued by forms of power unconstrained by publicity. The trend underscores a basic political problem: 'Power tends to hide itself. Power increases in strength the more it is hidden from view.'[12]

Bobbio was surely right about the dangers posed by what he variously called 'hidden powers', 'subgovernment', 'concealed power' and 'crypto-government'. Yet an odd feature of his remarkably prolific writings on the subject of power and democracy is that they so rarely discussed the paradox that in the age of communicative abundance hidden powers are typically encased within the shaping structures and dynamics of media.[13] It is not just that Bobbio's metaphor of invisibility

---

[12] Norberto Bobbio, 'Hidden Powers', in Norberto Bobbio and Maurizio Viroli, *The Idea of the Republic* (Cambridge, 2003), pp. 82–9. The words of Kant are taken from *Perpetual Peace: A Philosophical Sketch*, in Immanuel Kant, *Political Writings* (Cambridge, [1795] 1991), p. 126.

[13] The subject of democracy and media found its way to the table during a long, enjoyable and spirited lunch with Norberto Bobbio at his book-lined apartment in Turin, shortly after the publication of my *The Media and Democracy* (1991). At one point during the conversation, I asked him to explain why, despite publishing more than thirty books on the subjects of philosophy, politics and law, he had written next to nothing on the topic of communications media and power. Was this because he took for granted the potency of the written word that he favoured, for instance, in his roles as author of many books and essays, long-standing co-editor of *Rivista di Filosofia* and regular columnist for the Turin-based daily *La Stampa*? What about the political effects of television under democratic conditions, for instance? Bobbio replied sharply. He explained that pundits greatly exaggerate the influence of electronic media. Did he own a television set, I enquired? Yes, he owned a television set, but admitted to watching it rarely, as I later confirmed by observing its location in an obscure corner of his apartment, its old-fashioned wooden doors masking its screen. But, I continued, what about the millions of people who actually do watch television, and lots of it? Marshall McLuhan and others had surely put their finger on its epochal significance, its tangible power over our bodily senses? With an impatient wave of his hand, Bobbio insisted that there was little or no evidence for such propositions. The evidence, to the contrary, was that few people take it seriously. Most citizens keep a healthy distance from its programme schedules, formats and tropes. Bobbio then offered an amusing anecdote in support of his point about the impotence of contemporary electronic media. He explained that in his role as life senator he had recently agreed to a television interview. Next morning, he had made a scheduled visit to his barber, who welcomed him, proudly noting in the next breath that the previous evening he had seen his distinguished client featured on national public television. Bobbio casually asked him what he thought of the interview. 'Il Professore', exclaimed the barber, 'I have no idea what you said. I just kept thinking throughout how much you needed a haircut!' In view of later

is arguably tied too closely to presumptions about television and sight as the primary media of communication. More pertinent is the point that because power which is 'invisible' nowadays comes wrapped in publicity, it is imperative to rethink the subject of arbitrary power in terms of the dialectics of communicative abundance and media decadence analysed in this book. The point can be sharpened. Freedom of communication among citizens, that is, freedom *from* media decadence, is a good thing not only because it enables these citizens to live their lives democratically in freedom and dignity, as equals, without fear eating into their souls. It is a vital principle for a less obvious and more urgent reason: it is the most effective means of preventing *dangerous* accumulations of power, in the form of large-scale and high-risk business and government experiments in re-ordering the lives of citizens and their environment, sometimes with catastrophic consequences.

These adventures of power are nowadays described as 'megaprojects'.[14] Sometimes known through the anodyne euphemism 'major programme', megaprojects comprise a wide range of initiatives, from the construction and operation of under-sea tunnels, inter-city high-speed railway networks and airports through to liquid natural gas plants and nuclear power stations. These power adventures also encompass military innovations (the design and operation of UAVs or 'drones', for instance), as well as experiments in producing and marketing 'intangibles' within the business world, for instance, the global shadow banking system that in recent years has grown to rival mainstream banks by performing borrowing-and-lending functions based on securitisation, special purpose vehicles (SPVs), collateralised debt obligations (CDOs), credit default swaps and other unregulated instruments.

Megaprojects are distinguished by their astronomical design and construction costs (at least US$1 billion), and by their substantial complexity, scale and deep impact upon communities of people and their environment. In power terms, they are typically hybrid arrangements that involve consortia of variously sized companies, as well as funding

---

developments within the Italian mediascape, especially its contamination by the toxic spirit of Berlusconismo, Bobbio's joke now looks strangely complacent, the quaint attachment of a great public intellectual to a bookish world suited to just a few.

[14] See Bent Flyvbjerg, Nils Bruzelius and Werner Rothengatter, *Megaprojects and Risk: An Anatomy of Ambition* (Cambridge and New York, 2003).

and logistical support from governments. Megaprojects defy the conventional distinction between markets and states. Although sometimes initiated or signed off by elected governments, megaprojects resemble sizeable tumours of arbitrary power within the body politic of democracy. Details of their design, financing, construction and operation are typically decided from above; especially when it comes to military and commercial megaprojects, things are decided in strictest secrecy, with only limited monitoring by outside groups and almost no ongoing parliamentary scrutiny or active inputs by voters.

Megaprojects are a mixed blessing for monitory democracies. They create jobs and measurable wealth, exchangeable commodities, scientific-technical know-how and improved services. Many of these projects make our lives easier. Often a source of local and national pride, they generate large profits, but even when no golden harvest results they add hugely to the private fortunes of their managers and shareholders. Megaprojects make some people mega-rich. But all this comprises just half the story. Given their high sunk costs, their complexity and scale, measured in terms of the numbers of people whose lives are affected, megaprojects can have damaging effects. It is not just that they resemble predators that wreak havoc in a democratic environment; or, to switch similes, that megaprojects side-step and suspend democratic procedures through the enactment of permanent forms of emergency rule. When megaprojects malfunction, as they are prone to do, they destructively impact upon human beings and our biosphere on a scale unimaginable to our ancestors.

Scale provides a clue as to why this is the case. Megaprojects are highly concentrated systems of power whose footprints, or radius of effects, are without precedent in human history. Once upon a time, even when their fates were bound up with empire, most people on our planet lived and loved, worked and played within geographically limited communities. They never had to deal with all of humanity as a factor in their daily lives. Whenever they acted recklessly within their environment, for instance, they had the option of moving on, safe in the knowledge that there was plenty of Earth and not many other people. If bad things happened, they happened within limits. Their effects were local. When things went wrong elsewhere, at a distance, over their horizons, it was none of their concern or business. They could say (as the old Scots proverb has it) that 'what's nane o' my profit will be nane o' my peril'. Distance and time protected them from the trials and misfortunes of others.

The new adventures of power radically alter this 'out of sight, out of mind' equation in people's lives. Their size and connectedness with regional and global processes ensure that growing numbers of people and swathes of their environment are affected by things that happen in far-distant places. These projects pose potentially a double misfortune for our world. Their unparalleled ability to put in place systems of arbitrary power that enable some members of our species to lord over many others, and over our biosphere, is matched by the growing possibility that whenever their risky ventures go wrong, the disasters that result always have incalculable and potentially irreversible damaging effects, on a gigantic scale.

Powered by silence

Megaprojects do go wrong. During their design and execution phases they suffer construction problems, budget blow-outs and delayed completion schedules. The cost-inflation effects of Hong Kong's US$20 billion airport were so great that for a time they damaged the whole of its local economy. The Channel Tunnel project, whose completion costs were double the original forecasts, suffered several near-bankruptcies. In Australia, a land (it seems) of megaprojects, only one out of fifteen approved such projects during the past decade (Conoco Phillips' US$3.3 billion liquid natural gas project) has been completed on schedule, and within the targeted budget. When up and running, megaprojects are plagued by chronic operation problems and 'normal accidents' triggered by unforeseeable and irreversible chains of tightly coupled disruptions.[15] Sometimes the mishaps do irreparable damage. Hence, the household names: event sequences that include the Bhopal gas and chemical leak, nuclear meltdown at Chernobyl and gigantic oil spills courtesy of *Exxon Valdez* and *Deepwater Horizon* (Figure 5.1). Disasters of their type seem to be growing in number and frequency. They point to a grim future, one in which whole peoples and many parts of our planet are the potential victims of risky power experiments whose dysfunctions generate interconnected, cross-border, potentially life-or-death effects, some of them irreversible.

---

[15] Charles Perrow, *Normal Accidents: Living with High-risk Technologies* (Princeton, 1999).

Figure 5.1 Fire boat response crews at the off-shore oil rig *Deepwater Horizon* (April 2010).

Why do they happen? Why do megaprojects so often fail to measure up to the lavish claims made in their defence, often to the point where the dysfunctions they produce have devastating consequences? Is it because (as popular folklore and serious analysts sometimes propose) these projects are typically in the hands of alpha males, whose 'serial' thinking is inferior to women's capacity for 'parallel' thinking? Or due to the alleged fact that natural selection favours self-deception, or perhaps because humans have been turned loose on the world in the industrial age equipped with prehistoric brains that recognise only simple Newtonian causes and effects, and can think only in primitively visual terms?[16]

Reductionist explanations may contain insights, but they are implausible. There are multiple causes and causers of megaproject failures.

---

[16] The latter explanations are proposed, respectively, by Robert Trivers, *Deceit and Self-Deception: Fooling Yourself the Better to Fool Others* (London, 2011) and Gerhard Vollmer, 'Wissenschaft mit Steinzeitgehirnen?', *Mannheimer Forum* 86/ 87 (1986): 9–61.

Such forces as simple human miscalculation, the blind arrogance and impatience of leaders and inadequate 'hedging' for surprise events play a role. Bad decisions caused by poor coordination and diffused responsibility chains, systematic lying (what policy analysts sometimes call 'strategic misinformation') and unintended chain reactions also play their part in ensuring things go wrong, when they go wrong, as they sometimes do.

The gargantuan size and hyper-complexity of megaprojects predispose them as well to coordination problems and management failures, but more than their 'cognitive failure' is at stake.[17] Substantial evidence is mounting that their dysfunctions stem ultimately from their refusal of robust internal and external public scrutiny. Not all disasters are human and megaprojects do not always fail, it is true. Yet when they do fail, in the vast majority of cases, the proximate cause is the privatisation of risk. Those in charge of operations suppose, mistakenly, that their mega-organisations can be governed in silence – silence within and outside the organisation.

There is a paradoxical dynamic at work here, because the silence is *produced*, usually through intensive public relations campaigns, which have the effect of cocooning the power adventure, shielding it from rigorous public scrutiny by fabricating a positive sense of its necessity and perfection. The paradoxical production of silence through public relations campaigns is not understandable in the terms of Elisabeth Noelle-Neumann's well-known theory of the spiral of silence, which supposed individuals fall silent because they fear being outcasts from majority opinion. Megaprojects operate within media-saturated settings and the dynamics are different. Things closely resemble what anthropologists call the Rashomon effect (named after the 1950 Akira Kurosawa film, *Rashômon*).[18] The whole point is that the power of the megaproject comes wrapped in a canopy of multiple realities; hidden agendas are protected by various efforts at producing silence that

---

[17] Francis Fukuyama, 'Afterword', in Francis Fukuyama (ed.), *Blindside: How to Anticipate Forcing Events and Wild Cards in Global Politics* (Washington, DC, 2007), p. 170.

[18] Elisabeth Noelle-Neumann, *The Spiral of Silence: Public Opinion – Our Social Skin* (Chicago and London, 1984); James W. Fernandez, 'Silences of the Field', in Maria-Luisa Achino-Loeb (ed.), *Silence: The Currency of Power* (New York and Oxford, 2006), pp. 161–3.

functionally depends upon rhetoric, things being said and displayed to the outside public world.

When that happens, silent complacency and blind faith in complex operations get the upper hand, both within and outside the megaproject. Groupthink, wilful blindness and unchecked praise flourish.[19] Thinking the unthinkable, public questioning of the goals and *modus operandi* seems unnecessary, a taboo topic. Those in charge of operations discourage bad news from moving up the inner hierarchy. Troublemakers are ousted from the organisation. Contrarians are rebuked, or blanked. Discussing the undiscussable requires guts, which are usually in short supply. Silence encourages employees at all levels to distance themselves from its moral implications; they draw the conclusion that it is someone else's job to solve the problems or that problems will resolve themselves. Journalists play along; a standard combination of promises of access, sinecures and over-dependence on official handouts renders them obedient. They become 'plane spotters', cheerleaders of the power adventure, a cog in the 'compliant' or 'captive' machinery of culture within the organisation.

Silence

The great public silences produced by large-scale adventures of power are surely among the strangest, most paradoxical features of media-saturated societies, which otherwise thrive on high levels of open clamour and public hubbub that fuel demands for a new politics of noise reduction for the sake of 'our humanity, as well as of our beleaguered environment'.[20] So it is worth probing these silences in more depth.

---

[19] The foundational work on these subjects was done four decades ago by the American psychologist Irving Janis (1918–1990). He labelled as 'groupthink' the tendency of decision-makers operating in group settings to lie to others and to ignore counter-evidence in the interests of towing the line, getting things done and protecting their flanks. He showed in *Victims of Groupthink: A Psychological Study of Foreign-policy Decisions and Fiascos* (Boston, MA, 1972), how groupthink played a fundamental shaping (and ultimately disastrous) role in the American invasion of Cuba at the Bay of Pigs. See also Paul 't Hart, *Groupthink in Government: A Study of Small Groups and Policy Failure* (Baltimore, 1994); Paul 't Hart *et al.* (eds), *Beyond Groupthink: Political Group Dynamics and Foreign Policy-making* (Ann Arbor, MI, 1997).

[20] Stuart Sim, *Manifesto for Silence: Confronting the Politics and Culture of Noise* (Edinburgh, 2007).

Given the fundamental importance of silence as a power resource in the design, implementation and operation of megaprojects, it is unfortunate that a political treatise on silence and its various effects remains unwritten. It is as if a great political silence has descended on the subject of silence, that its study is reckoned properly to belong elsewhere, for instance, in the fields of semiotics, anthropology and sociolinguistics, where the analysis of human language has underscored the many ways in which 'the stupendous reality that is language cannot be understood unless we begin by observing that speech consists above all in silences'.[21] Just as the spaces, punctuation marks and patterns of aeration within any written text establish strategic silences that serve as signals that direct readers in their encounter with the text, so (it is pointed out) all communication with others rests inevitably on invisible beds and blocks of silence. Silence is not just the aftermath of communication. Every act of communication using words backed by signs and text is actively shaped by what is unsaid, or what is not sayable. Communication is the marginalia of silence – the foam and waves on its deep waters.

Proverbs and aphorisms pick up this theme of the interdependence of communication and silence. They stress the significance of the unsaid as a maker of meaning, the ways in which silence talks, the advantages of well-timed silence, even (as the old Swiss saying goes) the superiority of golden silence compared with silvern speech. In each case, silence is seen as a meta-linguistic strategy for positively managing communication. Backed by bodily gestures, silence produces meanings through halo effects. Theologians reinforce the point by emphasising the vitally important role played by sacred silence in all of the world's religions. Silence is a technique of self-discipline, a powerful solvent of worldly cares, a sign of respect for a deity, an acknowledgement of the inadequacy of words to capture the experience of sacredness.[22]

---

[21] José Ortega y Gasset, 'What People Say. Language. Towards a New Linguistics', in *Man and People* (New York, 1957); see also Stephen Tyler, *The Said and the Unsaid* (New York, 1978); George Steiner, *Language and Silence* (New York, 1967); Keith Basso, 'To Give Up on Words: Silence in Western Apache Culture', in *Language and Social Context* (New York, 1970), pp. 67–86; Edward T. Hall, *The Silent Language* (New York, 1959).

[22] The classic work is Gustav Mensching, *Das heilige Schweigen* (Giessen, 1926).

Historians chip in with reminders of the many long-standing efforts to codify etiquettes of everyday silence.[23] There are library shelves stuffed full with manuals on the delicate art of cultivating silence as a desirable way of communicating with others. In early modern Europe, for instance, silence was typically reckoned to be agreeable because of its binding effects. William Hazlitt observed that fools are those who have not yet seen that 'silence is one great art of conversation'. William Penn urged his children to love silence ('it is to the spirit what sleep is to the body, nourishment and refreshment').[24] Moralists backed their sermonising with citations from the classics. Among the favourites was the old anonymous Roman adage: *audi, vide, tace, si vis vivere in pace* (if you wish to live in peace, hear, see and be silent). Ethical inferences were drawn. Idle talk was condemned. The deliberate silence of respect was praised. There were warnings that what is said cannot be taken back. Lurking behind the moralising were fears of rebellion founded on what Auguste Comte first called 'conspiracies of silence'. He that is silent gathers stones, ran an old English proverb. It hit the mark: silence could be impolite, even expressive, speaking volumes, such that yawns could be silent shouts and underdogs could speak back to their masters by means of mocking silence, a practice later dubbed 'dumb insolence' by British army officers. If toothy silence could express scorn, then it followed that there were more than a few circumstances in which subjects had to learn when and when not to be silent. A much-cited example was the targeting of children, who were expected to understand that silence was a form of polite behaviour appropriate to beings of little status. Silence was certainly gendered: women were widely expected to wear the fine jewels of calculated quietude. Their faithful reserve and obedient hush, without appearing to be speechless, was deemed imperative. The same went for subjects of government. 'Silence is sometimes an argument of Consent', remarked Hobbes. The caveat was important, as the good bishop Beauvais (1731–1790) pointed out in his funeral oration for Louis XV. Monarchs must always keep in mind that 'the glory of the king is inseparable from the happiness of the people', and this is why their lugubrious toothless

---

[23] Peter Burke, 'Notes for a Social History of Silence in Early Modern Europe', in *The Art of Conversation* (Cambridge and Oxford, 1993), pp. 123–41.

[24] William Hazlitt, *Characteristics: In the Manner of Rochefoucault's Maxims* (London, 1837), p. 24, No. 59; *Advice of William Penn to his Children* (Philadelphia, 1881), p. 24.

silence should worry kings and queens just as much as their violent outbursts, or their false flattery. He was one of many courtiers and commentators convinced of the strategic importance of cultivating *respectful* silence among underlings. 'Tell not all you hear, nor speak all you know' ran advice to servants. Others advised that fools are wise as long as they are silent. The optimists added: silence seldom hurts.[25]

Catastrophes

How wrong that maxim proved. It is true that in political matters taciturnity can have civil effects, as happens when a call for silence precedes the entry of a judge into a court of law; or when crowds are requested by the authorities to observe a minute's respectful silence; or when jurors are obliged to remain publicly silent about their deliberations (as in the grand jury system in the United States). People politely rise, respectfully stand motionless, or they hold their tongues. The political effects are benign, and limited, certainly compared with the dilapidating effects that flow from the dysfunctions of megaprojects. When things go wrong within these large-scale adventures of power, many ancillary organisations and services grind to a halt. People are made homeless; some are killed. The daily lives of those who survive are disrupted and damaged, along with their habitats, which are often pushed beyond the limits of sustainability. They seize up, or break down.

Catastrophe is another term for such devilish outcomes. It is a potent word (originally from ancient Greek, *katastrophē*, 'sudden turn, over-turning') that cries out for definition and begs to be used carefully, especially because the numbers of large-scale misadventures are rising. To speak of catastrophes – unexpected, sensational events that inflict long-term ruinous damage on humans, or our biosphere, or both – is not to indulge apocalyptic thinking. It is not to be nostalgic for halcyon times when life was calm and peaceful. The new catastrophes of our age are not the climax of inevitable historical trends; they should not be understood, say, as markers of the final triumph and breakdown of

[25] Jean-Baptiste-Charles-Marie de Beauvais, *Oraison funebre de très-grand, très-haut, très-puissant et très-excellent prince, Louis XV, le bien-aimé, roi de France et de Navarre* (Paris, 1774), p. 32; Thomas Hobbes, *Leviathan, or The Matter, Forme and Power of a Common Wealth Ecclesiasticall and Civil* (London, 1651), bk 2, ch. 36.

Western metaphysics, as Heidegger proposed.[26] The new man-made catastrophes are not inevitable. More than a few are triggered by bizarre projects that should never have been attempted. With hindsight, had the megaproject been conceived and run differently, plenty of other catastrophes could have been avoided. That is why the trend towards catastrophes is not backwards. We are not returning in any simple sense to the vile events that paralysed the world from just before the outbreak of the First World War to 1950, a forty-year 'age of catastrophe' (Eric Hobsbawm) when whole societies stumbled from one calamity to another, through the wreckage of economic collapse, inter-state rivalries, total war, totalitarianism, murder and genocide.[27]

The catastrophes of our times have devastating effects, but they are different. Their slow-motion quality is striking. There is no Big Bang, but there are plenty of loud explosions whose numbers are growing in frequency. Our catastrophes are cumulative. Their sources are different. They are not products of fascism, capitalism or socialism. They are the effect of big adventures of power operating in many different settings, and at many different points on our planet. Our catastrophes cut deeper and more aggressively into our biosphere, and distinctive as well (thanks to communicative abundance) is that they stand centre stage in real-time media events that trigger fascination, fear and foreboding on a global scale. Catastrophes shatter the public silence that bred them in the first place. They attract millions of witnesses. They are also the raw material of business deals ('catastrophe bonds'[28]) and blockbuster movies and other forms of popular entertainment.

Catastrophes are difficult to capture in words; those who experience them first-hand are often unable to communicate their horror.[29] Silence is the currency of catastrophes both before and after they strike. Some part of their ugliness stems from their destruction of the ability to communicate with others. Their details are ugly, as can be seen in one recent troubling instance: the catastrophe that occurred at the

---

[26] Martin Heidegger, 'Letter on Humanism', in *Basic Writings*, ed. David Farrell Krell (New York, 1976), pp. 193–244.

[27] Eric Hobsbawm, *The Age of Extremes: A History of the World, 1914–1991* (New York, 1994).

[28] Tim Devaney, 'Investors Turn to "Catastrophe Bonds" as Hedge against Uncertain Market', *Washington Times*, 10 October 2011.

[29] Maurice Blanchot, *The Writing of the Disaster* (Lincoln, NE, 1995).

Fukushima-Daiichi nuclear power plant, on Japan's northeastern coast-
line, during March/April 2011.[30]

Fukushima quickly became the greatest industrial catastrophe in the
history of the world. Triggered by the largest-ever recorded earthquake
in the country's history (so large it made our planet spin faster on its
axis), and compounded less than an hour later by a vast pulse of water
that destroyed the plant's protective walls and choked its emergency
power generators under sea water, the disaster was not simply the effect
of 'natural' causes, as many observers initially claimed. The catastrophe
came covered in the fingerprints of organised silence. Fukushima
records show that warnings by experts and citizens about safety hazards
were swept aside, right from the beginning of the project. From the mid-
1950s, when, against the strong advice of the Japan Scientists Council,
the United States backed the policy of developing nuclear power in
Japan, using American-designed, enriched-uranium plants unsuited to
earthquake zones, voices of dissent were ignored, or silenced.

The silencing or 'blackout' policy was defended by successive governments, and by the Tokyo Electric Power Company (Tepco), which
became skilled at forging and doctoring safety data and issuing blanket
assurances through the media that their plants were invulnerable.
Harnessing the *kisha* club system of embedded journalism, a system,
as we have seen above, that rewards self-censorship and fosters bland
uniformity, the company acted to disprove the claim by philosophers
(Max Picard is the best-known example) that silence is 'valueless' and
'unproductive', that it is the only phenomenon today that 'stands outside the world of profit and utility'.[31] Silence was supposed to yield large
profits. In the lead up to the disaster, the company's organised dissimulation made it difficult to improve safety arrangements; even small-
scale tinkering implied the existence of unreported dangers. The old
habit of ignoring risks guaranteed, during the earliest phases of the
unfolding disaster, that reckless dissimulation retained its grip.
Company directors and government officials were determined to

---

[30] The following draws upon many contemporary media reports, including
contributions by Jonathan Soble and Mure Dickie, 'How Fukushima Failed',
Financial Times, 7/8 May 2011, p. 19; Dahr Jamail, 'Fukushima: It's Much
Worse Than You Think', available at: http://english.aljazeera.net/indepth/
features/2011/06/201161664828302638.html, accessed 16 June 2011; Evan
Osnos, 'The Fallout', *The New Yorker*, 17 October 2011, pp. 46–61.
[31] Max Picard, *The World of Silence* (South Bend, IN, 1952), p. 18.

Figure 5.2 Exclusion zone entrance at Minamisoma, 25 km north of the Fukushima-Daiichi nuclear power plant (14 January 2012), by Felicity Ruby.

speak with one voice, regardless of what was actually happening on the ground.

Unhappily for them, events pushed in other directions, mocking public reassurances by politicians and company spokespersons that everything was under control. Hemmed in by secrecy, media gaffes and bureaucratic incompetence (plant managers did not realise for eight hours that a back-up water cooling system had been shut down mistakenly), the crisis quickly turned into uncontrollable catastrophe. The president of the company crumbled under the strain; knowing (as the Japanese say) that the dog had fallen into the river, he stopped attending meetings and quarantined himself in silence in his office for five days and nights. Technicians meanwhile tried to prevent massive radiation leaks by releasing large quantities of radioactive steam into the atmosphere. Millions of television viewers soon witnessed fires and minor explosions, even a whole nuclear reactor flying apart in a cloud of dust and debris. There followed unsuccessful efforts to cool several reactors; a massive leak of radiation for several hours; the enforced withdrawal of emergency workers, then their redeployment after regulators more than doubled the acceptable limit for radiation exposure (from 100 millisieverts, the recognised level at which long-term detectable cancer risk jumps, to 250 millisieverts). Then came a highly controversial moment: the dumping of more than 10,000 tonnes of highly contaminated water into the nearby ocean. That move sparked protests from the wider region, especially from peoples living in South Korea and China, but the company carried on spraying seawater on several reactors and fuel cores, in the process generating many hundreds of thousands of tonnes of highly radioactive waste, for which it had no disposal plans.

With evacuation plans in disarray, and several reactors melting down, over 100,000 people were forced to flee the Fukushima area, many into temporary shelters, uncompensated and jobless, anxious about their exposure to contaminated food, water and soil, their futures tattered and torn. Japan's Nuclear Emergency Response Headquarters talked shut-down, but, as the first accredited journalists to visit the site quickly discovered, that was merely a fancy phrase. As radioactive steam and evaporated seawater continued to penetrate the atmosphere, confirmed reports of radioactive 'hot spots' around Japan began to make the news. There was also confirmation that a geographic area of nearly 1,000 square kilometres – an area roughly seventeen times the size of Manhattan – would remain uninhabitable for the foreseeable future; that quantities of strontium, caesium and plutonium isotopes, so-called hot particles, had been detected in local water tables and in car engine air filters as far away as Seattle; and that something worse than a meltdown had happened at the plant: a hot fuel 'melt through' of layers of the reactor plant cracked and compromised the bottom casing.

Three months into the disaster, nobody really knew what would happen next, or what could be done to reverse its deadly effects. Tepco, facing massive clean-up and compensation costs, tried to regain its media footing by outlining a roadmap for the future safe 'cold shut-down' of the plant. Tactful observers replied that full decommissioning and robotic clean-up of the wrecked and radioactive plant would take a decade at the minimum; the more prudent in their midst pointed out that nuclear disasters never end, and that the unknowable long-term impact of the disaster would almost certainly be shaped by future technical failures, unpredictable seismic shocks, human ignorance in the face of uncertainty and the willingness of decision-makers to open themselves up to robust public scrutiny.

Political effects

Those who coined the old proverb that silent people are dangerous people could never have foreseen just how dangerous those people who organise and manage public silence in the early years of the twenty-first century would be. Covered-up disasters on the scale of Fukushima are no laughing matter; and what ought to be especially worrying is that with the exponential growth of megaprojects, catastrophes caused by long strings of wilfully blind miscalculations are growing in frequency.[32] Catastrophes are becoming unexceptional. Tagged with names like AIG, Lehmann Brothers and *Deepwater Horizon*, they are a new normal.

To the list of actual or impending disasters should be added the 'slow-motion' catastrophes that come wrapped in public silence. Their piecemeal, step-by-step, bit-by-bit quality has numbing effects on mainstream media reporters, who typically turn a blind eye, complaining that it is all too complicated or, the flipside, not newsworthy enough because there is no 'event' to serve as a newsworthy 'hook'. The net effect goes beyond what is conventionally called 'gatekeeping': catastrophes in the making are so shrouded under canopies of silence that they become public non-issues. The numbers of slow-motion catastrophes are multiplying. The compound long-term social effects of economic stagnation within the Atlantic region are a case in point. Amartya Sen famously pointed out that no substantial famine has ever occurred in a country with a democratic form of government and a comparatively free press, but the large-scale personal devastation triggered by unemployment, pauperisation and what economists call 'hysteresis' (loss of motivation and work skills) within media-saturated rich countries seems less than newsworthy and undeserving of in-depth investigation by most professional journalists.[33] Slow-motion catastrophes are meanwhile brewing within the global manufacture and trade in weapons, 'a world of money, corruption, deceit

---

[32] The classic study of the catastrophe-prone global oil industry from the 1850s until around 1990 is by Daniel Yergin, *The Prize: The Epic Quest for Oil, Money, and Power* (New York, 1991).

[33] Jean Dreze and Amartya Sen, *Hunger and Public Action* (Oxford, 1989); compare the findings of Richard Wilkinson and Kate Pickett, *The Spirit Level: Why Equality is Better for Everyone* (London and New York, 2010).

and death'[34] connected to states, the United Nations, large listed corporations and covert operators in such intricate and unaccountable ways that most journalists do not seem to know where to begin their investigations, and so do not bother. The whole shadowy trade is fastened by middlemen, agents, brokers, lobbyists and so-called economic offsets in procurement decisions (promises by arms manufacturers to invest in a buying country's economy). It thrives on and protects itself in silence hidden by talk of 'transport and logistical services' and other euphemisms. Slow-burn catastrophes also encompass the field of the environment: the European Commission recently warned of the 'alarming decline' of biodiversity in lakes and rivers, and on land. Chemical pollution, industrial-scale fishing, habitat loss and the introduction of invasive species, all linked in one way or another with the advance of megaprojects, threaten at least a quarter (and sometimes nearly half) of all freshwater fish, molluscs and amphibians. More than 500 species of vascular plants are on the endangered list, and dragonflies, birds and animals that live near, or depend upon, increasingly dirty and receding sources of water are also suffering. Nearly 900 known species are now recorded as extinct in the wild, or as fully extinct, but the whole process of degradation receives limited media coverage.[35]

The list goes on, but these are cases enough to illustrate why the pockets of mediated silence that define the age of communicative abundance are among its most decadent features. But if catastrophes result from the misadventures of silent power linked to megaprojects, what are their probable political implications for democracy? The question is pertinent because past catastrophes typically triggered public mood

[34] Andrew Feinstein, *The Shadow World: Inside the Global Arms Trade* (London, 2011). According to monitory bodies such as Transparency International, the Stockholm International Peace Research Institute and Corruption Watch, the industry accounts for an estimated 40 per cent of corruption in all global trade. Profits run into the billions; losses are counted in human lives. Covert export deals worth around US$60 billion are annually signed, almost all of them (85 per cent) within the jurisdiction of the five permanent members of the UN Security Council (the United States, Russia, France, the United Kingdom and China), plus two other states, Germany and Italy.

[35] Details from the so-called European Red List, an ongoing environmental monitoring exercise of some 6,000 species conducted by the European Commission in conjunction with the International Union for Conservation of Nature (IUCN), are available at: www.iucnredlist.org, accessed 26 November 2011.

swings and reactions. In the world of medieval Europe, events such as the Black Death (which wiped out a quarter, perhaps a third of the population of Europe in the space of three or four years) and periodic outpourings of belief in the end of the world served several times as the spark that ignited the gunpowder of millenarian movements.[36] The gigantic earthquake that devastated Lisbon in 1755 ignited violent political tensions in the kingdom of Portugal, damaged the monarchy's colonial ambitions, inspired various innovations, ranging from the birth of modern seismology and earthquake engineering to Enlightenment criticisms of theodicy and fresh philosophical thinking about the sublime (Figure 5.3). Closer to our time, the battlefield slaughter of the First World War extinguished beliefs in one-way progress (think of Walter Benjamin's angel of history, turning its back on the future, gazing backwards on 'one single catastrophe that keeps piling wreckage upon wreckage'[37]). The catastrophe stoked fears of the end of the world twinned with hopes of universal redemption, often mixed with apocalyptic fantasies of violence, refusals of 'bourgeois' parliamentary 'chatter' and yearnings for strong political leadership.

The multiple catastrophes associated with the Second World War nearly destroyed parliamentary democracy. Monitory democracy was among their unintended offspring, but the catastrophes of that period produced few prophecies of perfection. For many, the world instead felt as if it had been punched in the face by Kafka, fully emptied of meaning and transcendent purpose, a nightmare reality, as Hannah Arendt noted, haunted hereon by the problem of how to understand and restrain human evil, for instance, through the invention of monitory democracy and its human rights organisations and cross-border open government and rule of law mechanisms.[38]

---

[36] Jean Delumeau, Le péché et la peur: la culpabilisation en Occident, XIIIe–XVIIIe siècles (Paris, 1983); Norman Cohn, The Pursuit of the Millennium: Revolutionary Millenarians and Mystical Anarchists of the Middle Ages (Oxford, 1970).

[37] Walter Benjamin, 'Theses on the Philosophy of History', in *Illuminations*, ed. Hannah Arendt (New York, 1969), p. 257.

[38] Compare the 1945 prediction of Hannah Arendt, 'Nightmare and Flight', in *Essays in Understanding 1930–1954* (New York, 1994), p. 134: 'The reality is that "the Nazis are men like ourselves"; the nightmare is that they have shown, have proven beyond doubt what man is capable of. In other words, the problem of evil will be the fundamental question of postwar intellectual life in Europe – as death became the fundamental problem after the last war.'

Figure 5.3 *The Ruins of Lisbon* (1755), a German copperplate engraving. The image depicts mayhem: tented survivors, criminal attacks and the hanging of earthquake survivors, under constabulary supervision and in the company of priests holding a crucifix and prayer book.

Freedom of communication: new horizons

While it is too early to forecast the long-term political impacts of the catastrophes of our age, they are bound to bring surprises. Viewed through the lenses of this book, what is certain is that catastrophes are symptoms of *democracy failure*. They are warnings that silent exercises of arbitrary power by manipulative human beings – the *absence* of monitory democracy – have harmful effects on citizens. Big power adventures are exercises in democracy destruction. By establishing spaces of arbitrary power that bear some resemblance to baronial fiefdoms ruling over medieval commoners, these misadventures take us backwards, into a future where mechanisms of freely chosen representation by citizens and keeping tabs on those who exercise power play a minor role in most people's daily lives. Big power adventures gone wrong have destructive effects on the spirit and substance of monitory democracy. They damage or permanently deform citizens' lives; and they have potentially hurtful effects upon the whole of humanity, and the rest of our biosphere. Not only do catastrophes turn patches of our planet into permanently uninhabitable zones; they pose worrying questions about irreversible tipping points. They prompt consideration of the possibility that the human species is passing through a door of no return, that we are falling victim to our own anthropocentrism and (a point forcefully made by Haruki Murakami when reflecting on the long-term significance of the Fukushima catastrophe) that we may be incapable hereon of living self-reflexively as 'uninvited guests on planet Earth'.[39]

Catastrophes fuelled by organised public silence are politically significant for another reason. They confront previous accounts of democracy and media with a new normative challenge. They force us to reflect on the possibility that human silence will so badly backfire on our world, sometimes with such devastating consequences, that the whole subject of media and democracy will become a dispensable luxury, perhaps even a relic from times when human citizens still believed in the democratic project of chastening and humbling the powerful, placing them under public control. The gloomy possibility has a bright implication: catastrophes fuelled by silence show not only that communicative abundance and media decadence greatly matter to the future of our world. They force us as well to rethink the reasons why the principle of 'free communication' is desirable – far more precious than our ancestors could possibly have imagined.

Is it possible to inject new energy and life into the old principle of freedom of communication, to effect its re-description so that it assumes a new and expanded political relevance in the early years of the twenty-first century? Can we leave behind the old arguments for 'liberty of the press' as well as move beyond the prevailing functionalist justifications of media freedom? Is there a way of regarding freedom of public communication as uniquely suited to the age of communicative abundance?

The shift of perspective in favour of monitory democracy proposed in this book pushes in this direction. When seen in terms of the perilous silences surrounding megaprojects, freedom of communication is much more than a means of informing and mobilising voters, investigating governmental power, providing intelligible frameworks of interpretation, lending different styles of life a stamp of public acceptability,

---

[39] Jared Diamond, *Collapse: How Societies Choose to Fail or Succeed* (New York, 2005); Haruki Murakami, 'As an Unrealistic Dreamer', speech upon receiving the Catalunya International Prize, Barcelona, 2011, available at: www.senrinomichi. com, accessed 10 January 2012.

binding disparate groups into common publics and educating them in the virtues of democracy.[40] The principle of freedom of public communication has a significance that runs well beyond these commonly cited functions. It is a means of damage prevention, an indispensable early warning mechanism, a way of enabling citizens and whole organisations and networks to sound the alarm whenever they suspect that others are causing them harm, or that calamities are bearing down on their heads, in silence. 'See something, say something', is a widely used motto invented by the New York Metropolitan Transit Authority and today used elsewhere, in many different settings. The motto captures the deepest significance of freedom of public communication. In principle, it rejects silent nonchalance in human affairs. 'Whereof one cannot speak, thereof one must be silent', wrote Ludwig Wittgenstein,[41] but the elegant last-sentence formula of his key early work must be revised. There are moments when silence is not an option. Refusal to hold one's tongue in the face of organised silence is necessary because it brings things back to earth. It serves as a 'reality check' on unrestrained power. It is a potent means of kick-starting action by citizens and their representatives, a vital way of ensuring that those in charge of organisations do not stray into cloud cuckoo land, wander into territory where misadventures of power are concealed by silence wrapped in fine words of trust, loyalty and progress.

When reformulated along these lines, the whole meaning of unfettered public communication is transformed. It no longer indulges bland fantasies of conjoining citizens into harmonious agreement, or luring them towards some form of global enlightenment based on a reasoned philosophical First Principle. It is a principle sceptical of all Principles. Freedom of public communication is not wedded to any particular form of life, be it Truth or Happiness or Human Rights or God or the Common Good. Quite the contrary: it is a precondition of the coexistence and flourishing of multiple ways of living.

It is in this revised sense that the early warning principle of communication has global implications. Suspicious of organised silences and arbitrary power, a champion of the weak against the strong, especially

---

[40] The range of prevailing consequentialist arguments for news media freedom is surveyed in Michael Schudson, 'How to Think Normatively about News and Democracy', unpublished paper, Columbia School of Journalism, New York, 2011.

[41] Ludwig Wittgenstein, *Tractatus Logico-Philosophicus* (London, 1922), p. 7.

when the weak find themselves silenced by the strong, freedom of communication is a norm whose universality stems from its active commitment to 'pluriversality', its defence of a multitude of different ways of living. Its role as an early warning device makes it meaningful in a wide range of contexts. It is on the lookout against all forms of arbitrary power, wherever they take root. The early warning principle is just as applicable to transport projects in China, multi-billion dollar tar sand extraction schemes in Canada and grandiloquent megaprojects in Turkey as it is to the 'modernisation' of military forces and credit and banking sector institutions elsewhere on the planet. Gripped by a strong sense of the contingency of things, the principle is a fair-minded defender of openness, a friend of perplexity when in the company of cocksure certainty. That explains its candour, its active commitment to return to the basics, to revisit with an open mind the old but vital question of why it is that the unfettered scrutiny of power through free communication is in principle a good thing.

Nothing about the behaviour of human beings comes as a surprise to the early warning principle of public communication. It doubts that human beings are straightforwardly 'gaffe-avoiding animals'.[42] It sees that humans are capable of the best, and the worst, including pleasurable acts of extreme violence against fellow human beings.[43] For that reason, the principle stands against hubris and the privatisation of risk. It considers that concentrated power is dangerous; it supposes that human beings are not to be entrusted with unchecked power over their fellows or their circumstances. It therefore rejects the utopia of a future world stripped of shadows, a fully 'transparent' world where nothing is misunderstood, where everything is bathed in the light of communicative reason, a world where arbitrary power cedes to happy 'rational' agreement among citizens and their representatives. The early warning principle seeks no easy answers to simple or difficult questions. It stands against stupidity and dissembling. It is opposed to silent arrogance and has no truck with bossing, bullying and violence. The

---

[42] Ernest Gellner, 'The Gaffe-Avoiding Animal, or a Bundle of Hypotheses', in *Relativism and the Social Sciences* (Cambridge and New York, 1985), pp. 68–82.

[43] Examples of dastardly acts of violence that give great pleasure to their perpetrators (raping women, strafing innocent civilians, witnessing mass shootings as if they were tourist entertainment) are cited at length in Sönke Neitzel and Harald Welzer, *Soldaten: On Fighting, Killing and Dying* (London and New York, 2012).

principle is sensitive to the pitfalls of hypocrisy, the double standards of those who preach freedom of communication, but violate that principle behind closed doors, or do so with blind eyes, deaf ears and hardened hearts. The early warning axiom is attuned to conundrums and alive to difficulties. It is serious about the calamities of our times; it tracks the calamities to come. The axiom understands that misadventures of power demand a powerful reply to the sceptics and outright opponents of monitory democracy and communicative abundance. The reply, simply put, is that societies plagued by pockets of public silence are asking for trouble. The absence of freedom of communication and its twin, monitory democracy, invites catastrophes. Their lack undermines much more than a supposed 'natural' or 'human' right to communicate such matters as the 'truth' of things. For when whole societies succumb to the unsaid, sweep things under the carpet, become victims of what some writers have called the *non-dit*, they flirt and dance with disaster.

Robust and rowdy mediated communication as a brake upon catastrophe: this way of thinking about the political problem of silence and the need for open public communication stands at right angles to those of a post-modernist persuasion whose abstract talk of 'contingency' and 'ambivalence' offers no remedies, instead treating catastrophes as fascinating dramas. With a sigh, some post-modernists find these catastrophes to be disabling proof of the rottenness of our 'modernity', its grand narratives and scientific and technological hubris; others of post-modernist persuasion treat catastrophes as marvellous challenges to the reigning banalities of mass culture, for instance, through doomsday movies.[44] The political wistfulness of both ways of thinking about catastrophes is anathema to the principle of open communication. It casts doubt as well on the conviction of political sceptics, who insist that catastrophe rhetoric is apocalyptic, that it encourages intellectual resignation and citizens' passivity. They say it implies a misery-guts view of the world that is bound to dampen people's enthusiasm for life, but that is misleading. Freedom of public communication is a positive principle: far from robbing them of hope, it has confidence in the capacity of wise citizens and their representatives to summon the courage to change things by putting pressure on arbitrary power, humbling it with the help of their elected and unelected representatives.

[44] Umberto Eco, 'Apocalyptic and Integrated Intellectuals', in Robert Lumley (ed.), *Apocalypse Postponed* (Bloomington, IN, 1994), p. 18.

The early warning principle of communication is positive and proactive in another sense. It questions the attitude of resignation recommended by those who have grown convinced that gloomy scenarios are our fate, and who then tread the path walked long ago by Kierkegaard, to declare that our media-saturated world is so diseased by catastrophes and so cluttered with decadent noise that what is now required is silken silence, the healing power of calm quietude, old-fashioned hush that breathes new life into a much-needed sense of the sacred.[45] Judged politically, appeals to silence are unappealing. They ignore the historic trend that carries us, without guarantees, not only towards catastrophes, but towards communicative abundance and monitory democracy. Patter about apocalypse and quietist calls for silence devalue the capacity of political thinking to 'name the unnameable, say the unsayable, conceive the unconceivable, pronounce the unpronounceable'.[46] Such calls for quietude sheepishly turn their back on democratic politics. They suppose that nothing can be done. They ignore the point that 'our lives begin to end the day we become silent about things that matter'.[47]

But what exactly does the early warning communication principle imply in practice? What is to be done about the organised silence that breeds catastrophes and their horrors, for instance? Can anything help to prevent them? Many things can and must be done; a political learning process is possible. Following the *Deepwater Horizon* catastrophe for which it has been held responsible, British Petroleum malpractices have been exposed through the courts and the company itself has launched a rudimentary programme of 'town hall' meetings for its employees and managers. Électricité de France SA, among the world's largest energy producers, operates a full media disclosure policy. The family-run global clothing retailer C&A has long embraced watchdog 'performance channels', close links with radical NGOs, annual citizenship seminars and sworn dependence upon a legally free-standing unit (SOCAM) responsible for monitoring questionable practices within the company. These companies take their cue from risk-management bodies such as the Oxford-based Major Projects Association (MPA), which urges large-

---

[45] Kierkegaard, *The Present Age*.
[46] Jean-François Lyotard, 'Endurance and the Profession', in *Political Writings* (London, 1993), p. 74.
[47] Martin Luther King Jr, 'A Time to Break Silence', in *I Have a Dream: Writings and Speeches that Changed the World* (New York, [1967] 1992), pp. 135 ff.

scale projects to adopt 'stand back reviews', periodic 'pulse checks', 'honest reporting' and an internal 'challenging' culture that draws upon 'intelligence' from multiple 'stakeholders'.[48] Parliamentary committees and public inquiries can meanwhile bare sharp teeth. Long-standing laws against 'wilful blindness' can be activated by courts.[49] Muckraking investigative journalism can serve as a counter to plane-spotting 'churnalism'. Wise citizens can help to build procedures designed to govern democratically during emergencies, as in the mutual aid networks of rural Saskatchewan.[50] Under great duress (to take one final example) they can invent radiation detection counter-systems and other power-monitoring networks, as happened in Japan after the Fukushima catastrophe.

The common thread running through these manifold efforts to scrutinise and restrain arbitrary power is as simple as it is demanding. These initiatives acknowledge that the revolution in favour of communicative abundance is by no means over. They maintain its momentum. In matters of politics, these initiatives recognise that arbitrary power protected by media decadence can get the upper hand. Their resistance to unchecked power doubts the claimed virtues of golden silence. These initiatives understand that pockets of silent power are both bad for democracy and dangerous, in that they have twisting and buckling effects on people's lives. That is why these experiments in the art of breaking the grip of arbitrary power are early warning signals. They call upon wise citizens to take advantage of communicative abundance, to get involved in public affairs, initially by making public noise, smart public noise, well-targeted din and disquiet loud enough to shatter the eerie silences that can so easily cause things to go so terribly wrong for so many people.

---

[48] Further details available at: www.majorprojects.org, accessed 10 December 2011.

[49] *Regina* v. *Sleep* (1861) 30 LJMC 170.

[50] Elaine Scarry, *Thinking in an Emergency* (New York and London, 2011).

Index